Historical Atlas of Arizona

University of Oklahoma Press Norman

Historical Atlas of Arizona

By Henry P. Walker and Don Bufkin

Books by Henry P. Walker:

*The Wagonmasters: High Plains Freighting from
the Earliest Days of the Santa Fe Trail to 1880*
(Norman, 1966)

(with Don Bufkin) *Historical Atlas of Arizona*
(Norman, 1979)

Library of Congress Cataloging in Publication Data
Walker, Henry Pickering.
    Historical atlas of Arizona.
    Bibliography: p.
    Includes index.
    1. Arizona—Maps.   2. Arizona—Historical
geography—Maps.   3. Arizona—History.
I. Bufkin, Don, joint author.   II. Title.
G1510.W3   1979   911'.791   78–58086
ISBN 0–8061–1489–4

PREFACE

ARIZONA HAS HAD a long and colorful history. From the late 1600's to 1821 it was a part of the northern frontier of New Spain, and from 1821 to 1848 it was part of the Mexican state of Sonora. In 1848 all of the present state lying north of the Gila River became the Territory of New Mexico, part of the United States. Five years later the area south of the Gila was purchased from Mexico. It took ten years of political maneuvering before Arizona Territory was established in 1863. There followed another long struggle before Arizona at last achieved statehood on February 14, 1912.

History is the story of man—his actions, his comings and goings, and his settlements. As most of man's actions and travels and the places he made his settlements are controlled by the natural setting—terrain, climate, geography, and even geology—an understanding of the land is essential to an understanding of history. It means little to know that it took three weeks for a member of the Arizona Territorial Legislature to ride from Tucson to the capital in Prescott if one does not know the distance traveled or appreciate the kind of terrain that had to be crossed. We hope that this historical atlas of Arizona will make it easier to understand the history of the state.

The first ten maps display some of the outstanding physical characteristics of the state that have affected man's behavior. In many ways Arizona is unique among the United States in its total ecology, particularly its climate and flora and fauna. Some aspects of these elements it shares with adjoining regions, so in order to show a complete picture, some of the maps cover areas outside the state's borders. For example, the Sonoran Desert sprawls across parts of Arizona and California and the Mexican states of Sonora and Baja California. In addition, some adjoining areas are much more closely allied with Arizona than with their home states; for example, Fort Yuma sits on the California bank of the Colorado River, but its history is tied completely to Arizona.

Following the maps of the natural setting, other maps are in more or less chronological order from the days of prehistoric man to the growth of modern urban complexes. There are some exceptions, such as the maps that show the development of the Indian reservations, which have been grouped to show the continuing changes. The cartographic presentations are accompanied by textual material that briefly sets each map in its historic perspective.

Arizona's prehistory goes back some ten thousand years, but its written history begins about the middle of the sixteenth century with the arrival of the Spanish missionaries and explorers. Until 1846 Arizona was essentially that part of the present-day state lying south of the Gila River, the northern limit of Spanish and Mexican settlement. Not until 1863 did settlement on any considerable scale begin in the central and northern portions of the state.

One of the problems encountered in preparing this atlas was the matter of the spelling of place names, especially those of Spanish origin. For example, consider those which contain the letter h or j, as Mohave, or Mojave. When official records or maps use the letter h, this form has been followed; however, when referring to the Indian tribe the j is used, in accordance with the preference of the Indians themselves. Older maps often disagree on spelling, as is the case of Solomonsville or Solomonville, now plain Solomon, the name given to the railroad station serving the town.

There are so many places, terrain features, and events involved in the history of the state that we were forced to be selective in what we present here. We have sought to offer those items which we feel are most significant historically.

We wish to express our appreciation to Sidney B. Brinckerhoff of the Arizona Historical Society, Bert M. Fireman of the Arizona Historical Foundation, John Bret Harte of the *Tucson Daily Citizen*, and Emil Haury, Bernard L. Fontana, Stanton B. Keith, and the late James R. Hastings of the University of Arizona, who read and commented on various parts of this work. Also, our thanks go to the staffs of the libraries of the Arizona Historical Society and the University of Arizona. Naturally, any errors herein are our own responsibility.

HENRY P. WALKER
DON BUFKIN

CONTENTS

Historical Atlas of Arizona

LOCATION of ARIZONA

1. LOCATION OF ARIZONA

ARIZONA IS LOCATED in the southwestern part of the United States, between the 109th and 115th meridians west of Greenwich; thus, it lies entirely west of the Continental Divide. It also lies between the thirty-first and thirty-seventh parallels north of the Equator, or at about the same latitude as Georgia and North and South Carolina. The eastern border of the state is a common line with New Mexico. At its northeastern corner Arizona shares a common point with New Mexico, Colorado, and Utah. This "Four Corners" area is the only place in the United States where four state lines come together at a single point. The northern boundary of the state is a common line with Utah. The western border is shared with Nevada in the north and California in the south. Except in the extreme north, this western border follows the channel of the Colorado River. The southern border is the international boundary between the United States and Mexico, specifically the Mexican state of Sonora.

The state measures 392 miles from north to south and 338 miles from east to west at its widest point. Its land area is 113,956 square miles, making it the sixth largest state in the Union.

Isolated from the Pacific coast and from the early settlements of Mexico by high mountains and many miles of desert, and from the eastern states by a thousand miles or more, Arizona developed slowly and under practically unique conditions.

During most of the period of Spanish control, the only legal port of entry was Vera Cruz, Mexico. All goods for the presidios and missions of Arizona had to be hauled by wagon or pack animal two hundred miles over the mountains from Vera Cruz to Mexico City and then northward for approximately twelve hundred miles. It is small wonder that development was slow under those conditions.

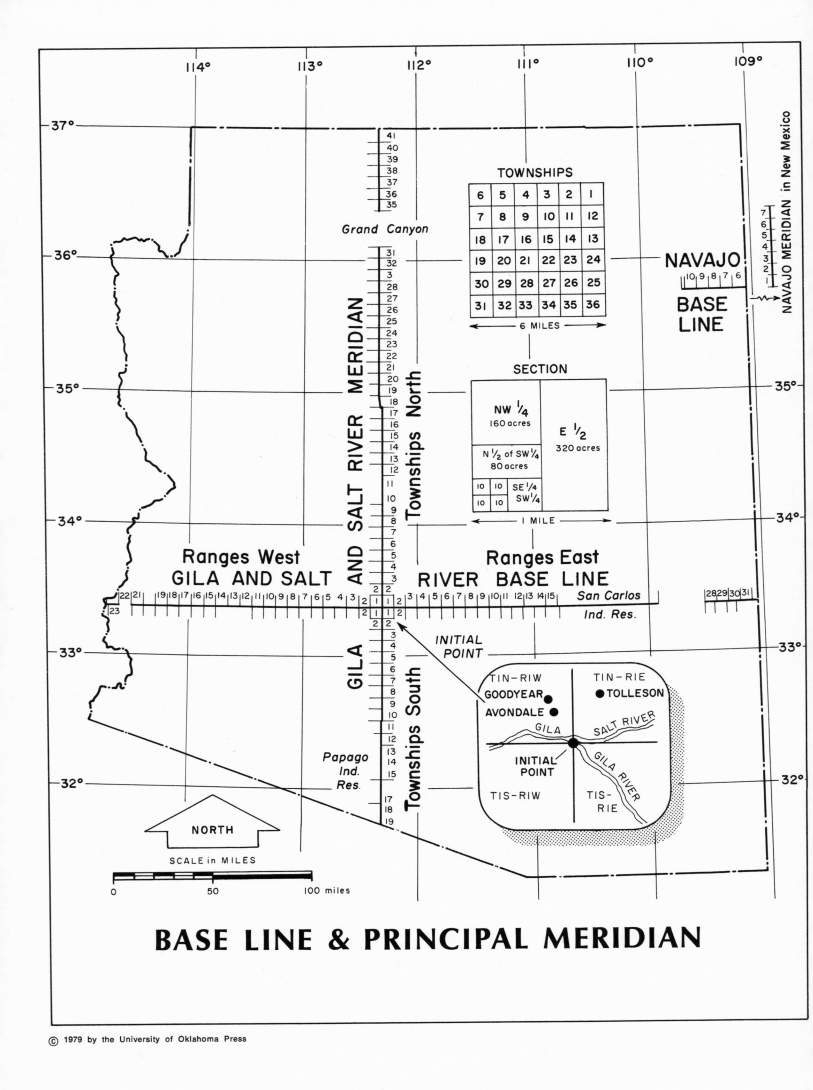

BASE LINE & PRINCIPAL MERIDIAN

2. BASE LINE AND PRINCIPAL MERIDIAN

THE BASIC SYSTEM of rectangular survey for the United States was prescribed by the Continental Congress in the Ordinance of 1785. The initial point of the survey was where the Ohio River left Pennsylvania. The system resulted in cadastral surveys—that is, surveys of public record showing the extent, value, and ownership of land for purposes of taxation. The General Land Office was set up in 1812 to direct the survey work and to handle the sale of land in the public domain. The first General Land Office in Arizona was opened in Prescott in 1868; others were opened in Florence (1873), Tucson (1880), and Phoenix (1905). Eventually all these offices were consolidated in Phoenix.

The Ordinance of 1785 called for townships six miles square, each township to be divided into thirty-six sections of 640 acres. In Arizona this basic grid starts from an initial point at the confluence of the Gila and Salt rivers. From this point the Gila and Salt River Meridian extends north and south, while the Gila and Salt River Base Line runs east and west. From the intersection of these two lines the land is laid off in six-mile squares. The north-south columns of squares are called *ranges*, while the east-west lines of squares are called *townships*. The squares are numbered outward from the intersection of the base line and the meridian and are distinguished by ranges east or west and townships north or south. Thus, Tucson is located at Township 14 South and Range 13 East (T14S R13E). Larger areas may be located by giving the inclusive points, such as T37–39N R10–11W.

A small section of northeastern Arizona uses the Navajo Base Line, which extend into Arizona from New Mexico, and the Navajo Meridian, which lies in New Mexico. Locations in this part of Arizona are distinguished by the letters NBL. For example, the Indian village of Nazini is located in T2N R9W NBL.

The sections within the townships are numbered beginning in the upper right-hand corner, from right to left. The second row is numbered left to right and so on until Section 36 appears in the lower right-hand corner. The sections in turn are divided into quarters, designated NE ¼, NW¼, SW ¼, or SE¼. Further subdivision may be described in such terms as the north half of the southwest quarter (N ½ SW¼), the southeast quarter of the northeast quarter (SE ¼ NE ¼), or the like. The large-scale topographic maps produced by the United States Geological Survey show the range and township lines of the basic grid.

In 1850 Congress decreed that "the meridian of the observatory at Washington shall be adopted and used as the American meridian for all astronomic purposes . . . that the meridian of Greenwich shall be adopted for all nautical purposes." This confusing situation was not entirely cleared up until 1912, when the act was repealed. Until then, most American maps showed longitude west of both Washington and Greenwich. When the Arizona state boundaries were surveyed, its north-south lines were based on the zero meridian of Washington, with the boundary between Arizona and New Mexico prescribed as 32° west of Washington. When it was decided in 1884 to standarize on the meridian of Greenwich, it was found that there was a three-mile difference between the meridians based on Greenwich and those based on Washington. As a result, Arizona's north-south boundary lines do not conform to lines of longitude west from Greenwich.

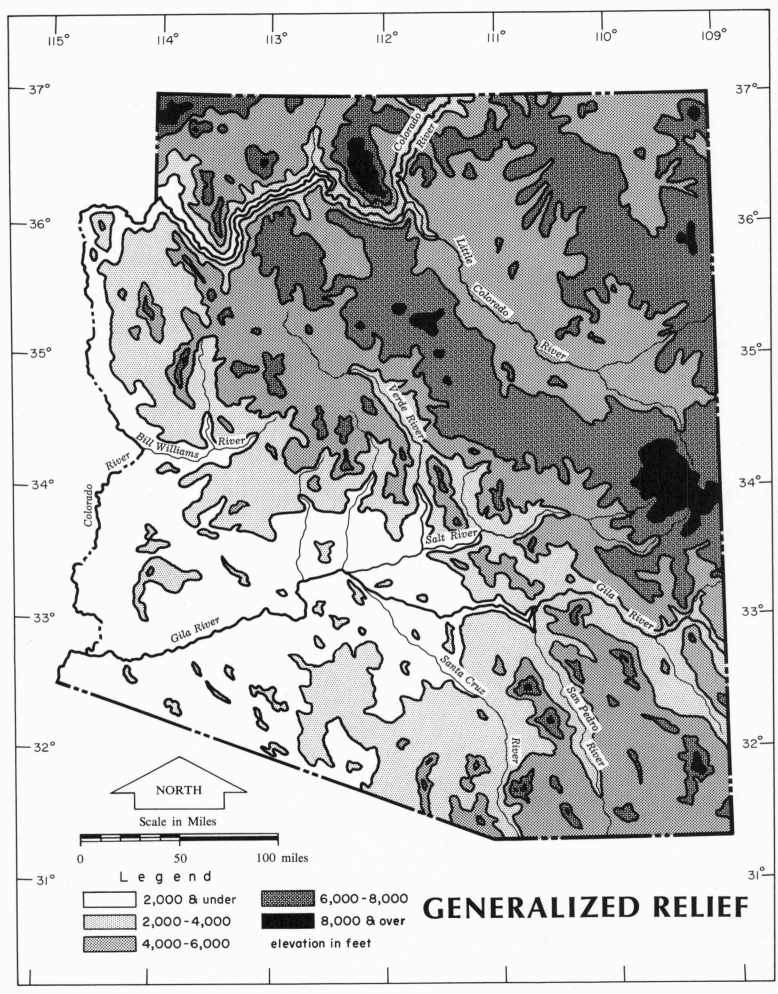

NORTH

Scale in Miles

0   50   100 miles

L e g e n d

2,000 & under	6,000 – 8,000
2,000 – 4,000	8,000 & over
4,000 – 6,000	elevation in feet

GENERALIZED RELIEF

3. GENERALIZED RELIEF

THE LAND SURFACE of Arizona may be visualized as a surface tipping from the northeast downward to the southwest. Elevation above sea level ranges from 141 feet at Yuma to 12,670 feet at Humphreys Peak in the San Francisco Mountains and 11,490 feet at Baldy Peak in the White Mountains. There are several other peaks that reach above 10,000 feet, and mountains with elevations over 8,000 feet are found scattered quite generally throughout the state. The average elevation for the state is about 4,000 feet.

Elevations above eighty-five hundred feet receive appreciably more precipitation and are cooler than the low desert country and have a resulting lower rate of evaporation. Thus, even isolated peaks such as Mt. Lemmon in the Catalina Mountains and Mt. Wrightson in the Santa Ritas are topped by coniferous forests.

The combination of elevation and precipitation gives Arizona the southernmost ski run in North America—the north slope of Mt. Lemmon, an hour's drive from Tucson.

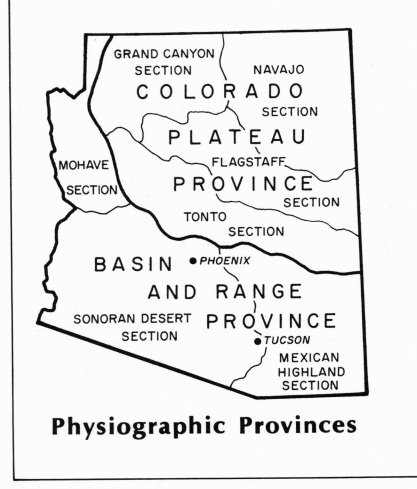

GRAND CANYON
SECTION

NAVAJO
SECTION

C O L O R A D O

P L A T E A U

MOHAVE
SECTION

FLAGSTAFF.

P R O V I N C E

SECTION

TONTO
SECTION

B A S I N

● *PHOENIX*

A N D   R A N G E

SONORAN DESERT
SECTION

P R O V I N C E

● *TUCSON*

MEXICAN
HIGHLAND
SECTION

Physiographic Provinces

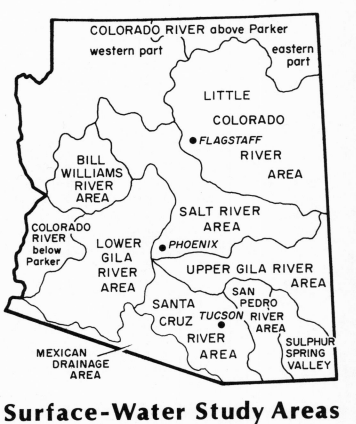

COLORADO RIVER above Parker
western part

eastern
part

LITTLE

COLORADO

BILL
WILLIAMS
RIVER
AREA

● *FLAGSTAFF*

RIVER

AREA

SALT RIVER
AREA

COLORADO
RIVER
below
Parker

LOWER
GILA
RIVER
AREA

● *PHOENIX*

UPPER GILA RIVER
AREA

SANTA
CRUZ

SAN
PEDRO

TUCSON RIVER
●   AREA

MEXICAN
DRAINAGE
AREA

RIVER

AREA

SULPHUR
SPRING
VALLEY

Surface-Water Study Areas

4A. PHYSIOGRAPHIC PROVINCES

PHYSIOGRAPHERS preparing maps of the physical geography of the United States show Arizona to be divided between the Colorado Plateau Province and the Basin and Range Province. The former covers approximately the northeastern half of the state; the latter covers the rest of its area. Other scientists have shown a third province between the other two—a transition zone called the Intermontane Province.

The Colorado Plateau Province extends east and north into New Mexico, Colorado, and Utah. This region is a generally level area cut by deep canyons such as those of the Gunnison River in Colorado, the Green River in Utah, and the Grand Canyon of the Colorado and the canyon of the Little Colorado in Arizona. Rising above the general level of the plateau are numerous volcanic cones ranging from some a few hundred feet tall to the San Francisco Peaks, which tower fifty-seven hundred feet above the surrounding country.

The Basin and Range Province extends eastward into New Mexico and west and northwest into California and Nevada. This area is also a generally level region, but it is cut up by numerous ranges of fault block mountains formed by the tilting of large blocks of the earth's crust. These mountains generally have a gentle slope on one side of the range and a notably steeper slope on the other. The broad valleys between the fault block mountains have been filled to a fairly uniform level by rocks and sand eroded from the mountains. Throughout Arizona's portion of this province the long axis of these blocks trends north and south.

Both major provinces have been subdivided for convenience. The Colorado Plateau Province has been broken up into the Navajo Section, which contains the Painted Desert and the Petrified Forest; the Grand Canyon Section; the Flagstaff Section, which has most of the timber country above the Mogollon Rim; and the Tonto Section of rough country below the rim. The Basin and Range Province has been divided into the Mexican Highland Section, where most of the good cattle ranges are found; the Sonoran Desert Section; and the Mohave Section. Both of these last two sections are parts of the Sonoran Desert (Map 8).

4B. SURFACE-WATER STUDY AREAS

BECAUSE LARGE AREAS OF ARIZONA are arid or semiarid, a thorough knowledge of its water resources is imperative if the best use is to be made of the meager supply. A great deal of water is pumped from underground basins, but that source is fixed in amount and very slow to replenish.

To facilitate the study of water resources, the state has been divided into eleven surface-water study areas, each representing the drainage basin of a river except for Arizona's part of the Colorado River basin, which has been broken into three study areas. There are 425 measuring stations throughout the state.

Because more than 95 per cent of the state's precipitation is lost through evaporation and transpiration by plants, the available supply of surface water is small and very difficult to measure and record.

Year-to-year variations in climate produce great disparity in surface-water flow. For example, while the average (1914–66) flow of the Gila River near Safford was about 300,000 acre-feet (one acre-foot being the amount of water required to cover one acre of land to a depth of one foot), the flow has been as low as 100,000 acre-feet and as high as 16 million. Such great differences emphasize the need for large storage reservoirs to hold the runoff of wet years for use in dry years. An indication of the general aridity of the state is the small number of natural lakes. In addition, there are a number of closed basins, such as the Willcox Playa (Map 6), which would be lakes if there were enough water to fill them.

Another important aspect of surface-water supply is the possibility of converting its energy to electric power. Power generation requires a large and fairly constant flow of water and a point of rapid descent of the river bed. With the exception of scattered points along the Colorado River and a short section of the Salt River above Roosevelt Lake, most of the available water-power sites are already in use to produce electricity for homes and industry.

Without radically new developments in the technology of water supply, such as an inexpensive method of desalting ocean water, it appears that there are definite limitations imposed by nature on the growth potential of Arizona.

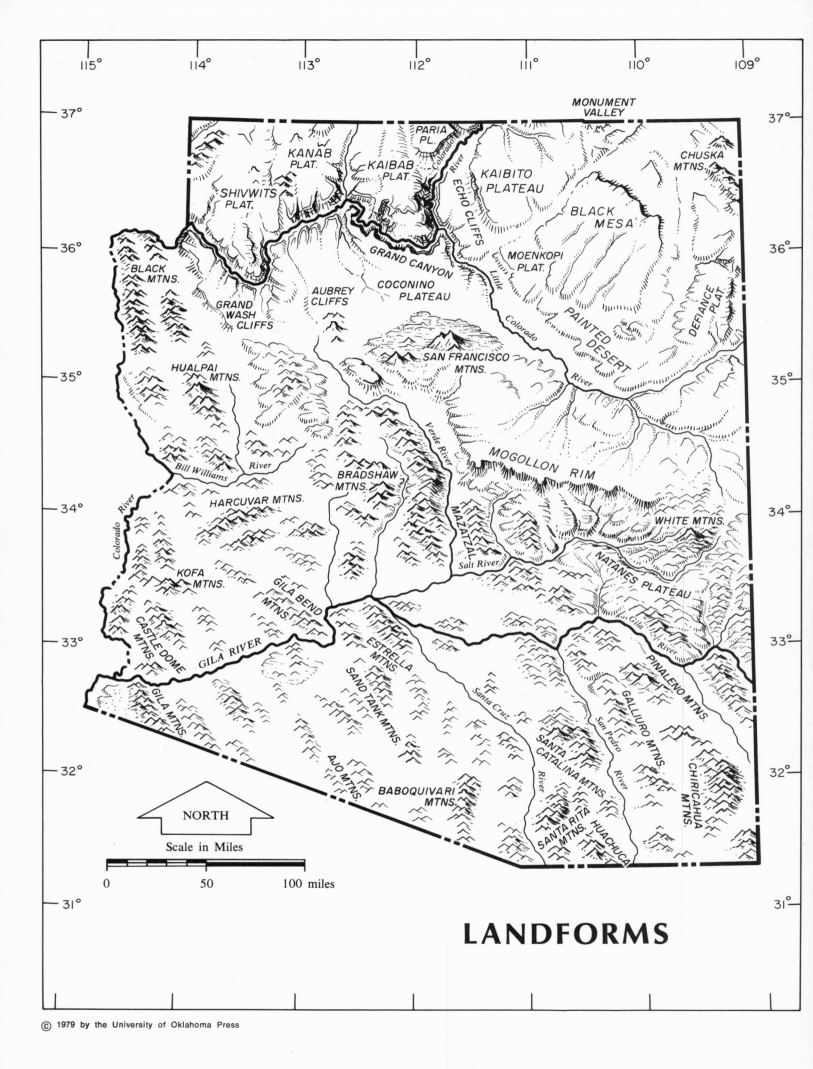

LANDFORMS

5. LANDFORMS

THERE ARE FEW STATES in the Union that display a greater variety of terrain than does Arizona. The landforms vary from broad, nearly flat valleys and mesa tops to very rugged mountains so tall that trees cannot grow on their peaks. Nearly every valley and every mountain, ridge, and peak have been officially named. As a result, only the outstanding features can be shown on a map of this scale.

The outstanding feature of the Colorado Plateau is the Grand Canyon of the Colorado River. Two hundred miles long, six to ten miles wide, and a mile deep, it is one of the great natural wonders of the world (Map 64). Only fifty miles away rise the San Francisco Mountains, the remnants of a vast volcano. Also in this region are found the Painted Desert of varicolored rocks, the Petrified Forest National Park, and the ruins of a number of prehistoric pueblos that are now protected as national monuments (Map 55). The canyons of the Little Colorado River made a serious barrier to Spanish and American explorers seeking an east-west route across the northern part of the state.

The Mogollon Rim is the southern edge of the Colorado Plateau, dropping sharply down to the Salt River to create exremely rough country where its edge has been cut by many streams. This area, a zone fifty to one hundred miles wide and trending from southeast to northwest, was for some centuries the stronghold of the Tonto subtribe of Western Apache Indians.

Much of the Arizona part of the Basin and Range Province is the northern portion of the Sonoran Desert (Map 8). Because most of the early travelers who passed through Arizona and wrote of their experiences used the southern route, the popular idea of Arizona was, and still is, that it is one vast desert. This idea overlooks entirely the region of tall timber and running water in the mountainous part of the state.

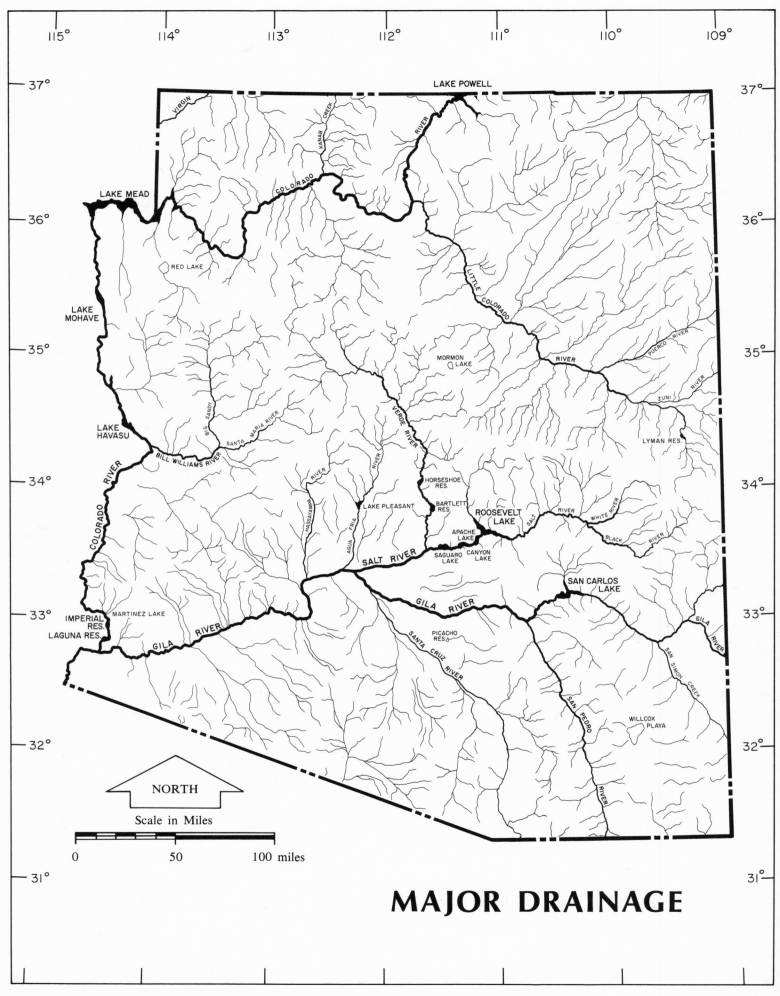

MAJOR DRAINAGE

NORTH

Scale in Miles

0   50   100 miles

© 1979 by the University of Oklahoma Press

6. MAJOR DRAINAGE

OVER 90 PER CENT of the land area of Arizona drains eventually into the Colorado River, which empties into the Gulf of California some eighty miles south of Yuma. The Colorado River and most of its major tributaries rise on the western slope of the Rocky Mountains in Wyoming, Colorado, Utah, and New Mexico, the so-called Upper Basin states. The river enters Arizona from Utah at about the midpoint of Arizona's northern border, then swings to the west to form most of the state's western boundary. Twenty-eight miles below Yuma the river enters Mexico en route to the Gulf of California. The Colorado River is one of the great rivers of the western United States. It played a vital role in the development of Arizona by providing a route of access by river steamer to much of the area of the state. The river is still very important to the state as a source of water to meet the needs of the rapidly growing cities of Phoenix and Tucson.

Since 1922 virtual war has raged between California and Arizona over the use of the Colorado River's water. In 1934 part of the Arizona National Guard was stationed at Parker to prevent the completion of the Parker Dam. The troops were withdrawn only after the United States Supreme Court decided that Arizona could not halt the work.

The whole matter of water use is most complex. Because of their growing economy, the Upper Basin states, source of most of the Colorado River's flow, are reluctant to see the water used elsewhere. The Lower Basin states of Nevada, California, and Arizona have the greater need for the water because of limited precipitation. Southern California has taken the lion's share of the Colorado water for Los Angeles and San Diego and the agricultural area of the Imperial Valley.

The Gila and its chief tributary, the Salt River, are vitally important to the state's economy, because they provide the water for most of the irrigated agricultural land and for the urban center of Phoenix. Ground water in the basin of the Santa Cruz River valley provides most of the water for the urban center of Tucson and for agricultural lands along its course. In 1846 the Santa Cruz carried water for seven to nine miles north of the city, but today, because of human demands, running water is seldom found less than ten miles south of the city.

At present, Arizona has put to use most of its water resources, with the exception of its share of the Colorado River, only a small portion of which is used for irrigating a narrow strip along the east bank of the river. The pumping of underground water in the Phoenix and Tucson areas has seriously lowered the water table, causing shallow wells to go dry and even resulting in subsidence of the land surface—as dips in some highways indicate.

Along the Mexican border there are two areas that drain into Mexico. The larger of these, located to the west of Nogales, drains a large portion of the Papago Indian Reservation. The other area lies to the east of Douglas. In addition, there are two small areas that have no drainage. In these areas evaporation balances precipitation. In the northwest corner of the state is the so-called Red Lake, and in the southeast is Willcox Playa.

All three major rivers of Arizona, the Colorado, the Little Colorado, and the Gila, at various points flow through spectacular deep and narrow gorges. Of these, the Grand Canyon of the Colorado is by far the largest and best known.

Flooding of the major rivers has presented a recurrent problem. A levee has been built along the Colorado River south of Yuma to protect the irrigated land on the east bank. The Slough Dam on the Little Colorado River, built by local farmers at a cost of $200,000 in 1886, was washed out in 1903 and again in 1915.

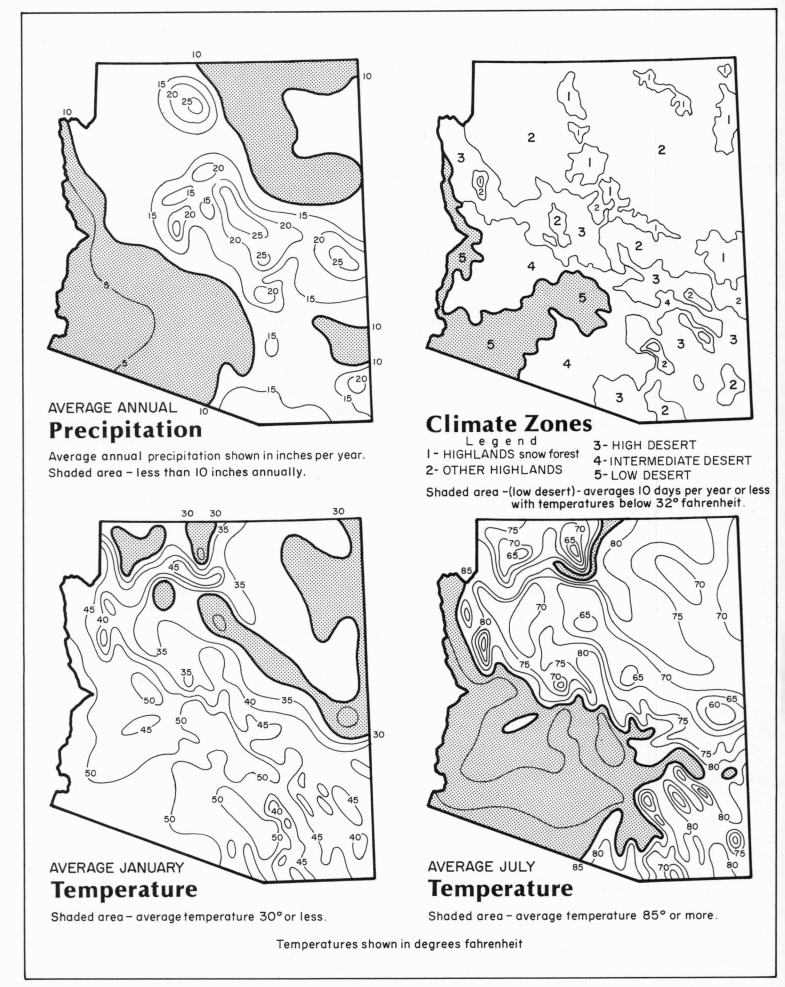

AVERAGE ANNUAL
Precipitation
Average annual precipitation shown in inches per year.
Shaded area – less than 10 inches annually.

Climate Zones
Legend
1 - HIGHLANDS snow forest
2 - OTHER HIGHLANDS
3 - HIGH DESERT
4 - INTERMEDIATE DESERT
5 - LOW DESERT

Shaded area –(low desert)– averages 10 days per year or less
with temperatures below 32° fahrenheit.

AVERAGE JANUARY
Temperature
Shaded area – average temperature 30° or less.

AVERAGE JULY
Temperature
Shaded area – average temperature 85° or more.

Temperatures shown in degrees fahrenheit

7. CLIMATE

ARIZONA'S CLIMATE is classified as arid or subhumid. Nowhere in the state does rainfall reach the thirty inches per year that is generally felt necessary for farming without irrigation. The annual average precipitation ranges from less than five inches near Yuma and up the Colorado River valley to a little over twenty-five inches along the Mogollon Rim and in a small area north of the Grand Canyon.

The moisture comes in two "rainy" seasons. The winter rain, or snow, comes as widespread storms between December and March. The rainfall is gentle, allowing the water to soak into the ground, and the cool weather reduces loss by evaporation. Summer thundershowers occur during July and August. They account for 60 to 70 per cent of the annual total in the southwest and about 45 per cent in the northeast. About 97 per cent of the thundershowers have a diameter of less than three miles. The heavy downpours often cause dangerous flash floods in normally dry stream beds, and the water does not have much chance to soak into the ground. Also, because of the high summer temperatures much of the water is lost through evaporation. Lightning during the storms causes numerous fires in the brushlands and forests which damage the watersheds and destroy forage for cattle and wild animals.

Periods of severe drought are not uncommon. Some anthropologists hold that it was such a period about A.D. 1200 that caused the abandonment of most of the large prehistoric settlements. A drought from 1889 to 1892 forced Arizona cattlemen to dump their livestock on the market.

In general, the average annual temperatures are a function of elevation. There is usually a drop of about three to three and a half degrees fahrenheit for each 1,000-foot increase in elevation. This drop could amount to a difference of forty degrees from Yuma (142 feet above sea level) to the top of Humphreys Peak (12,670 feet above sea level). There is also a decrease in temperature as one goes from south to north, but it amounts to only one and a half to two and a half degrees fahrenheit for every degree of latitude, or roughly seventy miles. In Arizona this decrease amounts to about five and one-half degrees of temperature from south to north.

Because of the variations in precipitation and temperature, Arizona has a variety of climatic zones which support many forms of life. So delicately does climate control vegetation that the appearance of certain plants may vary by as much as 1,000 feet on the northern and southern slopes of the same mountain. On the northern slopes, protection from the sun's direct rays results in lower temperatures, which in turn allow moisture to remain longer in the ground. Even the mass of a mountain can affect the shielding of the plants. On the bulky San Francisco Peaks, spruce grows 410 feet lower than on nearby, but smaller, O'Leary Peak which does not provide as much shade for the vegetation.

The high summer temperatures and mild winters make for a long growing season, which varies from 240 days per year without a killing frost around Yuma to 100 days in the northern part of the state. This generally mild weather has, over the years, drawn many health seekers and retired persons from all over the nation, largely to the Phoenix and Tucson areas. It is not unusual for the temperature to swing thirty degrees from the heat of late afternoon to the cool of early morning. The relatively recent development of refrigerated air conditioning has made life tolerable in the summer heat of southern Arizona.

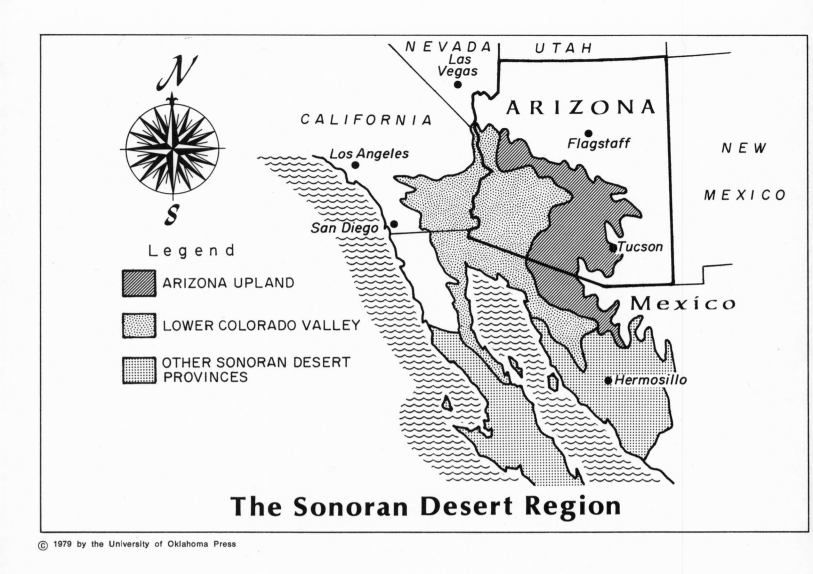

The Sonoran Desert Region

8. THE SONORAN DESERT REGION

THE SOUTHWESTERN ONE-THIRD of Arizona is a biologically unique area, the northern part of the Sonoran Desert. Because the desert blends gradually into other climatic classifications, there is no consensus about its exact limits. Some scientists include certain bordering areas and exclude others. This book, in general, follows the work of Forrest Shreve in defining this region.

The Sonoran Desert is a roughly wedge-shaped area of some 120,000 square miles, or a territory about the size of New Mexico. Thus, it is among the dozen largest deserts in the world. On the east the desert is bounded by the Sierra Madre Occidental of Mexico and the northward extension of this range in New Mexico and Arizona. These mountains tend to wring the moisture out of the summer rain clouds which originate in the Gulf of Mexico. To the west, the mountains of California and Baja California greatly reduce the rainfall from the winter clouds that come from the Pacific Ocean. In a north-south direction the Sonoran Desert extends from about Needles, California, to the Río Mayo in southern Sonora—roughly 800 miles. At its greatest width it reaches from the vicinity of Hayden, Arizona, to

Palm Springs, California, approximately 320 miles.

The desert is usually divided into seven regions, all having a desert climate but differing vegetational characteristics. Of these regions, only two are represented in Arizona: the Lower Colorado Valley and the Arizona Upland. The other regions are found in Sonora or Baja California.

The Lower Colorado Valley is the larger of Arizona's two desert regions. It straddles the lower Colorado River and reaches into Mexico on both shores of the Gulf of California. It is a region of nearly flat land broken by widely scattered, low mountain ranges. The total annual rainfall is, in general, less than five inches. The typical vegetation of this region is creosote bush and white bur sage in open stands. There are occasional stands of mesquite along the channels of ephemeral streams. In sheltered canyons in the mountains there may be a few native palm trees.

The Lower Colorado Valley region is the home of many species of lizards, the kangaroo rat, and the Yuma antelope squirrel. One also finds several kinds of skunks and the kit fox, which hunts kangaroo rats and various insects. Larger and more mobile animals, such as the coyote and the puma, or mountain lion, may range the region. A few small herds of bighorn sheep can be found in some of the more remote mountain ranges of the desert.

The terrain of the Arizona Upland is essentially one of alternating rugged mountain chains and broad, flat valleys. The average annual rainfall there ranges from seven to twelve inches. This region is the desert of cacti: cholla, barrel cactus, prickly pear, and the giant saguaro whose blossom is the state flower of Arizona. There is also a great variety of shrubs and small trees, such as the palo verde, mesquite, and ironwood. The two rainy seasons (see Map 7) are reflected by two distinct groups of flowering plants. The winter rains bring out plants that are closely related to the flora of California. The plants that spring up after the summer rains are more Mexican in type.

Just as this region has a greater diversity of plant life, so it also has a greater variety of animal life. In the Arizona Upland one can find both the desert mule deer and the Sonora white-tailed deer. The peccary, or javelina, roams the valleys, while the bobcat and the ringtail prefer the rough foothills of the mountains. The occasional running streams and ponds in the desert provide living conditions for plants, and their associated animals and birds, of types that are usually found only in damper climates.

The adaptation of plants and animals to life in a country of high temperatures and low and uncertain humidity is truly amazing. The seeds of many small plants may lie dormant on the ground for several years until climatic conditions are right. Then they germinate, grow a few inches, flower, go to seed, and die all in the space of a few days. Some plants, such as most of the cacti, through extensive root systems pick up water and store it in a spongy interior protected by spines. Other plants, such as the ocotillo, shed their leaves in dry seasons and put them out during rainy periods, sometimes several times a year. Still other plants coat their leaves with a waxy substance that reduces transpiration, or evaporation from the leaf surface.

The Yuma antelope squirrel avoids the heat of the desert, where ground temperatures can reach 150° F. by retreating into its burrow and going into a deathlike trance called estivation. In this condition its respiration and loss of body moisture are greatly reduced. The bannertail kangaroo rat of the Arizona Upland needs very little free water because its digestive system can, through complex chemical processes, manufacture water from its normal diet of dry seeds. In addition, this rat plugs the entrance holes to its burrow during the heat of day, sealing out the heat and sealing in its body moisture. To gain better traction on soft sand, the kit fox has developed hair on the soles of its feet, and the fringed lizard has flaps on the edges of its feet. The sidewinder, or horned rattlesnake, has developed a strange sidewise movement over the ground. Most animals and birds of the Sonoran Desert either restrict their summer daytime activities to the early morning and late afternoon hours or they are strictly nocturnal.

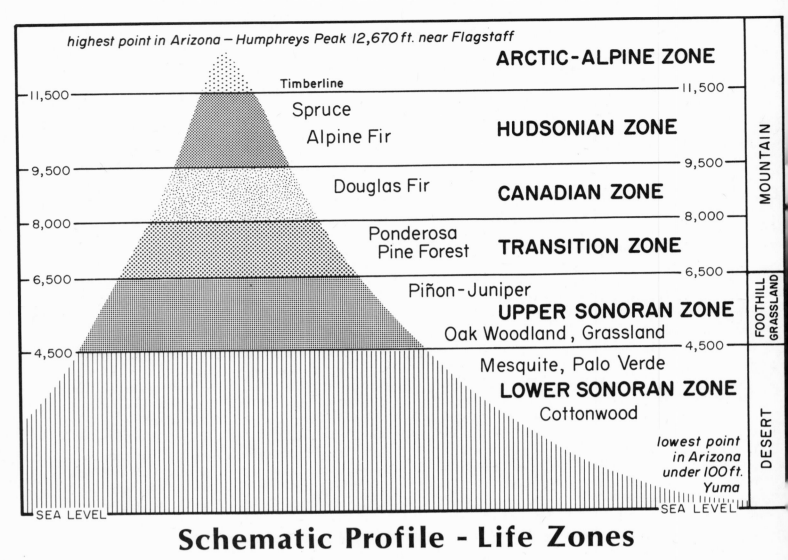

highest point in Arizona – Humphreys Peak 12,670 ft. near Flagstaff

ARCTIC-ALPINE ZONE

Timberline — 11,500 —

— 11,500 —

Spruce
Alpine Fir

HUDSONIAN ZONE

— 9,500 —

Douglas Fir

CANADIAN ZONE

— 8,000 —

Ponderosa
Pine Forest

TRANSITION ZONE

— 6,500 —

Piñon-Juniper

UPPER SONORAN ZONE

Oak Woodland, Grassland

— 4,500 —

Mesquite, Palo Verde

LOWER SONORAN ZONE

Cottonwood

*lowest point
in Arizona
under 100 ft.
Yuma*

MOUNTAIN

FOOTHILL GRASSLAND

DESERT

SEA LEVEL

SEA LEVEL

Schematic Profile - Life Zones

9. LIFE ZONES

SCIENTISTS HAVE DEVELOPED a number of sets of names for the different environments found in Arizona as typified by specific species of plants and animals. As plants are dependent on climate and climate is greatly affected by elevation, within broad limits the different life zones begin and end at certain elevations above sea level. To some extent animals are dependent on plants and so may be restricted to certain zones. Unfortunately for the general reader, these elevations are not exact and vary considerably according to various authorities. This book follows the work of C. Hart Merriam in this section. Another factor is that during prolonged periods of drought or of above-average precipitation the boundaries shift upward or downward. This book, in general, uses the popular or more descriptive names.

Desert vegetation is prevented from moving to higher elevations by its inability to function in colder temperatures. Plants normally found in higher elevations cannot move downward because of their year-round dependence on available moisture in the soil and their inability to resist drought.

The lower elevations, from one hundred feet to about four thousand feet, occur in the Sonoran Desert and have been given special treatment (Map 8). Above the Arizona Upland, at elevations of four thousand to five thousand feet, in the southeastern part of the state and below the Mogollon Rim is a temperate steppe zone where the average rainfall is ten to fifteen inches a year. Here are located the grasslands that supported large herds of cattle as early as the 1820's. Beginning in the 1880's, these grasslands have been badly degraded by the invasion of mesquite and other woody plants and by deep erosion of the stream beds. This erosion has drained most of the *ciénagas*, or wet meadows. This zone is the range of mule deer, whitetailed deer, and a few pronghorn antelope.

Above the desert grassland, in some parts of the state, is the Chaparral Zone, a belt of closely spaced shrubs that range from three to seven feet tall. They are so closely spaced that it is almost impossible to ride through the area. In the southern part of the state, oak woodlands are found above the grassland. In this zone the rainfall varies from twelve to twenty-three inches a year. Deer and antelope hide under the small trees, and scaled quail and the Sonora spiny lizard may be found.

Still higher, in the northern part of the state, is the Evergreen Woodland of juniper and piñon. This zone is approximately the upper limit of the range of the mountain lion (Puma, Cougar) and javelina (Peccary, Wild Pig). It is also the lower limit of the few bears still to be found. The harlequin quail is native to this zone. According to some scientists, this is the upper limit of the Upper Sonoran Desert.

Above the Juniper-Piñon Zone one enters the Transition Zone, where the dominant tree is the ponderosa pine and precipitation ranges from eighteen to twenty-six inches. The pines may be as much as 500 years old, and when mature they may reach 125 feet in height. The ponderosa pine is the primary support of the state's logging industry. In this zone one finds the wild turkey.

Still higher occurs the Canadian Life Zone or Fir Forest, whose dominant tree is the Douglas fir. These trees may reach a height of 150 feet and attain an age of 200 to 400 years. As the environmental tolerances of fir, spruce, and pine overlap, it is often difficult to locate the dividing line between these last two zones. In general, the Canadian Life Zone extends from eight thousand to ninety-five hundred feet, and the annual precipitation is approximately twenty-five to thirty inches. This is the upper limit of the range of the mule deer and white-tailed deer.

Still higher, at elevations ranging from 9,000 to 11,500 feet, is the Hudsonian Life Zone, or Spruce-Alpine Forest, which receives about thirty to thirty-five inches of precipitation a year. The primary trees are the Engelmann spruce, blue spruce, and bristlecone pine. Here the trees reach a height of only some 80 feet, but may be more than 250 years old.

At the upper limit of the Hudsonian Zone one passes the timberline—that line above which trees cannot grow. Above the timberline is the Arctic-Alpine Zone. This zone appears only atop the San Francisco Peaks near Flagstaff. Low temperatures, very rocky soil, and strong ground winds restrict plant life to herbs, grasses, and lichens. Only one vertebrate is native to this zone—the water pipit, a small and very hardy bird.

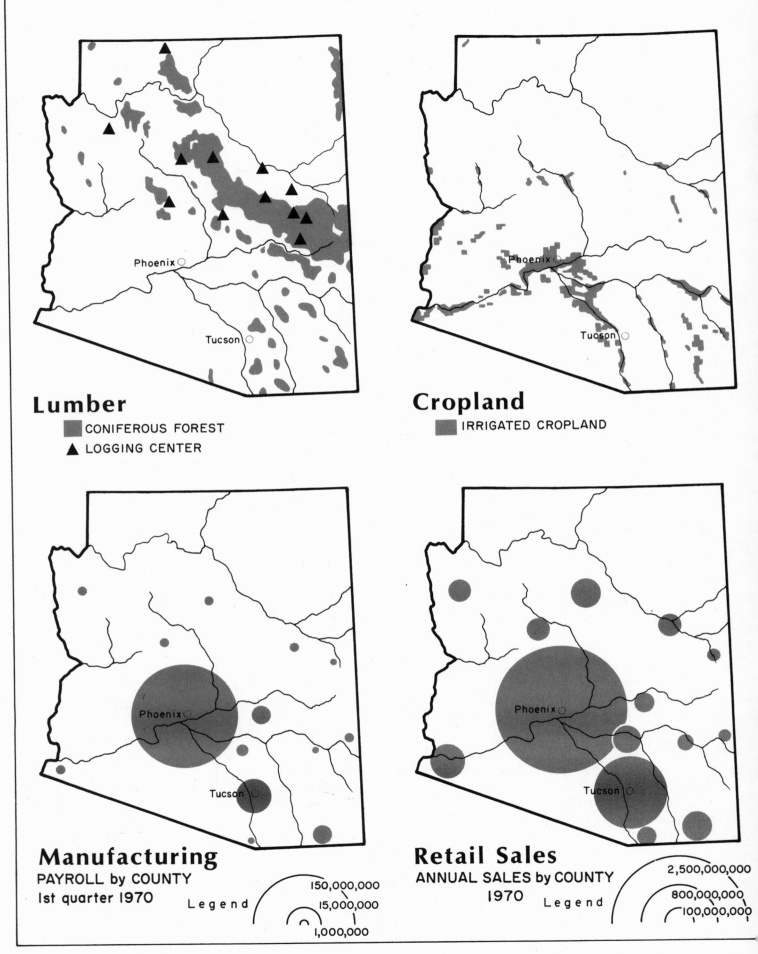

Lumber

▨ CONIFEROUS FOREST
▲ LOGGING CENTER

Cropland

▨ IRRIGATED CROPLAND

Manufacturing
PAYROLL by COUNTY
1st quarter 1970

Legend

150,000,000
15,000,000
1,000,000

Retail Sales
ANNUAL SALES by COUNTY
1970

Legend

2,500,000,000
800,000,000
100,000,000

10. ECONOMY

MANY OF THE EARLY INDIANS of Arizona were agriculturists, raising corn, beans, squash, melons and cotton on irrigated plots along the Gila River and its tributaries. Along the Colorado River the natives relied on the spring floods to moisten the soil for planting. On the Colorado Plateau the Indians raised only small crops of corn. As early as 1697 Father Eusebio Francisco Kino brought cattle, sheep, horses, and European fruits and vegetables into southern Arizona.

The availability of water controls the amount and distribution of agriculture. There are a few areas where underground water is close enough to the surface to warrant pumping. The chief crops of the irrigated river valleys are citrus of several varieties, dates, pima longstaple cotton, alfalfa, grain sorghum, and barley.

Cattle raising has always been an important sector of Arizona's agriculture. During the early 1800's, large ranches developed in the southern part of the state, but Apache depredations forced their abandonment. The demand for beef in California, after 1849, resulted in large herds being driven from Texas and Sonora. Some of the animals were sold in Tucson. This ranching peaked in the 1880's. The Aztec Land and Cattle Company, or "Hashknife" outfit, operated on the railroad land grant of the Atchison, Topeka & Santa Fe Railroad in the northern part of the state.

Sheep raising on a large scale began in 1866 when Juan Candelaria imported a large flock from New Mexico. These animals usually wintered in the valleys south of the Mogollon Rim and spent the summer on higher mountain pastures. The United States Forest Service set aside special trails for this seasonal migration.

The early period of Arizona industry was largely extractive: mining, lumbering, and cattle raising. Manufacturing was restricted to the processing of local raw materials. The census of 1870 listed eighteen manufacturing establishments with a capital of $15,700; they consumed $110,090 worth of raw materials, turned out $185,410 worth of products, and employed eighty-four persons who were paid $45,580 in wages. Sawmills and flour mills made up the majority of the manufactories.

Since World War II there has been a boom in light industry. Taking advantage of the mild climate, a number of large corporations such as Motorola, General Electric, Reynolds Metal, and Hughes Aircraft have opened branches in the Phoenix and Tucson areas. A few lumber product and machine tool producers are located in the northern part of the state. Between 1946 and 1968 manufacturing output tripled to an estimated $2 billion, and manufacturing employment reached 93,200.

Arizona's logging and lumber industry is small but has been vital to the development of the state. Saw timber consists essentially of ponderosa pine (western yellow pine), Douglas fir, and Englemann spruce. About 82 per cent is ponderosa pine, whose soft, fine-grained texture makes it excellent for sashes, doors, flooring, and general mill work.

As early as 1857 timbers for mines in the Tubac area were dragged from the Santa Rita Mountains. Later, the Catalina Mountains provided lumber for the growing city of Tucson. The lumbering industry got its real start when Edward E. Ayer brought to Flagstaff a mill with a daily capacity of 150,000 board feet. This mill was close to the coniferous forests of the Mogollon Rim and provided lumber for the Atlantic and Pacific Railroad, which was then building across the northern part of the state. The burgeoning of the lumber business came at a time when the United States was setting up the national forests, and thus the ruthless destruction of the forests that happened elsewhere was avoided in Arizona. By 1966 the output of the lumber industry reached a value of some $67 million, and the number of employees stood at about forty-two hundred. Of the total output, about half came from Coconino County.

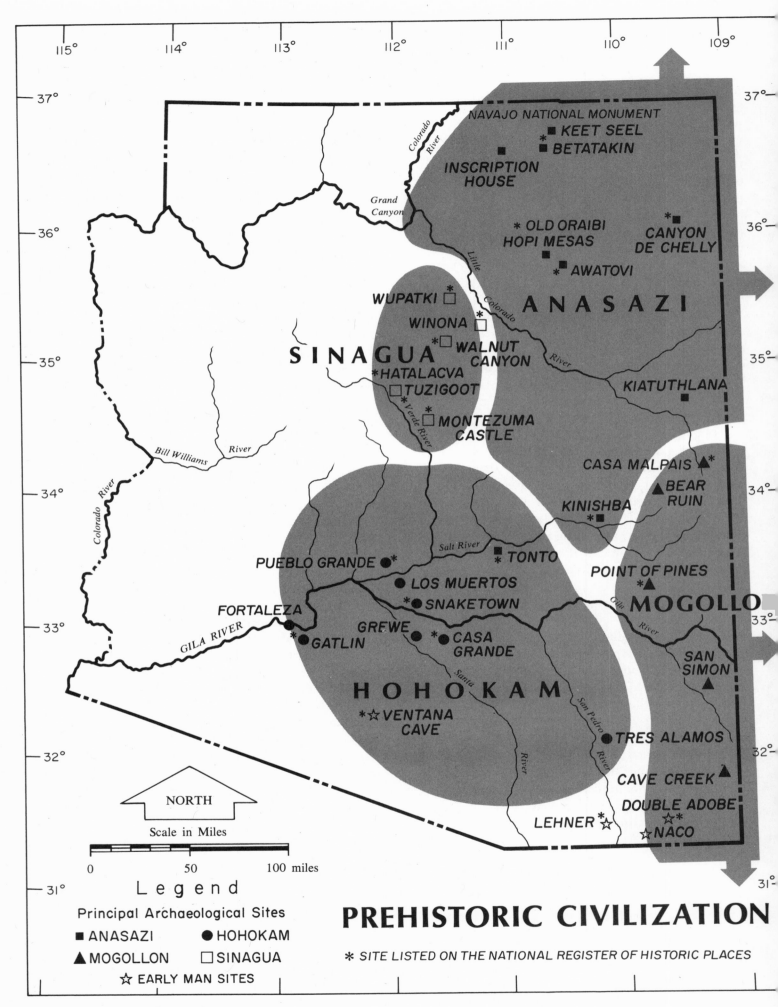

NAVAJO NATIONAL MONUMENT

■ KEET SEEL
＊
■ BETATAKIN
INSCRIPTION ■
HOUSE

＊ OLD ORAIBI
HOPI MESAS ■

＊ AWATOVI

CANYON
DE CHELLY ＊■

A N A S A Z I

WUPATKI ＊
□

WINONA ＊
□

S I N A G U A ＊□ WALNUT
CANYON

＊ HATALACVA
□ TUZIGOOT

□ MONTEZUMA ＊
CASTLE

KIATUTHLANA ■

CASA MALPAIS ▲＊

BEAR ▲
RUIN

KINISHBA
＊■

PUEBLO GRANDE ● ＊

● LOS MUERTOS

＊● SNAKETOWN

Salt River
■ ＊ TONTO

POINT OF PINES
＊▲

M O G O L L O

FORTALEZA
＊● GATLIN

GREWE
● ＊● CASA
GRANDE

Gila River

SAN
SIMON
▲

GILA RIVER

H O H O K A M

＊☆ VENTANA
CAVE

● TRES ALAMOS

CAVE CREEK ▲

DOUBLE ADOBE
☆＊

LEHNER ＊
☆

☆ NACO

NORTH

Scale in Miles

0   50   100 miles

L e g e n d

PREHISTORIC CIVILIZATION

Principal Archaeological Sites

■ ANASAZI   ● HOHOKAM

▲ MOGOLLON   □ SINAGUA

＊ SITE LISTED ON THE NATIONAL REGISTER OF HISTORIC PLACES

☆ EARLY MAN SITES

11. PREHISTORIC CIVILIZATION

THE FIRST KNOWN human inhabitants of America were members of a hunting culture that spread from the Great Plains through New Mexico into eastern Arizona. These people are known chiefly by kill sites where spear points and scrapers of chipped stone have been found in conjunction with the bones of the extinct mammoth, tapir, horse, bison, and camel. Several sites have been found in the southeastern part of the state, and similar artifacts have been found in stream beds in the valley of the Little Colorado River. The finds have been dated as ranging from ten thousand to thirteen thousand years old. It has been postulated that the large animals were exterminated by human hunters rather than by drought, as had been thought earlier.

Possibly at the same time, or slightly later, there developed the Desert Culture in the region lying to the west of the area of the Hunter Culture. The people of the Desert Culture gathered plants and seeds for their food more than they hunted. Most of the artifacts found were for the grinding of seeds, though a few were of a type associated with the chase. Beginning about 5000 B.C., the Cochise Culture was the best representative of the Desert Culture. In some areas, at least, Cochise Man seems to have persisted until the beginning of the Christian era. The first appearance of corn dates at about 3000 B.C. During the eight thousand to nine thousand years of its existence Cochise Culture seems to have made little progress.

An evolution from Cochise Culture was the Mogollon Culture. About 200 to 300 B.C. simple houses and pottery began to appear. The stone implements were of the Cochise type, and the pottery was red-brown in color and undecorated. About the time of Christ the Mogollon Culture was well established. Simple decorations appeared on the pottery, and more varied forms were produced. The atlatl, or spear throwing stick, was the chief hunting instrument, though the bow and arrow seem to have been introduced about this time. The people lived in pit houses and built large ceremonial structures. By about A.D. 1000 this culture was in decline.

The Hohokam Culture evolved in the area generally to the west of the Mogollon, with which it was linked in its early days. This culture was based almost exclusively on irrigated agriculture. Traces of an extensive network of irrigation canals have been found along the Salt and Gila rivers near Phoenix.

On the northern plateau there developed, between 5000 B.C. and A.D. 1400, the Anasazi Culture. Shortly after the time of Christ these people began weaving excellent baskets. Cottonseed and cotton cloth appeared in the area about A.D. 700 to 900. By about A.D. 1000 the early Pueblo Culture was well established, and two hundred years later it had spread south as far as the valleys of the Salt and Gila rivers.

By A.D. 1400 the prehistoric Pueblo Culture was beginning to break up, possibly under pressure from more warlike and nomadic Athapascan people. The people tended to concentrate in larger pueblos where there was enough water to raise crops. Between A.D. 900 and 1000 another regional culture, called Sinagua, evolved near Flagstaff. It was a blend of Mogollon, Hohokam, and Pueblo cultures. About A.D. 1066 a small volcano, Sunset Crater, erupted, spreading a layer of volcanic ash over the countryside. This ash conserved the moisture in the soil and made agriculture very simple. But eventually the wind piled the ash into dunes and exposed the underlying clay soil to dehydration, and the people began to move away.

By the time the early Spaniards arrived in the 1600's, the local Indians knew nothing of the people who had built the great structures like Casa Grande or the amazing cliff dwellings.

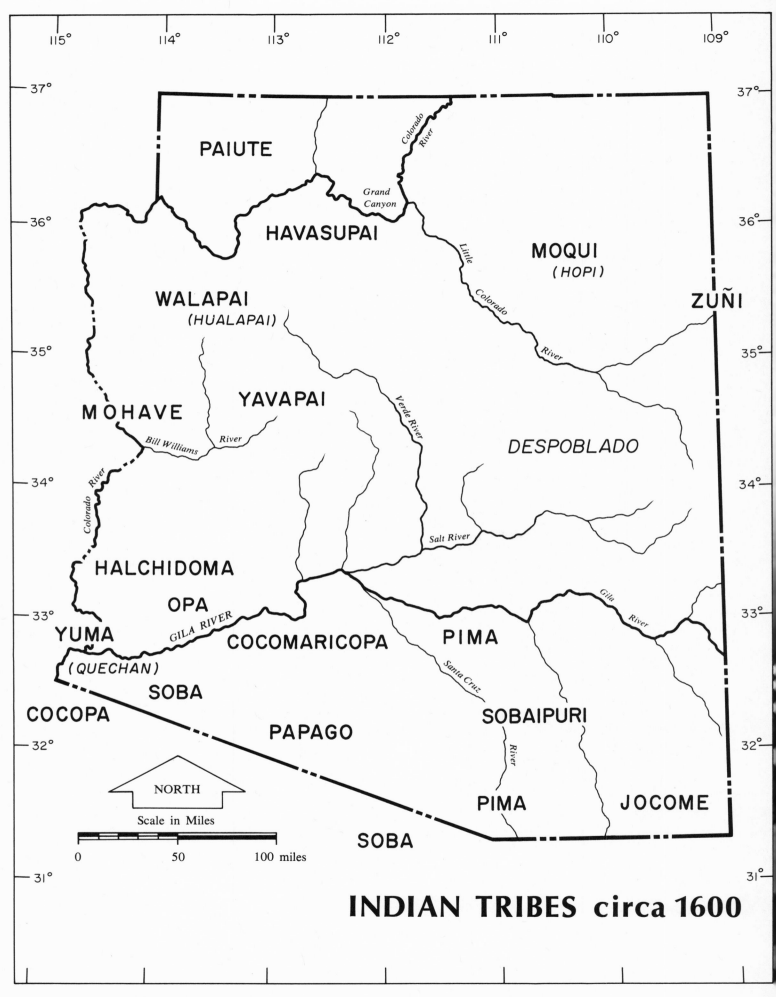

PAIUTE

HAVASUPAI

Grand Canyon

MOQUI
(*HOPI*)

ZUÑI

WALAPAI
(*HUALAPAI*)

Colorado
River

Little

MOHAVE

YAVAPAI

Colorado

River

Bill Williams   *River*

Verde River

DESPOBLADO

Colorado   River

HALCHIDOMA

Salt River

Gila
River

OPA

GILA RIVER

COCOMARICOPA

PIMA

YUMA
(*QUECHAN*)

SOBA

Santa Cruz

SOBAIPURI

COCOPA

PAPAGO

River

PIMA

JOCOME

NORTH

Scale in Miles

0   50   100 miles

SOBA

INDIAN TRIBES circa 1600

ONE OF THE GREATEST PROBLEMS facing the beginner in the study of the Indians of Arizona is the matter of names given the different groups. The early Spanish explorers soon found that there were at least eight different languages spoken by the Indians they met. Many Indian groups identified themselves simply by various words meaning "the people" and other bands or tribes by "the others" or "the enemy." When different writers tried to reduce those words to phonetic spelling, the confusion was doubly confounded. The early Spaniards gave three different names to the Yavapai, Americans have used two distinctly different names, and neighboring tribes have applied six different titles. In almost all cases the areas occupied by different tribes were not clearly defined.

In general, the area south of the Gila River was occupied by people speaking the Piman language, though with different dialects. In the valleys of the San Pedro and Santa Cruz rivers were the Sobaipuris. The Spaniards moved the Sobaipuris from the San Pedro valley about 1762 to replace the Pimas who had died in the unhealthy climate of Guevavi Mission. It was thought that this move would strengthen the Santa Cruz valley missions and rancherias against the Apaches. Instead, it merely opened the door to raiders from the north. The Sobaipuris either died or became mixed with the Pimas.

In the middle Santa Cruz valley were the Pimas. Only among these people did the Spaniards have even limited success in their efforts to civilize and Christianize the native peoples. In the desert west of the Santa Cruz lived the Papagos, a distinct branch of the Pimas.

North and west of the Pimas were some six tribes, all speaking the basic Hokan languages. Along the western portion of the Gila were the Cocomaricopas. From south to north in the Colorado River valley were the Cocopas, Yumas (this tribe now prefers the name Quechan), Halchidomas, and Mojaves. Around Cataract Canyon, a branch of the Grand Canyon of the Colorado, live the Havasupais. In the high country of the central part of the state were the Pai Indians, who later separated into two very closely allied groups, the Yavapai and the Walapai. North of the Grand Canyon dwelt the Uto-Aztecan–speaking Paiutes. On their bleak mesas in the northeastern corner of the state were the Hopis (called Moquis by the Spaniards), also of Uto-Aztecan stock.

The first contact with the tribes of the lower Colorado River was made in 1540 by Hernando de Alarcón, who commanded the supply ships that were supposed to support Coronado's army. Alarcón traveled up the river, possibly as far as Yuma. In 1605 Juan de Oñate's party from New Mexico struck the Colorado at the mouth of Bill Williams River and marched south to the Gulf of California. In his report Oñate mentions two tribes that were probably named by Alarcón, though with different spellings.

From Coronado's entry into Arizona in 1540 until his return to Mexico two years later the area between the Gila and Little Colorado rivers was known as the Despoblado—the uninhabited land. However, by 1775 that area was one of the strongholds of the Western Apaches, who were raiding the settlements of the agricultural Indians of the Gila and San Pedro valleys.

If there were any Navajos in the northeast, they were in such small, nomadic bands that they escaped notice of the early Spaniards of New Mexico. There is reference, as early as 1627, to "Apaches de Navaju" in northwestern New Mexico.

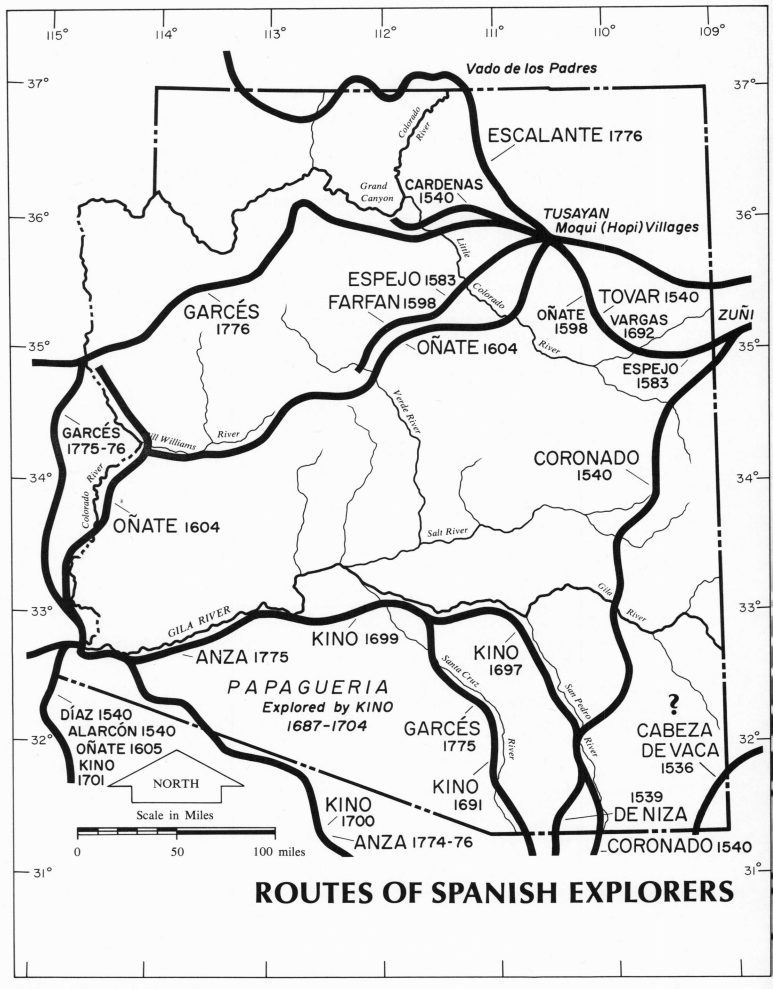

ROUTES OF SPANISH EXPLORERS

Vado de los Padres

ESCALANTE 1776

CARDENAS 1540

Colorado River

Grand Canyon

TUSAYAN
Moqui (Hopi) Villages

Little

Colorado

ESPEJO 1583
FARFAN 1598

GARCÉS 1776

TOVAR 1540

OÑATE 1598

VARGAS 1692

ZUÑI

OÑATE 1604

River

ESPEJO 1583

GARCÉS 1775-76

Bill Williams River

Verde River

Colorado River

CORONADO 1540

OÑATE 1604

Salt River

Gila River

GILA RIVER

KINO 1699

KINO 1697

Gila River

ANZA 1775

PAPAGUERIA
Explored by KINO
1687-1704

Santa Cruz

San Pedro

?

DÍAZ 1540
ALARCÓN 1540
OÑATE 1605
KINO 1701

GARCÉS 1775

River

River

CABEZA
DE VACA
1536

NORTH

KINO 1691

Scale in Miles

KINO 1700

1539
DE NIZA

0   50   100 miles

ANZA 1774-76

CORONADO 1540

13. ROUTES OF SPANISH EXPLORERS

POSSIBLY THE FIRST Spanish penetration into Arizona was that of Álvar Núñez Cabeza de Vaca and three companions who had been shipwrecked on the Texas coast in 1528 and after six years of servitude among the coastal Indians made their escape. On foot they crossed Texas and New Mexico and swung through the southeastern corner of Arizona before reaching Culiacán in Sinaloa. As a result of Cabeza de Vaca's stories of vast riches to the north, the viceroy of New Spain sent Fray Marcos de Niza with Esteban the Moor, one of Cabeza de Vaca's companions, to check the tales. Esteban, going in advance, was killed at a Zuñi village, and Fray Marcos returned south.

The reports of Fray Marcos, added to those of Cabeza de Vaca, caused the viceroy to send out an expedition commanded by Francisco Vásquez de Coronado. Marching north from Culiacán, the army entered Arizona via the San Pedro Valley, crossed the Mogollon Rim, and marched up the Zuñi River to the westernmost Zuñi pueblo, Háwikuh, which they reached in July, 1540. From there Coronado sent out exploring parties. Captain Pedro de Tovar led a small group to visit the Moqui towns. García López de Cárdenas later was sent to investigate a great river to the west reported by Tovar. These were the first white men to see the Grand Canyon. Meanwhile, Melchior Díaz had left the intermediate camp near Corazones (Ures), Sonora, in an attempt to contact the supply vessels commanded by Alarcón in the Gulf of California. Díaz reached Yuma only to learn that the ships had sailed away. After two years in New Mexico, Coronado returned to Mexico by the route he had used going north.

Not until 1583 was there another *entrada*. In that year Don Antonio de Espejo, governor of Nuevo México, led an expedition westward from Santa Fe in search of mineral wealth. The most extensive exploration in the seventeenth century was made by Don Juan de Oñate in 1604–1605. Marching west from New Mexico, he reached the Colorado River and followed it downstream to tidewater.

The first Spanish explorer who left a moderately accurate record of his travels was the Jesuit missionary Father Eusebio Francisco Kino, who had been trained as a mathematician and cartographer. Kino traveled extensively in the triangle bounded by the San Pedro and Gila rivers and the present international boundary. Based on these trips, between 1691 and 1702, Kino prepared maps that showed most of the Indian rancherias.

In 1692 Alférez (Lieutenant) Juan Matheo Ramírez descended the San Pedro as far as Benson in search of horses stolen from a Sonoran mission. In the same year Don Diego de Vargas visited the Moqui villages from Santa Fe.

In 1774 the viceroy sent Captain Juan Bautista de Anza from Tubac along the Camino del Diablo to Yuma and on to Mission San Gabriel in California. In the following year Anza led a colony of California-bound settlers along the Santa Cruz and Gila rivers. Traveling with the captain on both trips was the restless Franciscan missionary Fray Francisco Garcés. Returning from California in 1774, Garcés left the party and traveled into northern Arizona to visit the Yavapais. On the 1775 trip Garcés recrossed the Colorado River near present-day Needles and visited the Moqui town of Oraibi before returning to San Xavier by way of the Colorado.

In an attempt to open a land route between Santa Fe and California, Fathers Silvestre Vélez de Escalante and Francisco Atanasio Dominguez traveled into western Colorado and southern Utah before returning to Santa Fe across northeastern Arizona.

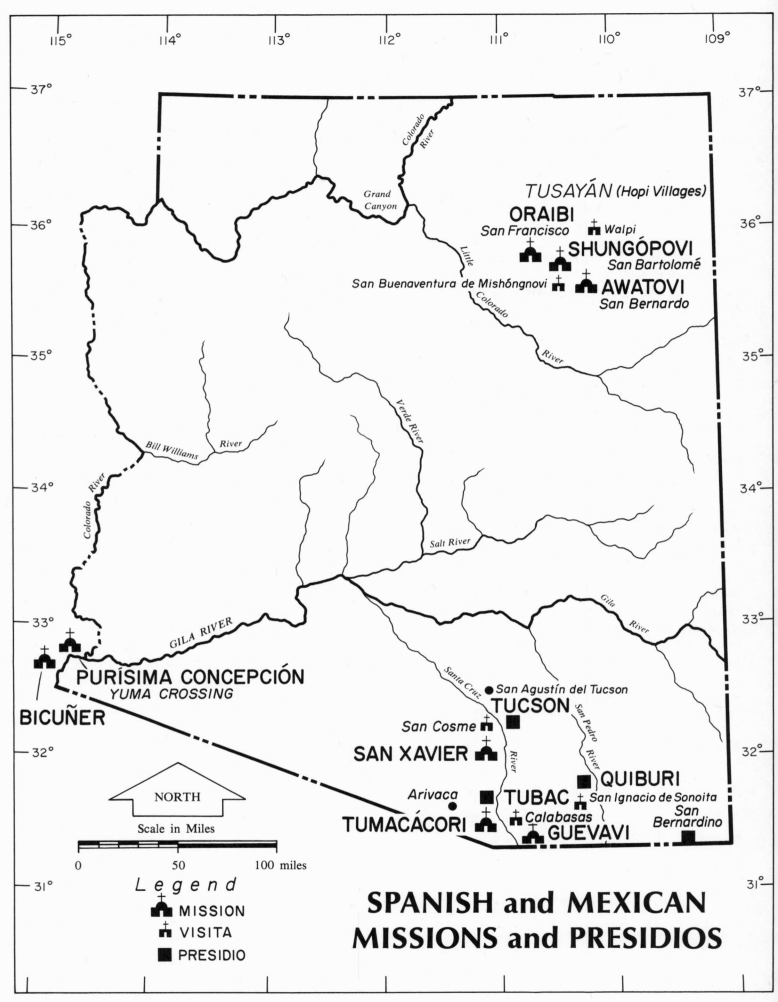

TUSAYÁN (Hopi Villages)

ORAIBI
San Francisco ☩ Walpi
SHUNGÓPOVI
San Bartolomé
San Buenaventura de Mishóngnovi ☩
AWATOVI
San Bernardo

Grand Canyon

Colorado River

Little

Colorado

River

Bill Williams   River

Colorado River

Verde River

Salt River

Gila River

GILA RIVER

Gila River

PURÍSIMA CONCEPCIÓN
YUMA CROSSING

BICUÑER

Santa Cruz

● San Agustín del Tucson
TUCSON
San Cosme ☩ ■
SAN XAVIER

San Pedro River

River

QUIBURI ■
Arivaca
● TUBAC ■ ☩ San Ignacio de Sonoita
☩ Calabasas San Bernardino
TUMACÁCORI ☩
GUEVAVI ■

NORTH

Scale in Miles

0   50   100 miles

Legend
MISSION
VISITA
PRESIDIO

SPANISH and MEXICAN
MISSIONS and PRESIDIOS

14. SPANISH AND MEXICAN MISSIONS AND PRESIDIOS

THROUGHOUT THE PERIOD of her rule in North America, Spain sought to Christianize and civilize the native population to make them worthy citizens of her new empire. The two great institutions employed were the ecclesiastical mission and the military presidio. Missions formed the forward line of northward expansion until contact was made with more warlike Indians in the American Southwest; then the presidios moved to the front.

The first missions in Arizona were planted among the Hopi Indians by Franciscans (Order of Friars Minor) from Santa Fe in 1629. The Hopis resisted conversion, and several missionaries earned the crown of martyrdom. The effort was terminated by the Pueblo Revolt of 1680 in New Mexico. Also, the Jesuits complained that the Franciscans were proselyting in their territory.

The early explorers were accompanied by priests, but it was not until Father Eusebio Francisco Kino reached Sonora in 1687 that missionary work began in earnest. From Mission Nuestra Señora de los Dolores, Father Kino visited many of the Indians living south of the Gila River. Shelters for saying Mass and houses for visiting priests were built, cattle and sheep were given to the Indians, and crops of grain were planted. Thus, when priests could be assigned, there would be the wherewithal for their support.

Following Kino's death in 1711, the missions of Arizona were neglected for twenty-five years while Spain was involved in Europe's War of the Spanish Succession. The Arizona missions were visited occasionally by priests from Sonora.

When the Jesuits were expelled·from the Spanish Empire in 1767, the Franciscans took over and made some changes in mission organization. Tumacácori became a *cabacera*, a mission with a resident pastor, and Guevavi became a *visita*, a chapel visited from time to time. The present Tumacácori church was completed about 1822 and was abandoned in 1848. The present church at San Xavier was started about 1783, completed in 1797, and staffed continuously until 1828. Bernardo Middendorff, S. J., founded a mission at San Agustín del Tucson in 1757, but it was a transitory effort.

When the Pima Indians revolted in 1751, San Xavier and Guevavi were plundered, but the missionaries escaped. As a result, a new presidio was established at Tubac. This fort, manned by fifty soldiers, became the center of the first recorded white settlement in Arizona. Late in 1775 or early in 1776 the Tubac garrison was moved to a new presidio at Tucson to protect Mission San Xavier. The authorized strength of 106 officers and men was seldom filled. A few years later Tubac was regarrisoned by a company of Pima Indians. The fort was abandoned in 1848, and the population of the town was moved to Tucson.

To block Russian expansion south along the Pacific coast, missions were established in Alta California in the 1760's. A land route had to be established and the crossing of the Colorado River had to be secured. For reasons of economy, the new settlements were to combine mission, presidio, and pueblo. This close proximity of priests, soldiers, and settlers was something new on the Spanish frontier. Two missions were established on the California bank of the Colorado in 1780—La Purísima Concepción opposite Yuma and San Pedro y San Pablo de Bicuñer some four leagues downstream. Disregard of the rights of local Indians led to a revolt by the Yumas in the following year. The four priests, including Father Francisco Garcés, the most active Franciscan missionary, and most of the male Spaniards were killed and the missions plundered. This was the only effort to take control of the crossing.

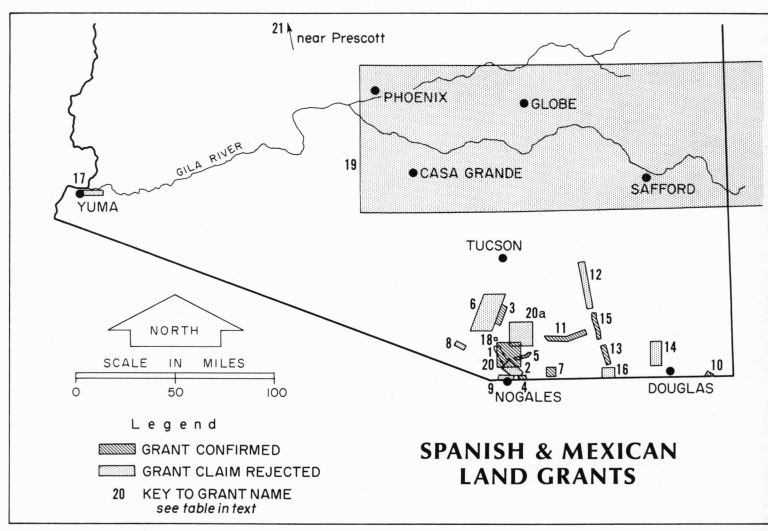

SPANISH & MEXICAN
LAND GRANTS

In the 1890's, the Court of Private Land Claims considered the following claims:

NUMBER ON MAP	NAME OF GRANT CLAIM	ACREAGE CLAIMED	ACREAGE APPROVED OR REJECTED	SUCCESSFUL CLAIMANT
1. Tumacácori		81,350	rejected	
2. Calabasas				
3. San Ignacio de la Canoa		46,696	17,204	Maish & Driscoll
4. Buenavista (María Santísima del Carmén)		17,354	5,733	Maish & Driscoll
5. San José de Sonoita		7,593	5,123	Santiago Ainsa
6. El Sopori		141,722	rejected	
7. San Rafael de la Zanja		152,890	17,352	Colin Cameron
8. Aribaca		8,677	rejected	
9. Los Nogales de Elías		32,763	rejected	
10. San Bernardino		13,746	2,383	John Slaughter
11. San Ignacio del Babocomari		123,069	33,792	Robert Perrin
12. Tres Alamos		43,385	rejected	
13. San Rafael del Valle		20,034	17,475	Juan Pedro Camoul
14. Agua Prieta		68,530	rejected	
15. Ranchos de las Boquillas		30,728	17,354	William R. Hearst
16. San Pedro		38,622	rejected	
17. Algodones		21,692	rejected	
18. Otero (Tubac claim)		1,199	claim not filed	
		850,050	116,416	
19. Peralta-Reavis		11,280,000	rejected	fraudulent claim
20. Baca Float Number 3			94,289	Lieu Land selection
21. Baca Float Number 5			99,000	Lieu Land selection
		12,130,050	309,705	

15. SPANISH AND MEXICAN LAND GRANTS

As the frontier of New Spain moved northward, close behind the missions and presidios came the *haciendados* (farmers) and *rancheros* (ranchers). Spain encouraged settlement by making large grants of land to potential settlers, and Mexico followed the same policy.

On application for a grant, a minimum value was placed on the land, it was surveyed, and a public auction was held. An original grant for stock raising was for four *sitios*, or four square leagues (17,350 acres). However. if a grantee could prove that he needed more land for his herds, he could purchase, as "overplus," adjoining lands at the original purchase price.

Most of the petitions for grants in southern Arizona were filed between 1820 and 1833, although the Los Nogales de Elías petition was filed in 1841. These grants were largely for former mission lands. The boundaries were very vaguely stated. Sometimes the *titulo* (deed) merely granted so much land within a larger tract. At other times the limits were set by settlement, possession, or other acceptable evidence. These vague descriptions caused trouble when Americans sought to settle on or near these grants.

The Gadsden Treaty stipulated that claimants to the grants must find evidence in Mexican archives. The surveyor general of the territory investigated the claims and reported on their validity to the secretary of the interior, who then referred the matter to Congress for final action. By 1888 thirteen claims had been approved and two rejected, but Congress had not acted on any. In 1891 the Court of Private Land Claims was set up by the federal government to settle such cases in Arizona and New Mexico. When the court finally went out of business in 1904, it had confirmed title to 116,400 acres out of 850,100 acres claimed in Arizona.

By the middle of the nineteenth century the pre-sidio system in Sonora had deteriorated under the impact of civil war in Mexico, and most of the ranches were abandoned because of Apache attacks. By 1848 the only white settlement left was Tucson. Not until the 1870's, when the Apache menace had been well subdued, did Americans feel safe on isolated ranches. Many of the abandoned ranches were then claimed by California speculators who had bought out the descendants of the original grantees. This absentee ownership caused much bitterness among settlers who wanted to start working the idle land.

An additional problem appeared when the Baca family of New Mexico was granted the right to select land in the public domain of Arizona and New Mexico in lieu of land granted to the town of Las Vegas, New Mexico. The Bacas selected three tracts, called "floats," in New Mexico and two in Arizona. Originally, Baca Float Number 3, comprising 94,289 acres, overlay most of the Tumacácori claim and much of the Calabasas and San José de Sonoita grants. In 1866 the float was moved northeastward about five miles. Although the floats were not supposed to include mineral lands, the new location neatly blanketed the mining areas of the Santa Rita Mountains. The case was not settled by the United States Supreme Court until 1914. Baca Float Number 5 centered on Francis Creek in Yavapai County and was confirmed for 99,000 acres.

The most widely known claim was the fraudulent Peralta-Reavis claim. James Addison Reavis had worked in the St. Louis land office where he handled many old documents. With this experience he forged a series of papers to support his claim. For a while he sold quitclaim deeds to settlers in the Salt River valley and taxed the Southern Pacific Railroad for running its trains over his land. In June, 1895, the Court of Private Land Claims disallowed the claim, and Reavis went to prison for forgery.

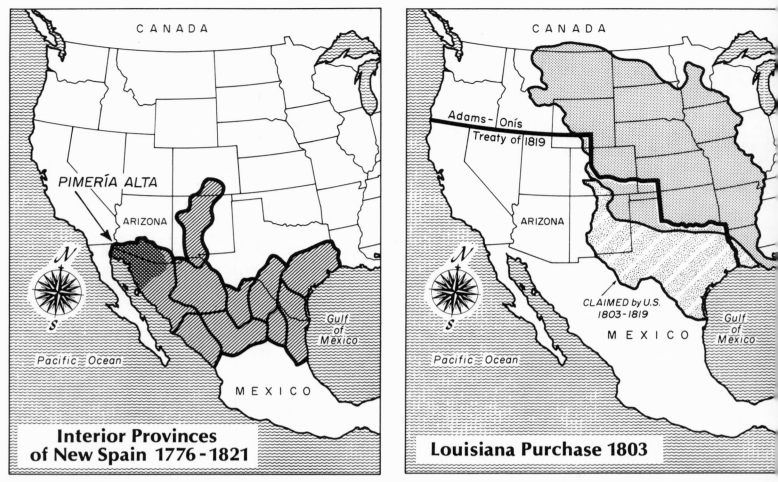

Interior Provinces of New Spain 1776-1821

PIMERÍA ALTA
ARIZONA
Pacific Ocean
Gulf of Mexico
MEXICO
CANADA

Louisiana Purchase 1803

Adams-Onís Treaty of 1819
ARIZONA
CLAIMED by U.S. 1803-1819
MEXICO
Pacific Ocean
Gulf of Mexico
CANADA

16A. INTERIOR PROVINCES OF NEW SPAIN, 1776–1821

ARIZONA WAS NEVER a province with its own government under Spanish or Mexican rule, as was New Mexico. The white-inhabited area, that part lying south of the Gila River, was a portion of a larger subdivision of New Spain or Mexico. In the northeast, the area around the Moqui pueblos was thought to be part of Nuevo México, though no effective administration was ever established.

Based on the discoveries of Columbus, the Papal Line of Demarkation of 1493, and the Treaty of Tordesillas with Portugal in 1494, Spain claimed all the Western Hemisphere except the bulge of South America—Brazil. Spain never bothered to indicate how far north Sonora extended or how far west New Mexico reached. These provinces were assumed to extend indefinitely into the uninhabited regions. Only California had a vague boundary with Sonora—the Colorado River.

The first map showing southern Arizona was Kino's "Teatro de los Trabajos Apostolicos," drawn in 1695–96. This map shows Pimería, the land of the Pima Indians, as an ill-defined area astride the Santa Cruz River between the Gila and the Río Sonora. Later, Pimería was separated into Pimería Alta and Pimería Baja, with the Río Altar in Sonora as the dividing line.

In 1693 Sonora was separated from the province of Sinaloa and given a *capitan-gubernador* who was responsible to the governor of the province of Nueva Viscaya. A governmental unit called Sinaloa y Sonora was formed in 1734. The new province was answerable to Mexico City.

Because of the long delay in getting administrative action from Mexico City, the northern provinces from Texas to California were, in 1776, formed into what amounted to a new viceroyalty, the Provincias Internas, or Interior Provinces, directly responsible to the crown in Spain. The great extent of the Interior Provinces led to their division into three districts, the westernmost comprising Sinaloa, Sonora, and California. Eight years later a reorganization dropped some of the provinces and consolidated the rest into a single unit. This arrangement held until the Mexican Revolution in 1822.

The new government separated Sinaloa and Sonora, with the capital of the latter at Ures. It soon proved to be a hasty measure, as Sonora needed the help of wealthier Sinaloa to combat the Yaqui Indians. A decree of February, 1824, recombined the two provinces as the Estado Interno de Occidente. The state of Occidente was dissolved in 1851, and Sonora was again a separate province.

16B. LOUISIANA PURCHASE, 1803

AS THE UNITED STATES expanded westward, trouble arose with Spain over the borders. When Napoleon sold Louisiana to the United States in 1803, the boundaries were merely stated as those "as acquired from Spain." However, Spain had never laid down the northern boundaries of her claim. Finally, in 1819 the Adams-Onís Treaty drew the first clear border. By the treaty Spain ceded Florida to the United States and gave up a shadowy claim to the Oregon country. At the same time, the United States surrendered a rather weak claim that Texas had been included in the Louisiana Purchase.

All of Texas, New Mexico, Arizona, California, Nevada, and Utah, as well as parts of Colorado, Kansas, Oklahoma, and Wyoming, remained under the nominal control of Spain. Spanish settlements in all this area consisted of a line of villages along the Río Grande as far north as Taos, some missions and presidios in southern Arizona, and a string of missions and villages along the coast of California up to San Rafael, north of San Francisco Bay.

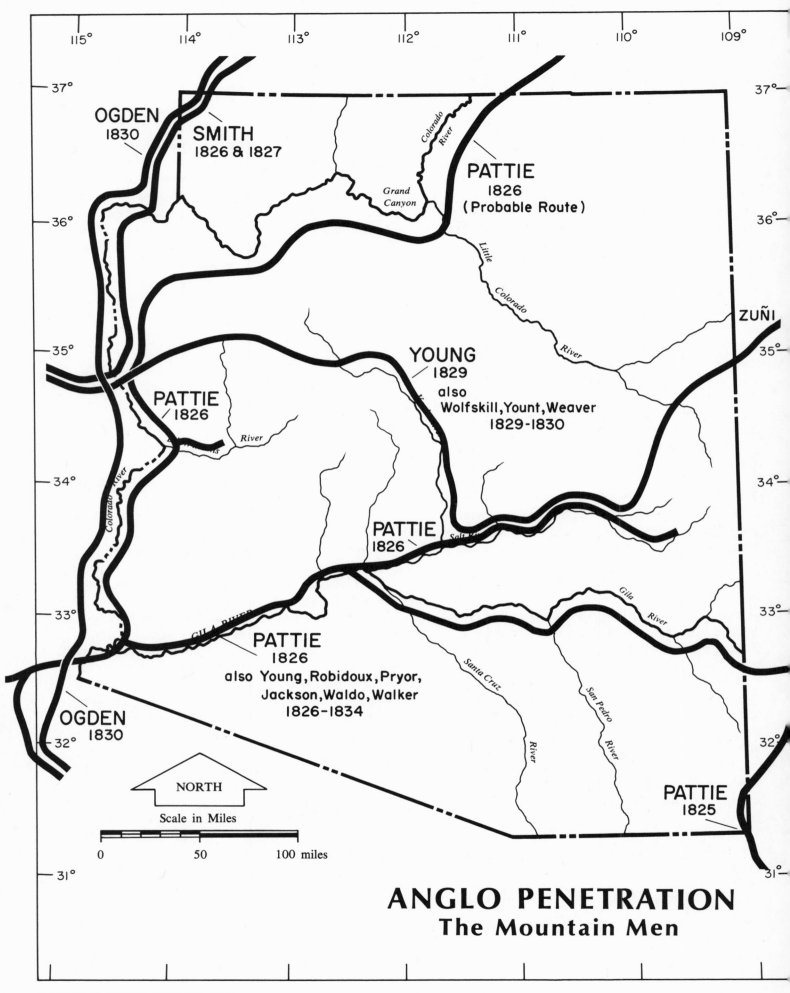

OGDEN
1830

SMITH
1826 & 1827

Colorado River

PATTIE
1826
(Probable Route)

*Grand
Canyon*

*Little
Colorado
River*

ZUÑI

PATTIE
1826

River

YOUNG
1829
also
Wolfskill, Yount, Weaver
1829-1830

Colorado River

PATTIE
1826

Salt River

*Gila
River*

OGDEN
1830

PATTIE
1826
also Young, Robidoux, Pryor,
Jackson, Waldo, Walker
1826-1834

GILA RIVER

*Santa Cruz
River*

*San Pedro
River*

PATTIE
1825

NORTH

Scale in Miles

0   50   100 miles

ANGLO PENETRATION
The Mountain Men

© 1979 by the University of Oklahoma Press

17. ANGLO PENETRATION: THE MOUNTAIN MEN

THE FIRST RECORDED PENETRATIONS by Anglo-Americans into Arizona were those of the fur traders and trappers—the "mountain men"—operating westward out of Santa Fe and Taos, New Mexico.

The first penetration was made in 1825 when Sylvester Pattie and his son, James Ohio Pattie, with a party of about a dozen men, trapped a section of the Gila River. In 1826 the Patties again entered Arizona along the Gila. While trapping the middle Gila most of the party were killed by Indians. Three survivors joined a party of about thirty men led by Ewing Young that was also working the Gila and some of its tributaries. The Young party moved up the Salt River to its junction with the Verde. Here the party divided, part following the Verde to its source and the others following the Salt to its headwaters in the White Mountains. The two sections rejoined and trapped down the Salt and Gila rivers to the Colorado. Trapping up along the Colorado, the men left Arizona with the river. In 1827 both Patties led another party down the Gila to the Colorado. Here the party split, with some, under William Workman, returning to New Mexico; the rest, under the Patties, pushing on to the Pacific Coast. In the following year Ewing Young and a small party again trapped the upper Gila. In 1829 Young, with forty men, including Kit Carson, trapped down the Salt and up the Verde. There Young's party divided, with part returning to New Mexico and the rest, including Young and Carson, setting off for California.

Occurring at the same time as the activities of the Patties was the penetration made in 1826 by Jedediah S. Smith, who left the trappers' rendezvous at Bear Lake on the Idaho-Utah line and entered Arizona by traveling down the Virgin River to the Colorado. He then made his way down the latter river to the vicinity of present-day Needles, California, and then struck westward to the Pacific Coast. In the following year Smith again traveled from Bear Lake to California over a route lying a bit to the east of his earlier route.

In 1830 William Wolfskill, in an attempt to open a profitable trade between Santa Fe and California, traveled through southern Colorado and Utah and entered Arizona by the Virgin River. Leaving the Colorado near Needles, he proceeded to the Pacific Coast.

Two parties followed the Gila Trail in 1831 (Map 40). David E. Jackson took a party to California to buy horses and mules, and Ewing Young again worked the Gila and Colorado rivers. During the decade of the 1830's, several parties traded with the Apaches along the Gila River near where Safford stands today. In 1836 a group led by James Kirker traded guns, powder, and lead for horses, which they sold in New Mexico. Some of the men also panned for gold.

Besides the mountain men and others of whose entries into Arizona we have a written record, several hundred unknown travelers undoubtedly moved back and forth through the area. By 1846 the Gila Trail was a well-known route across the territory, and other sections had been traversed by parties of trappers. There was considerable knowledge of Arizona geography stored away in the heads of these mountain men, but little, if any, of this knowledge was committed to paper. It was from this body of knowledgeable mountain men that the United States Army surveyors and engineers obtained the guides they needed to show them the trails and water holes. In this group were such men as Kit Carson and Antoine Robidoux, who guided General Stephen Watts Kearny's Army of the West, and Antoine Leroux and Pauline Weaver, who guided Lieutenant Colonel Philip St. George Cooke's Mormon Battalion, served the United States–Mexican Boundary Commission, and worked for Captain Lorenzo Sitgreaves and Lieutenant Amiel W. Whipple in the northern part of the state.

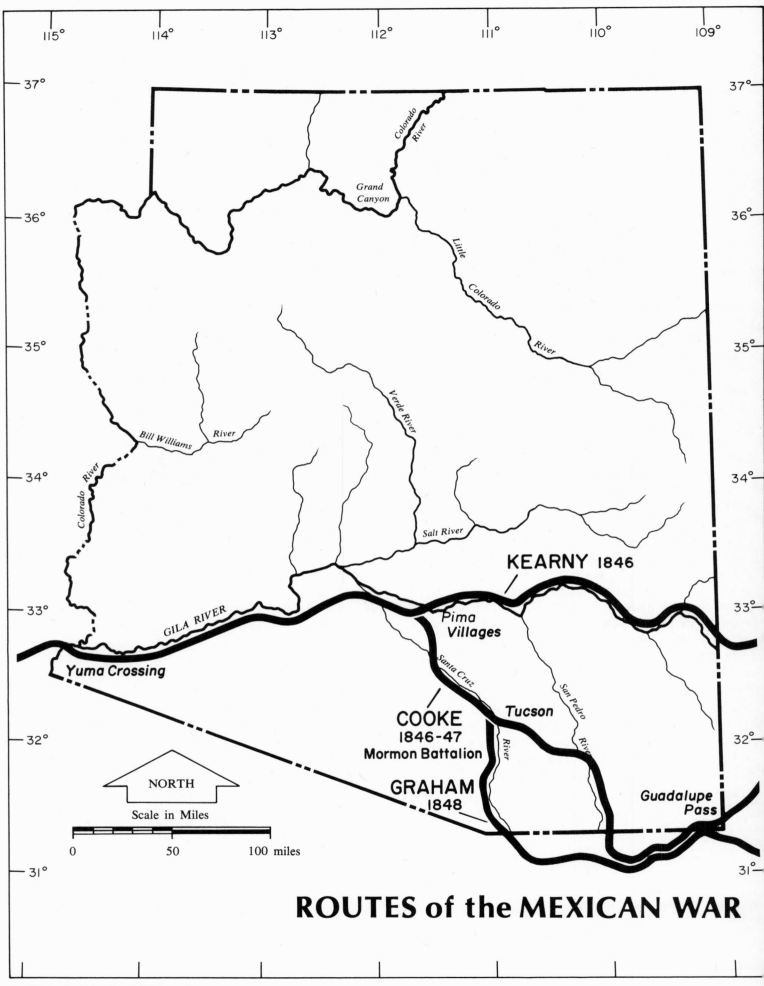

ROUTES of the MEXICAN WAR

KEARNY 1846

Pima Villages

COOKE
1846-47
Mormon Battalion

GRAHAM
1848

Yuma Crossing

Tucson

Guadalupe
Pass

GILA RIVER

Colorado River

Bill Williams River

Verde River

Salt River

Little Colorado River

Grand Canyon

Santa Cruz River

San Pedro River

NORTH

Scale in Miles

0   50   100 miles

18. ROUTES OF THE MEXICAN WAR

WHEN WAR WITH MEXICO broke out in 1846, a small military force, designated as the Army of the West, was collected at Fort Leavenworth, Kansas, under the command of Colonel Stephen Watts Kearny. The army consisted of some three hundred regulars of the First Regiment of Dragoons, the First Missouri Mounted Rifles (volunteers), three independent companies of volunteers, one company of Indian scouts, and one battalion plus two batteries of volunteer artillery—a total of 1,650 men with sixteen artillery pieces. The mission of this force was to conquer New Mexico and California and establish United States control over the vast area of the American Southwest.

Following the bloodless conquest of New Mexico in August, Kearny, who had been promoted to brigadier general, set out for California with three hundred dragoons and two mountain howitzers. Marching south from Santa Fe along the Río Grande, the general met Lieutenant Christopher "Kit" Carson, who was traveling to Washington with dispatches announcing that Commodore Robert F. Stockton of the navy and Lieutenant Colonel John C. Frémont had accomplished the conquest of California. Since his orders required Kearny to establish military government in the conquered area, he decided to push on. Sending most of his soldiers back to Santa Fe, and keeping only an escort of a hundred dragoons and the two howitzers, Kearny marched westward.

From the Río Grande Kearny crossed southwestern New Mexico to the headwaters of the Gila River, followed that stream down to its junction with the Colorado, and passed into California. The conquest of the Pacific coast was not complete, and there were several more months of fighting before permanent peace settled over California.

Kearny had with him Lieutenant William H. Emory of the Corps of Topographical Engineers, whose map of the route of the march was the first relatively accurate map of the Gila Trail, which in a few years would carry thousands of gold seekers to California.

Reinforcements for the Army of the West left Fort Leavenworth a month or so after the main body. They consisted of the Second Missouri Mounted Rifles and a five-hundred-man infantry battalion. The latter was an unusual organization; it was made up of volunteers from among the Mormons, who were then moving westward from Nauvoo, Illinois, to eventual settlement in Utah. The first commander of the Mormon Battalion, Captain James Allen, First Dragoons, died before reaching Santa Fe, so Kearny put Captain Philip St. George Cooke in command. Cooke was ordered to march to California and build a wagon road as he went.

Cooke followed Kearny's route to a point near the Burro Mountains in southwestern New Mexico. Here, because of the extremely rough going on the upper Gila, which was impractical for wagons, and limited supplies of water until the river could be reached, he changed his direction of march from west to south-southwest and entered present-day Arizona through Guadalupe Pass in the Peloncillo Mountains. Striking the San Pedro River just south of the present international boundary, the battalion marched north along the river to about the site of Benson and then swung westward to Tucson. After a short pause to obtain supplies, the battalion marched northwest to the Pima Villages on the Gila River. From that point on, Cooke followed Kearny's route into California.

In 1848, after the peace treaty, a battalion of the Second Dragoons, commanded by Major Lawrence Pike Graham, was ordered from Chihuahua, Mexico, to California. Marching south of the present border via Janos and the presidio of Fronteras, the battalion struck the Santa Cruz River and marched northward down the river to Tucson. From that point they followed Cooke's route to California.

It should be noted that all the troops were en route to California; none of them stayed in Arizona.

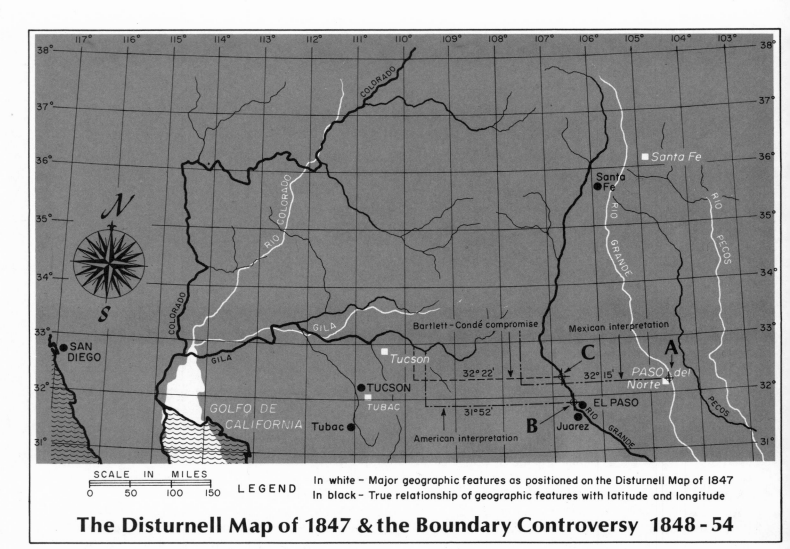

The Disturnell Map of 1847 & the Boundary Controversy 1848-54

19. THE DISTURNELL MAP OF 1847 AND THE BOUNDARY CONTROVERSY, 1848–54

ACCORDING TO the Treaty of Guadalupe Hidalgo, which ended the war with Mexico, the southern boundary of the Mexican cession was described as the Río Grande from its mouth to the southern boundary of the Mexican province of Nuevo México, then westward along that line to the western limits of New Mexico, thence north to the first branch of the Gila River and along that stream to its junction with the Colorado River. From the junction the boundary was to run in a straight line to a point on the Pacific shore one marine league (roughly three and one-half miles) south of the southern end of San Diego Bay.

The western end of the line, between California and Baja California, was run by Brevet Major William H. Emory without any trouble. Lieutenant Amiel W. Whipple and Andrew Gray, a civilian surveyor, completed the survey of the Gila, and Emory supervised the survey of the Río Grande below El Paso.

When the American and Mexican boundary commissioners met in El Paso in December, 1850, they found that the map used in drawing up the treaty was badly in error. The map was "Mapa de los Estados Unidos de México" printed by J. Disturnell of New York in 1847. According to the treaty, the southern boundary of Nuevo México started where the Río Grande struck the "southern boundary of New Mexico (which runs north of the town called Paso)." When the longitude and latitude of the town were taken from the map and compared with astronomical observations, it was found that the map was in error by about 130 miles east and west and some 30 miles north and south.

The Mexican commissioner, General Pedro García Conde, in order to save as much land as possible for his country, insisted that the initial point be set according to the longitude and latitude taken from the map, about 130 miles east of the river (Point A) and about 30 miles north of El Paso. The American surveyors insisted that the initial point be set on the river nine miles north of the actual town (Point B). Finally the American commissioner, John R. Bartlett, and General Conde agreed on a compromise. The initial point would be on the river about 35 miles north of El Paso (Point C). The American surveyors refused to sign the compromise, and a deadlock ensued. When word of this impasse reached Washington, funds for the American part of the commission were cut off, and the problem remained in limbo until the Gadsden Purchase of 1854 (Maps 21–22).

Both commissioners were satisfied with the compromise. General Conde had saved the Mesilla Valley, a rich agricultural part of the Río Grande Valley to the north of El Paso. Bartlett felt that he had saved valuable mineral land in the mountains of southern New Mexico, particularly the Santa Rita del Cobre mine near present-day Silver City, New Mexico.

It is worthy of note that if the junction of the Gila and Colorado rivers had been as the Disturnell map showed, Arizona would have access to the sea. For years after the Gadsden Purchase, officials of Arizona Territory urged that the United States annex more land from Mexico in order to give the territory a seaport. As late as the 1960's an Arizona legislator suggested that the United States lease from Mexico a large tract of land on the gulf coast where a port could be established—the port to be under complete United States jurisdiction similar to the treaty ports of China before World War II.

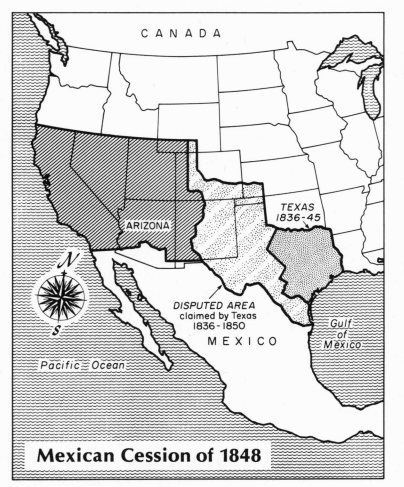

Mexican Cession of 1848

ARIZONA

TEXAS 1836-45

DISPUTED AREA claimed by Texas 1836-1850

MEXICO

Gulf of Mexico

Pacific Ocean

CANADA

Proposed State of Deseret 1849

ARIZONA

MEXICO

Gulf of Mexico

Pacific Ocean

CANADA

20A. MEXICAN CESSION OF 1848

THE ADAMS-ONÍS TREATY of 1819 (Map 16B) did not stop the westward and southwestward push of citizens of the United States. Beginning in 1821 Mexico had encouraged immigration from the United States in order to populate the vast and nearly empty reaches of Texas. However, in 1836 these new settlers rose in revolution and established the Republic of Texas. There followed ten years of desultory war between Texas and Mexico.

Texas claimed all the territory between the Adams-Onís line on the northeast and the Río Grande to its headwaters and thence north to forty-two degrees north latitude. The Mexican province of Texas had never been so extensive. Mexico stubbornly refused to recognize the Republic of Texas, although she could not reconquer the rebellious territory.

After a great deal of political maneuvering in Washington, by joint resolution of both houses of Congress, and to the joy of Texans, the United States annexed Texas in 1845. At the same time, the United States also "annexed" a war, and fighting broke out in the following year. By September 14, 1847, American troops had entered Mexico City.

The Treaty of Guadalupe Hidalgo of 1848 acknowledged the annexation of Texas by the United States and, in addition, ceded a vast tract of land comprising the present states of New Mexico, Arizona, California, Nevada, and Utah along with portions of Wyoming, Colorado, Kansas, and Oklahoma. Altogether, Mexico surrendered approximately two-thirds of its prewar territory. At the same time, the United States agreed to pay $15 million to Mexico and to assume some $3 million in claims of United States citizens against Mexico.

It was not until the Compromise of 1850 that the boundary line between Texas and New Mexico was settled as it stands today.

20B. PROPOSED STATE OF DESERET, 1849

THE MORMONS were hardly settled in the Salt Lake Valley, after their trek from Illinois in 1847–48, before they set about expanding the boundaries of their colony. Between 1849 and 1856 colonies were planted in arable valleys in present-day Utah forming what has been termed "the inner cordon of settlements." At the same time, an outer cordon was established from Lemhi in east central Idaho to the Carson Valley and Las Vegas in Nevada, San Bernardino, California, and Fort Bridger, Wyoming. This outer cordon embraced an area extending a thousand miles north and south and eight hundred miles east and west, or roughly one-sixth of the area of the contiguous United States.

Even before the settlements had been well established, the Mormon colony, in 1849, set about organizing the "Provisional Government of the State of Deseret" and proposed boundaries for the new state that were of truly imperial proportions. The bounds included all of the present states of Nevada and Utah, Arizona north of the Gila River, large portions of California including several hundred miles of seacoast and the port of San Diego, New Mexico, Colorado, Wyoming, and small areas in southern Idaho.

Congress refused to grant statehood, but as part of the Compromise of 1850 it formed Utah Territory with greatly reduced boundaries which still included all of Utah and Nevada and parts of Colorado and Wyoming. Despite the fact that northern Arizona was no longer under political control from Salt Lake City, a large number of Mormons moved into Arizona in the 1870's and 1880's. Their settlements reached from Fredonia in Coconino County, less than five miles below the Utah border, through St. Johns and Springerville to St. David in the San Pedro Valley. The largest settlement grew up at Mesa in the Salt River Valley.

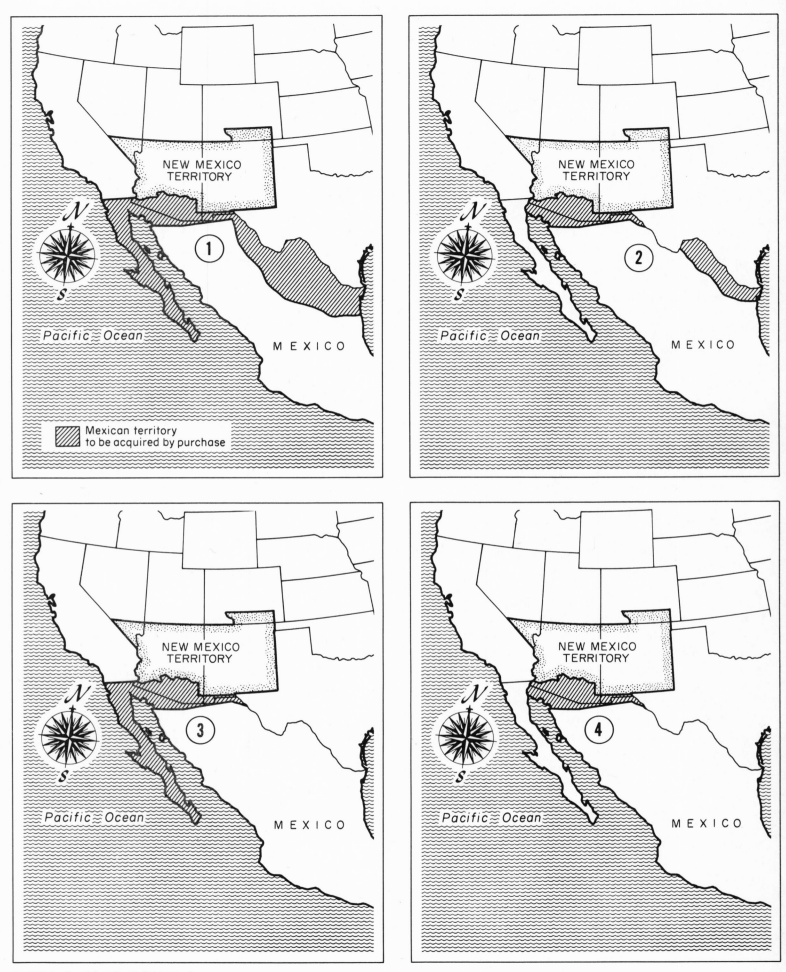

Gadsden Treaty Proposals

21. GADSDEN TREATY PROPOSALS

SECURED TO THE UNITED STATES by the Treaty of Guadalupe Hidalgo (1848), California became a center of world attention following the gold rush of 1849. When it was admitted to the Union as a state under the Compromise of 1850, attention turned to the problem of overland communications with the older states far to the east. Since the early 1830's there had been discussion of a transcontinental railroad, and during the 1840's and 1850's interest in such a project grew rapidly. From the reports of boundary commission surveys and travelers over the Gila Trail it became obvious that the valley of the Gila River would be impassable for a railroad, and the country to the north was thought to be too rough and mountainous. It was also clear that the country sixty to a hundred miles south of the Gila presented few obstacles to railroad building. In addition, the United States wanted control of the land through which ran Cooke's Wagon Road.

After a short exile in disgrace after his defeats during the Mexican War, General Antonio López de Santa Anna was again president of Mexico. The authorities in Washington knew that Santa Anna was in financial difficulties, so President Franklin Pierce sent James Gadsden to Mexico City to present to Santa Anna five different proposals, each with a different price tag.

The first proposal would have added to the United States large portions of the Mexican states of Coahuila, Chihuahua, and Sonora and all of Baja California. For this cession of 120,000 square miles the United States would pay up to $50 million. This line was considered by President Pierce to be the boundary that would be most easily defended and guarded by both countries.

The second proposal did not extend as far south into Mexico, nor did it include Baja California. Such a cession was estimated to involve 50,000 square miles of Mexican territory, for which the United States would pay $35 million.

Proposal number three, still farther north, excluded Coahuila and most of Chihuahua but did include Baja California. The area was estimated to encompass 68,000 square miles at a price of $30 million.

Proposal four was the same as number three except that it did not include Baja California; the cession now would only cost $20 million and would involve only 18,000 square miles.

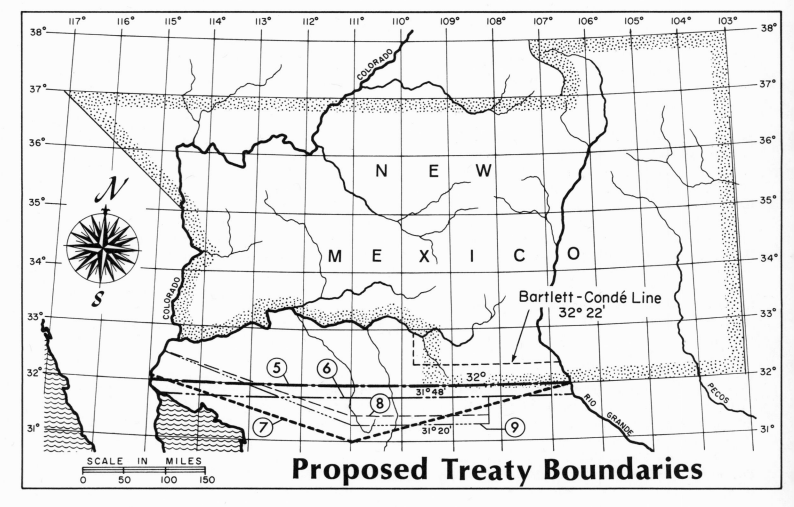

Proposed Treaty Boundaries

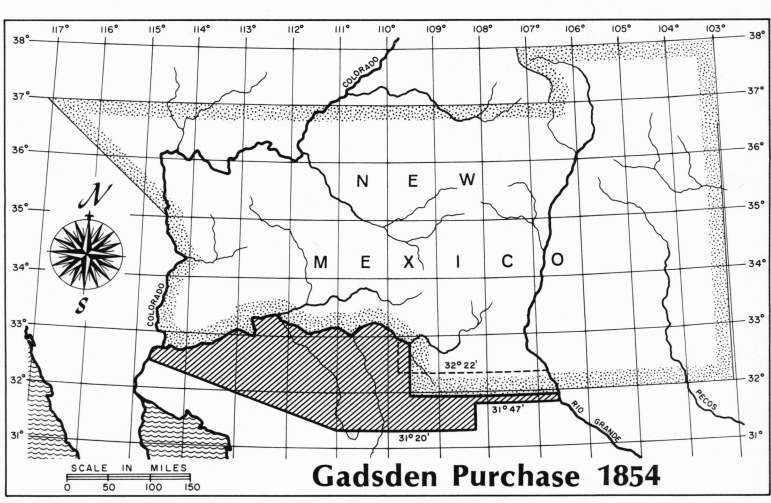

Gadsden Purchase 1854

22. GADSDEN PURCHASE, 1854

IF NONE OF THE FOREGOING plans were acceptable Gadsden was to negotiate for a possible railroad route from the Río Grande to California. A line along 31° 48′ (Line No. 6 on map) or 32° (Line No. 5) north latitude would be considered satisfactory. For either of these lines, a price of $15 million would be paid.

All of these plans were designed to include a port on the Gulf of California. If Disturnell's map had been correct, the United States could have had a port at the junction of the Colorado and Gila rivers with the Gulf of California (Map 19). As it turned out, the junction of the two rivers was some eighty airline miles from the Gulf.

While President Santa Anna needed money to equip the Mexican army and was anxious to avoid another war with the United States, he made it clear to Gadsden that he would negotiate only for cession of enough land to assure the United States of a railroad route. During the negotiations, Mexican Foreign Minister Manuel Díaz de Bonilla convinced the American that Mexico would not sell any land unless assured of a land connection with Baja California. As a result, the boundary of the purchase, as set forth in the treaty signed December 30, 1853, was to end on the Colorado River six miles above its mouth (Line No. 7).

When the treaty was submitted to the United States Senate, the atmosphere was still heated as a result of the debate on the Kansas-Nebraska Bill. Many northern senators were opposed to the acquisition of more territory in which slavery might be permitted and to the building of a transcontinental railroad through southern states. Other senators complained that the treaty did not acquire enough land.

During the debate an alternate line (Line No. 8) was proposed and rejected. Meanwhile the Mexican minister to Washington, Juan Nepomunceno Almonte, convinced influential senators that the western end of the boundary was poorly placed. He pointed out that because of the tidal bore (the meeting of river current and ocean tide) and floods on the river, the lowest point on the Colorado where a bridge could be built with reasonable chance of standing was at a place twenty English miles south of Yuma. This point was accepted in the final treaty (Line No. 9), the area acquired was reduced by nine thousand square miles, and the amount to be paid to Mexico was reduced to $10 million. The treaty was ratified by the Senate on June 24, 1854.

The Gadsden Purchase embraced some 29,640 square miles. Of this, approximately 27,305 square miles were added to Arizona, the rest to New Mexico. The addition to Arizona was equivalent to about 24 per cent of the land area of the present state.

The new boundary was surveyed and marked by a joint commission. Major William H. Emory, a member of the earlier unsuccessful boundary commission, was the American commissioner. Between 1891 and 1894 another joint commission reran the boundary to verify the accuracy of the Emory survey and to replace many of the monuments that had been destroyed by hostile Apaches.

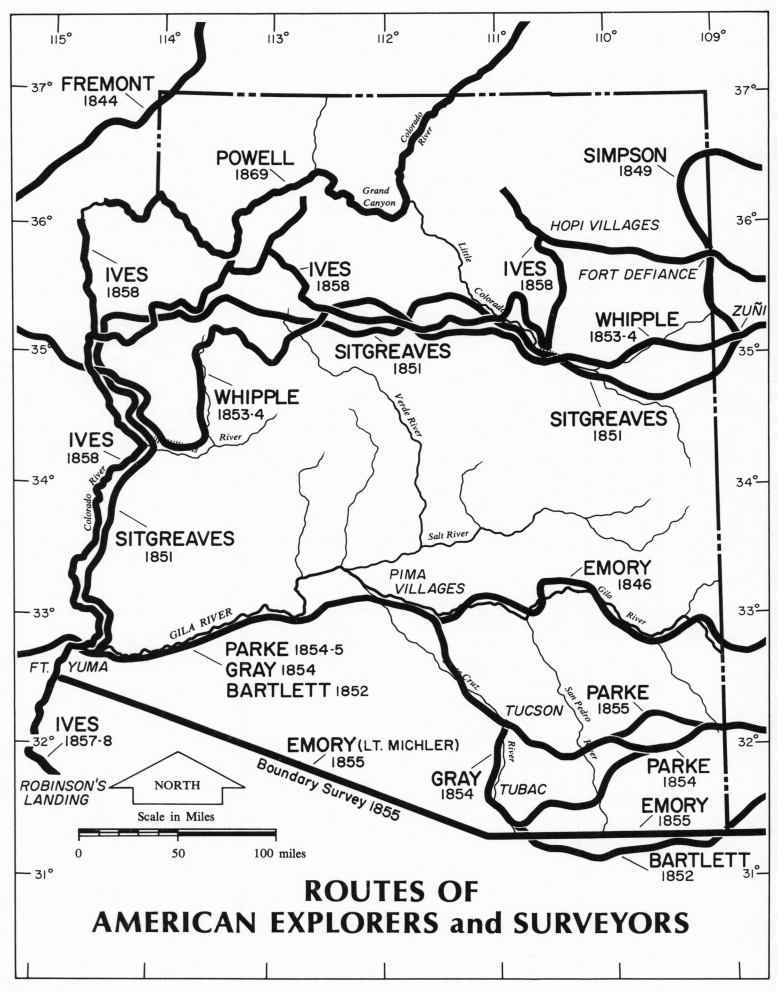

ROUTES OF
AMERICAN EXPLORERS and SURVEYORS

THE INK WAS HARDLY DRY on the Treaty of Guadalupe Hidalgo (1848) when the United States government took steps to learn something about the vast tract of land it had acquired from Mexico. In 1849 Lieutenant James H. Simpson had accompanied an expedition against the Navajos in Canyon de Chelly. Based on an interview with the mountain man François X. Aubrey, Simpson reported that a wagon road west from Zuñi to California was feasible. Captain Lorenzo Sitgreaves of the Army Corps of Topographical Engineers was sent to seek out this road in 1851. Sitgreaves' work produced a careful study of a hitherto unknown area.

Because of the great interest in possible routes for a transcontinental railroad, Lieutenant Amiel W. Whipple, who had served on the boundary commission, was sent out to survey along the thirty-fifth parallel from Fort Smith, Arkansas, to Los Angeles, California. As with most of the early exploring parties, Whipple had with him a geologist, a naturalist, a botanist, and an artist to record the wonders of nature along the route. Whipple left Zuñi on November 29, 1853, and crossed the Colorado on February 28, 1854. His final report concluded that a feasible railroad route lay across the northern part of the state.

While Whipple was making his way across the northern part of the state, Andrew B. Gray, also formerly of the boundary commission, was hired by the Texas Western Railroad to run a preliminary survey across Mexican territory south of the Gila. Gray completed the work in 1854.

It was realized in Washington that more information was needed on the railroad possibilities of the southern route. Lieutenant John G. Parke in 1854 resurveyed the area between the Pima Villages and the Río Grande. With the permission of the Mexican government, his route took him through Tucson and Apache Pass in the Chiricahua Mountains to a junction with Cooke's Wagon Road in New Mexico. A year later Parke again covered the route and found a pass between the base of Mount Graham and the Chiricahuas that cut thirty miles from the distance and reduced the number of summits to be crossed.

By 1858 the Colorado River was the last major stream in the United States still to be explored. Steamers were already running from the river's mouth to Fort Yuma when the army sent Lieutenant Joseph C. Ives, formerly a companion of Whipple, to determine the head of navigation of the Colorado. A few days before Ives reached Fort Yuma in the government vessel *Explorer*, Captain George Johnson went north in his own steamer, the *General Jesup*. At the mouth of Black Canyon, above the point at which Johnson had turned back, Ives divided his party. Half returned down-river on the steamer, and the lieutenant took the other half overland to Fort Defiance. The reports of these pre–Civil War explorations provided a great amount of knowledge about the geography, geology, plant and animal life, and native Indians.

Because of the Civil War, it was not until 1869 that another government-sponsored exploring party entered Arizona. By this time only the extreme northwestern part of the state was still marked "unexplored" on the maps. In 1869 Major John W. Powell, supported largely by private funds, descended the Colorado by boat from Green River, Wyoming, to Callville, Nevada (now under Lake Mead). In the following year Powell crossed the Shivwits Plateau and reached the Colorado in the lower Grand Canyon. In 1871 Powell crossed the Colorado Plateau many times, while his assistant, Almon H. Thompson, made another descent of the river to Lee's Ferry.

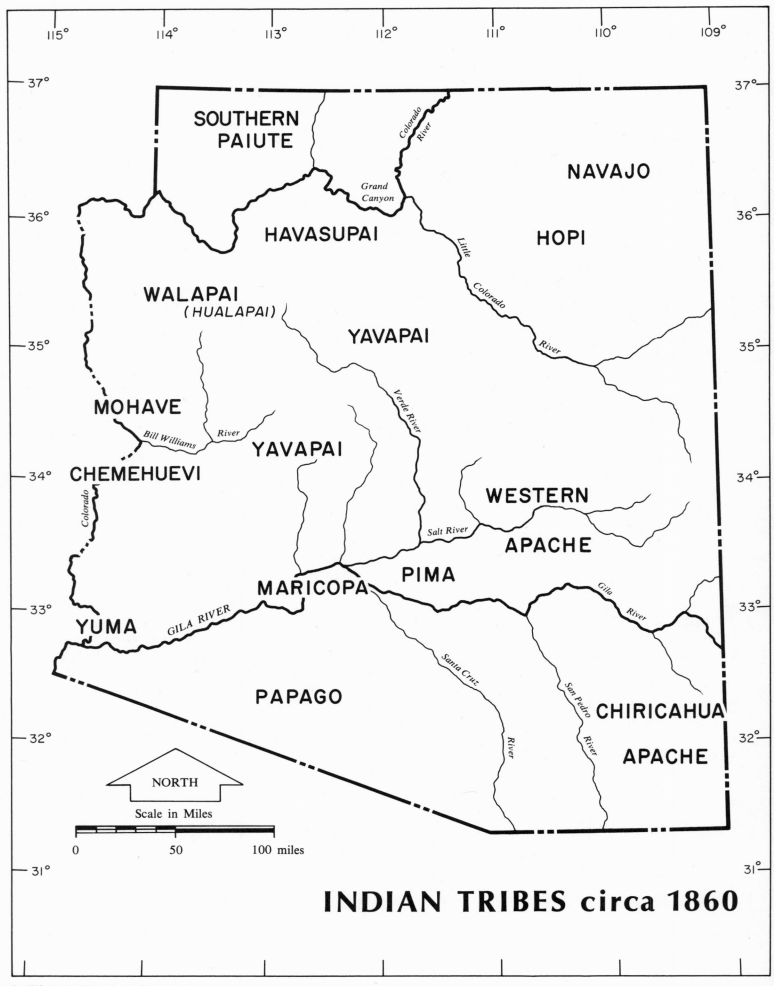

SOUTHERN
PAIUTE

Colorado River

Grand Canyon

HAVASUPAI

NAVAJO

HOPI

Little

Colorado

WALAPAI
(HUALAPAI)

YAVAPAI

River

MOHAVE

Bill Williams   *River*

Verde River

YAVAPAI

CHEMEHUEVI

Colorado

WESTERN

Salt River

APACHE

MARICOPA

PIMA

Gila

River

YUMA

GILA RIVER

Santa Cruz

San Pedro

River

CHIRICAHUA

PAPAGO

River

River

APACHE

NORTH

Scale in Miles

0   50   100 miles

INDIAN TRIBES circa 1860

BETWEEN THE FIRST EXPLORATIONS by the Spaniards, and their reports on the indigenous population of Arizona, and the appointment in 1863 of Charles D. Poston as the first United States Indian Agent for Arizona Territory there had been a number of changes in the tribal distribution of the Indians.

On the Colorado River various Indian groups were in an almost continuous state of war. During the first half of the nineteenth century the Halchidomas, Kohuanas, and Kavelchadoms were driven eastward up the valley of the Gila River by pressure of the Mojaves from the north and the Yumas from the south. By 1858 these bands had merged with the Maricopa Indians and had settled on Pima land along the river. In 1857 the Pimas joined the Maricopas in a successful pitched battle against a combined force of Yumas and Mojaves.

The eastward movement of the Maricopas left a large tract of land in the Colorado River valley, near present-day Parker, unoccupied. Into this tract moved some of the Chemehuevis from the Mojave Desert of California.

The Sobaipuris of the San Pedro Valley, a division of the Piman people who had long served the Spaniards as a buffer against the raiding Apaches from the north, were not supported by the white man. Many were moved to San Xavier del Bac and to Sonora; the rest finally gave way before the attackers and moved westward to mingle with the Papagos, another division of the Piman people living in the Santa Cruz Valley and westward.

A clear differentiation between the Papagos and their cousins the Pimas seems to have come about when Americans first moved into southern Arizona. The name "Pimo," later "Pima," came to be applied exclusively to the sedentary, farming Indians who lived on the Gila River. The name Papago was applied to the seminomadic people living west of Tucson and south of Casa Grande and to the Sobaipuri and Pima descendants in the Santa Cruz Valley. In the desert the Indians had to move twice a year. In the summer they took advantage of the summer rains to plant crops at spots in the desert where water stayed close to the surface. In the winter they moved to rancherias at the foot of the mountains where water could be found in seepage springs.

The Athapaskan-speaking Navajos seem to have moved into the northwestern part of the state in the 1700's, when they occupied their great fortress, the Canyon de Chelly. Over the years their reservation has been expanded several times, until today it completely surrounds the Hopi Reservation, a cause of intertribal strife to present times. The earlier name "Moqui" for Hopi came from the derisive Navajo word meaning "dead." It was used because of the Hopis' peaceful ways. The name was changed officially in the early twentieth century.

The record indicates that the Western Apaches and Chiricahua Apaches spread across New Mexico and into southeastern Arizona from the Texas plains during the seventeenth century, settling largely in the area called by Coronado the "Despoblado." These Athapaskan-speaking people were basically hunters and raiders, though they did grow small amounts of food. They were fragmented into as many as twenty different bands, which often were at war with each other. A problem for the historian arises in the number of different names given to each band by the early explorers and travelers.

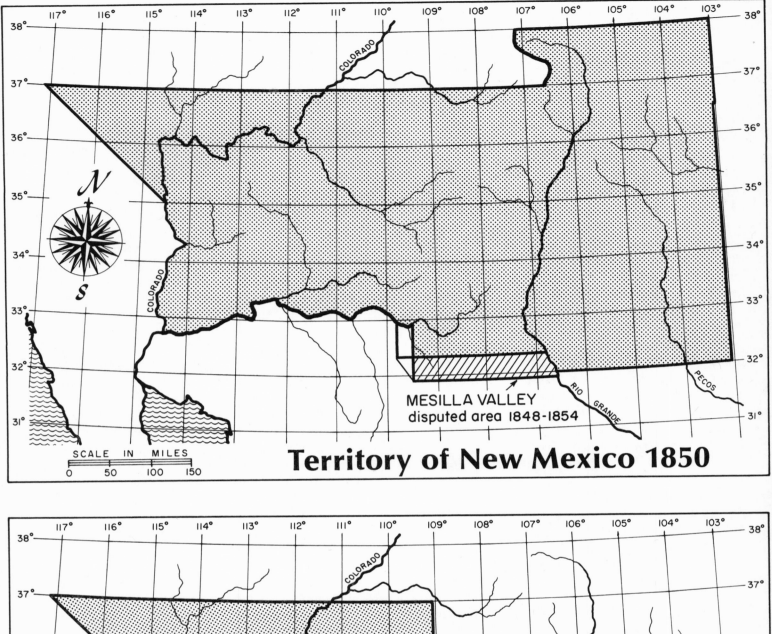

Territory of New Mexico 1850

MESILLA VALLEY
disputed area 1848-1854

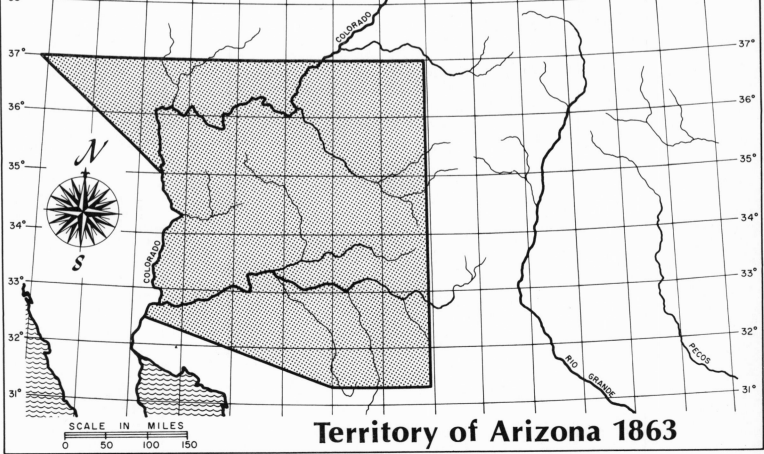

Territory of Arizona 1863

WHEN GENERAL STEPHEN WATTS KEARNY occupied the Mexican province of New Mexico in 1846, the province consisted essentially of a string of settlements in the Río Grande Valley stretching north from El Paso to Taos. Kearny established a civilian government for the territory, but the Taos Revolt of 1847 and the murder of several civilian officials, including Governor William Bent, resulted in the imposition of military government. At the same time, Texas was claiming the upper Río Grande, including Santa Fe, as its western boundary.

Congress was faced with the problem of what to do with the vast area ceded by Mexico, especially in view of the great westward migration of the California Gold Rush of 1849. After considerable debate, a group of bills were passed that are generally called the Compromise of 1850. California was admitted to the Union as a state, the eastern boundary of New Mexico was settled, and Utah and New Mexico were established as territories. The Territory of New Mexico covered all of the present state of New Mexico, part of south-central Colorado, all of present-day Arizona north of the Gila River, and that portion of Nevada lying south of 37° north latitude. Santa Fe was the territorial capital.

When the joint United States–Mexican Boundary Commission started to survey the new international boundary, a dispute arose over the interpretation of the Treaty of Guadalupe Hidalgo concerning the southern boundary of New Mexico, and a stalemate resulted (Map 19).

The stalemate left unresolved the fate of the Mesilla Valley, a thirty-mile-long strip of the Río Grande Valley, valuable agricultural land, inhabited by Mexicans who had no great desire to become American citizens. At one time tension reached the point that the governor of New Mexico threatened to call out the militia and take the area by force. The fate of the area was settled by the Gadsden Treaty in 1854 (Maps 21–22).

Only a year after the Gadsden Purchase, a motion was introduced into the territorial legislature of New Mexico to divide the area into two territories along an east-west line. The southern portion of New Mexico, dominated largely by Anglos from Texas, felt that it was being discriminated against by the northern portion, which was generally under the control of a large Mexican population. The politically active Anglos called a convention in Mesilla, organized a territorial government, and elected a delegate to Congress. Washington refused to recognize this unauthorized government but did authorize a new judicial district for the area south of the Gila. There is no sign that this district ever functioned.

By February, 1860, ten bills had been introduced into Congress calling for a division of New Mexico Territory along an east-west line. All these bills failed because Congress was deeply involved in the sectional controversy that led to the outbreak of the Civil War in 1861. Finally, in 1863, a bill was passed and signed by President Abraham Lincoln which separated Arizona from New Mexico along a north-south line. Southern Arizona and New Mexico were thought to favor the Confederacy, and a north-south line would break up this potentially hostile bloc.

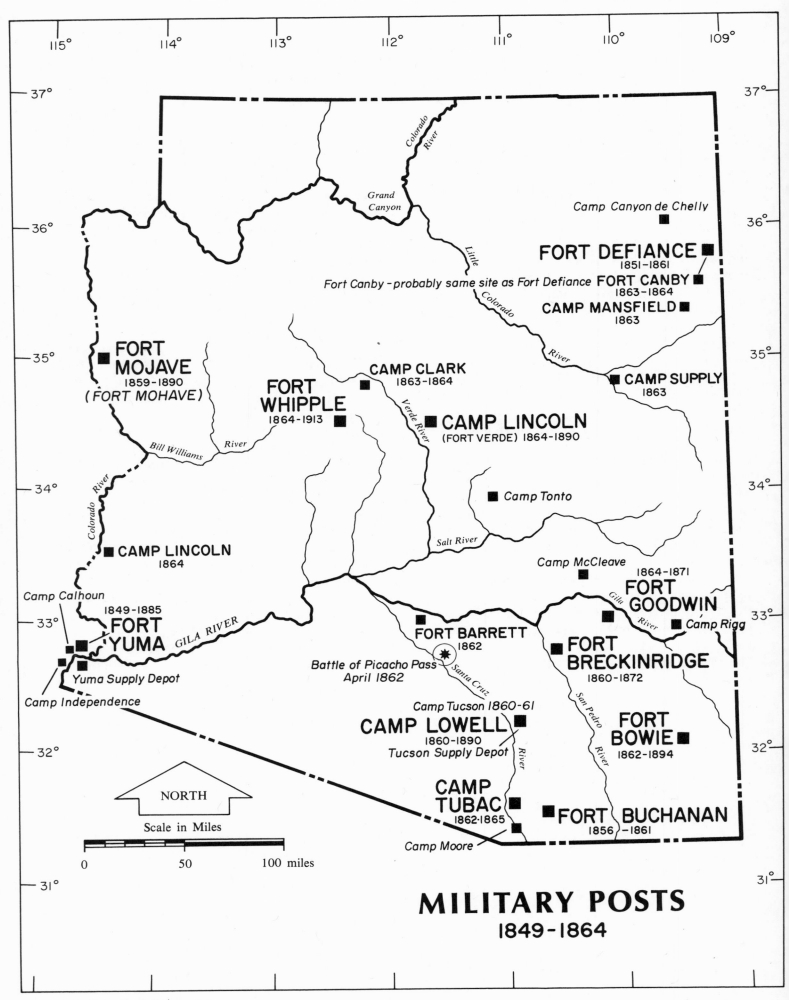

Camp Canyon de Chelly

FORT DEFIANCE
1851–1861

Fort Canby – probably same site as Fort Defiance   FORT CANBY
1863–1864

CAMP MANSFIELD
1863

FORT MOJAVE
1859–1890
(FORT MOHAVE)

CAMP SUPPLY
1863

CAMP CLARK
1863–1864

FORT
WHIPPLE
1864–1913

CAMP LINCOLN
(FORT VERDE) 1864–1890

Camp Tonto

Camp McCleave

CAMP LINCOLN
1864

Camp Calhoun

1849–1885
FORT
YUMA

Yuma Supply Depot

Camp Independence

GILA RIVER

FORT BARRETT
1862

Battle of Picacho Pass
April 1862

1864–1871
FORT
GOODWIN

Camp Rigg

FORT
BRECKINRIDGE
1860–1872

Camp Tucson 1860-61

CAMP LOWELL
1860–1890
Tucson Supply Depot

FORT
BOWIE
1862–1894

CAMP
TUBAC
1862–1865

Camp Moore

FORT BUCHANAN
1856   –1861

NORTH

Scale in Miles

0   50   100 miles

MILITARY POSTS
1849–1864

© 1979 by the University of Oklahoma Press

ALTHOUGH SITUATED on the California bank of the Colorado River, Fort Yuma played a vital role in the history of Arizona. Camp Calhoun was established at the crossing of the Southern Overland Trail in 1849. However, not until supply by river steamer was assured in 1852 was Camp Yuma firmly established. The name was changed to Fort Yuma in 1861. The Yuma Supply Depot was opened on the Arizona shore in 1864.

The first army post in Arizona was Fort Defiance, set in the middle of the Navajo country in 1851. Usually garrisoned by infantry, its impact on the marauding Indians was slight. The post was abandoned in 1861 when the troops were concentrated in the Río Grande Valley to meet the Confederates. The site was reoccupied by New Mexico Volunteers in 1863 and named Fort Canby.

Following the Gadsden Purchase, four companies of the First Dragoons reached Tucson in 1856. The first site for a post was the Calabasas Ranch on the Santa Cruz River. Here Camp Moore was set up. Next year Major Enoch Steen was ordered to select a site nearer Tucson. The best that could be found with adequate water and grazing for the horses was at the head of Sonoita Creek, where Fort Buchanan was established. The troops were ordered east in 1861, and the fort was burned.

A post was established at the Colorado River crossing of Beale's Wagon Road to control the local Indians and to provide a resting place for emigrants before crossing the Mojave Desert. The regulars left Fort Mojave (now Mohave) in 1861, and a contingent of California Volunteers took over in 1863.

Fort Arivaypa, soon called Fort Breckinridge, was founded in 1860 in hopes of controlling the Apaches. The post was put to the torch in July, 1861. For six months of 1863 the site was occupied by some of the California Volunteers and was called Fort Stanford in honor of the governor of California. In October the name Breckinridge was revived, and in 1865 the post was renamed Camp Grant.

The spring in Apache Pass was a vital point on the Southern Overland Trail. It was the only reliable water supply for thirty or more miles east or west. After a battle in June, 1862, between Apaches under Mangas Coloradas and Cochise and California Volunteers, Camp Bowie was set up to guard the spring and passing wagon trains.

When gold was discovered near Prescott in 1863, troops were sent from New Mexico to protect the miners. The first site of Fort Whipple was twenty-two miles north of the mining camp. In May, 1864, the post was moved closer to the town. The name was later changed to Whipple Barracks.

During the Civil War a number of small posts were opened. Fort Barrett at the Pima Villages was described as "earthworks thrown around a trading post." A temporary camp, called Goodwin, was set up on the Gila River until a permanent location was found thirty-two miles to the west and named Camp Goodwin. Camp Lincoln was a subpost of Fort Yuma. Camp Tubac was a reoccupation of the old Spanish presidio. Camps Tonto, McCleave, and Rigg, which appear in official papers, seem to have been no more than camping places for troops on the move. As a result, their exact locations are matters of speculation.

Camp Tucson was established in what is now downtown Tucson in 1860, but it was closed in 1861. Next year the California Volunteers opened the Tucson Supply Depot, but the depot was moved to Fort Whipple in 1864. A temporary camp was opened on the Rillito for better grazing, water, and wood, but the troops were moved back to town in 1865.

During the Civil War there was one small skirmish between thirteen Union and sixteen Confederate soldiers at Picacho Pass between Tucson and Phoenix. While total casualties were small—five killed and three taken prisoner, the approach of a force of California Volunteers caused the Confederates to retire east from Tucson.

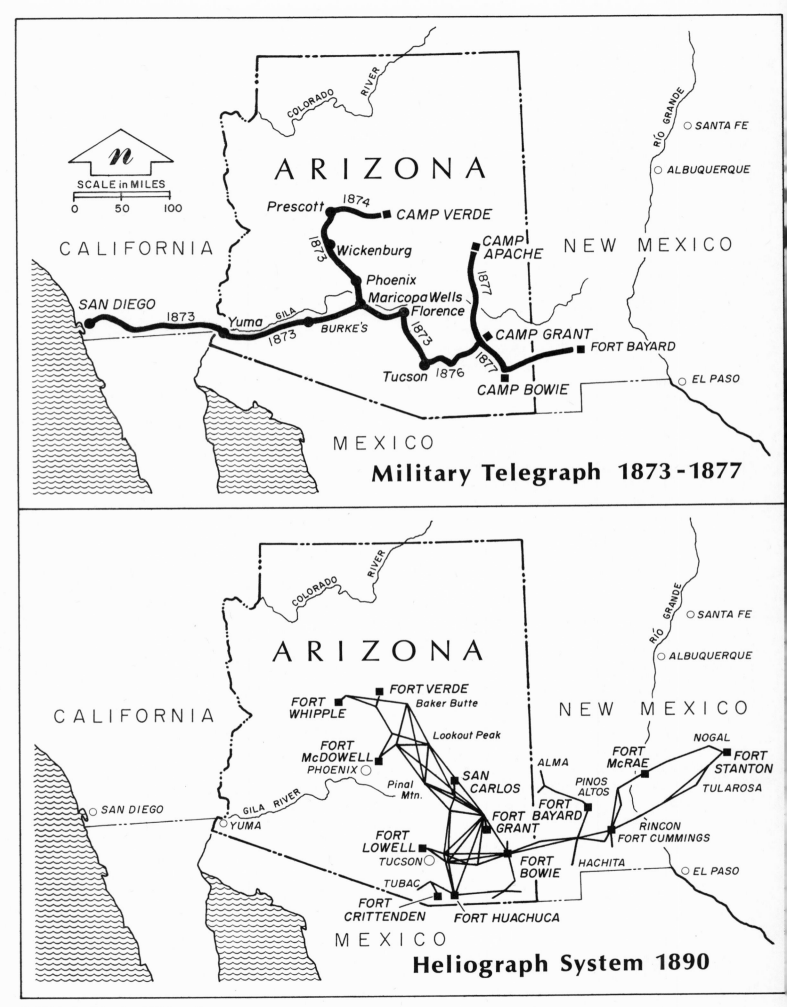

Military Telegraph 1873-1877

Heliograph System 1890

27A. MILITARY TELEGRAPH, 1873–77

THE FIRST transcontinental telegraph line connecting San Francisco with the East was completed in 1861. A line from San Francisco to Los Angeles had been built in 1860, and San Diego was tied in in 1870. There had been talk of a telegraph in Arizona as early as 1866, but nothing was done.

General George Crook, in his first annual report in 1871, urged the construction of a line from California to Arizona, with branches to the more important posts. Next year Crook noted that the nearest telegraph office was in Los Angeles—several days away by mail. Congress appropriated $120,000 in 1873 for a line to Yuma and on to Prescott and Tucson. Construction began in August at San Diego and in September in Prescott. The line from Prescott to Yuma was opened on November 11 and to San Diego on November 18.

The posts were set and the wire strung by details of soldiers under the technical superviison of civilians hired by the army for that work. Most citizens took great interest in the work. The town of Florence provided a number of poles free; they wanted the line to pass through town.

While the telegraph system was primarily for military purposes, civilian messages were accepted. This policy was a great boon to the commercial interests of the territory. Goods could be ordered from wholesale houses in San Francisco much faster than by stagecoach. Also, the rates charged by the military were much lower than those charged by commercial telegraph companies. Some companies, in order to insure privacy, employed their own codes for their business messages.

By the time the Southern Pacific Railroad and Western Union reached Yuma in 1877, there were about one thousand miles of line in operation in Arizona. As commercial telegraph became available, the military lines were abandoned. In 1882 there were only 532 miles of the military system in use. In a few years all telegraph communication was commercial.

27B. HELIOGRAPH SYSTEM, 1890

THE HELIOGRAPH was a device which, by the use of mirrors, could direct a beam of rays from the sun in any desired direction. By interrupting the beam with a shutter, messages could be sent with the device, using the dots and dashes of the Morse code.

The United States Army began experimenting with the heliograph at Fort Myer, Virginia, in 1877. Other experiments were carried out in Montana, Oregon, and Arizona. The telegraph required a fixed installation of poles and wire which was subject to interruption by storms or unfriendly Indians, but the heliograph was simple and very mobile. On the other hand, it could not be used at night or during storms; intermediate stations were required, as the flash could not be read at distances much over forty miles. In dangerous country extra guards had to be provided for the two operators at each station.

When General Nelson A. Miles succeeded General George Crook in command of the Department of Arizona and New Mexico in 1886, he requested the best instruments and operators that could be provided. A heliograph network would provide a faster means of communication with troops in the field than the usual combination of telegraph and mounted courier. In addition, the stations could observe and report any movements in a large area.

By August, 1886, an extensive network had been set up. The Arizona Division comprised fourteen stations manned by sixty-five soldiers. The New Mexico Division had thirteen stations manned by twenty-nine men.

Although each station was supposed to keep a file of all messages handled, no files have been found. Some idea of the importance of the system may be gained from the fact that when General Miles set up his headquarters at Fort Bowie, 802 messages were sent between May 1 and September 30, 1886.

Following the surrender of Geronimo in early September, 1886, the major part of the system was dismantled. However, during departmental maneuvers held in late 1887, at least part of the network was reestablished. In 1890 a major field test was conducted with fifty-two stations extending from Fort Whipple east to Fort Stanton, New Mexico. Short sections were used to connect various forts with the telegraph until it was replaced by the telephone.

27A. MILITARY TELEGRAPH, 1873–77
27B. HELIOGRAPH SYSTEM, 1890

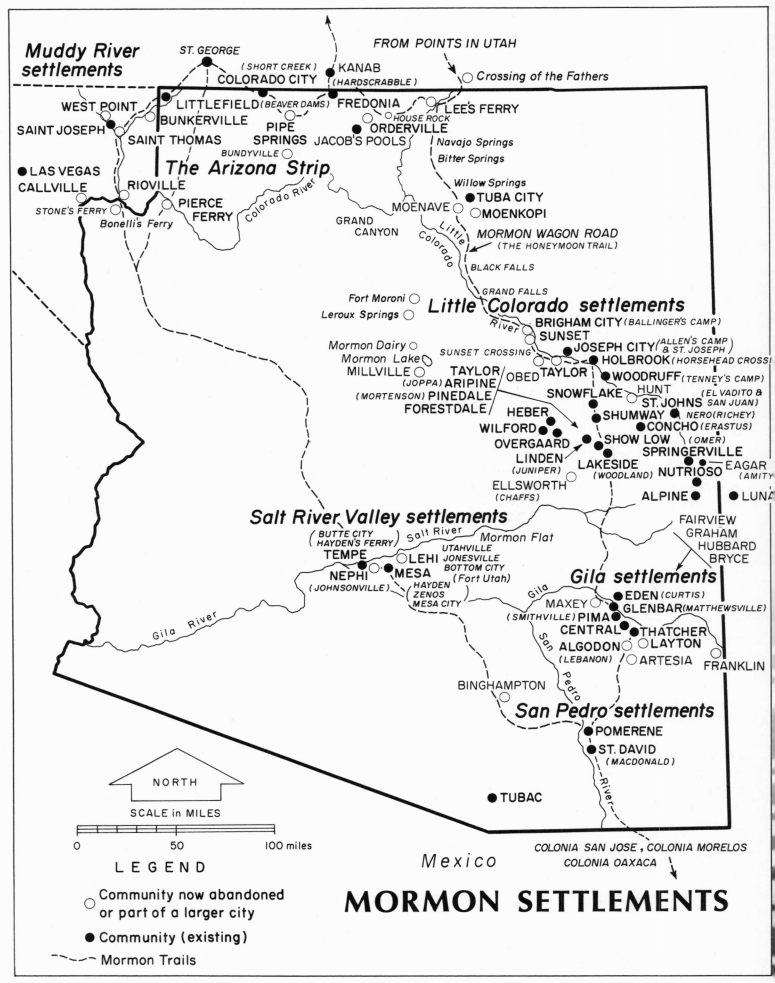

Muddy River settlements

FROM POINTS IN UTAH

ST. GEORGE

(SHORT CREEK) KANAB
COLORADO CITY (HARDSCRABBLE)

○ Crossing of the Fathers

WEST POINT
LITTLEFIELD (BEAVER DAMS) FREDONIA
BUNKERVILLE
SAINT JOSEPH
SAINT THOMAS
PIPE SPRINGS
JACOB'S POOLS

LEE'S FERRY
HOUSE ROCK
ORDERVILLE

LAS VEGAS
CALLVILLE
RIOVILLE
BUNDYVILLE

The Arizona Strip

Navajo Springs
Bitter Springs

STONE'S FERRY
PIERCE FERRY

Willow Springs

MOENAVE
TUBA CITY
MOENKOPI

Bonelli's Ferry

Colorado River

GRAND CANYON

Little Colorado

MORMON WAGON ROAD
(THE HONEYMOON TRAIL)

BLACK FALLS

GRAND FALLS

Fort Moroni
Leroux Springs

River

Little Colorado settlements

BRIGHAM CITY (BALLINGER'S CAMP)
SUNSET

Mormon Dairy
Mormon Lake
MILLVILLE

SUNSET CROSSING

JOSEPH CITY (ALLEN'S CAMP & ST. JOSEPH)
HOLBROOK (HORSEHEAD CROSS)

TAYLOR (JOPPA)
ARIPINE (MORTENSON)
PINEDALE
FORESTDALE

OBED TAYLOR
WOODRUFF (TENNEY'S CAMP)

SNOWFLAKE
HUNT
ST. JOHNS (EL VADITO & SAN JUAN)

HEBER
WILFORD
OVERGAARD
LINDEN (JUNIPER)

SHUMWAY NERO (RICHEY)
CONCHO (ERASTUS)
SHOW LOW (OMER)
SPRINGERVILLE

LAKESIDE (WOODLAND)
NUTRIOSO
EAGAR (AMITY)

ELLSWORTH (CHAFFS)

ALPINE
LUNA

Salt River Valley settlements

FAIRVIEW
GRAHAM
HUBBARD
BRYCE

(BUTTE CITY HAYDEN'S FERRY)
Salt River
Mormon Flat

TEMPE
UTAHVILLE
JONESVILLE
BOTTOM CITY
(FORT UTAH)
LEHI

NEPHI (JOHNSONVILLE)
MESA
HAYDEN
ZENOS
MESA CITY

Gila settlements

Gila

EDEN (CURTIS)
GLENBAR (MATTHEWSVILLE)
MAXEY (SMITHVILLE)
PIMA
CENTRAL
THATCHER
ALGODON (LEBANON)
LAYTON
ARTESIA
FRANKLIN

San Pedro

Gila River

BINGHAMPTON

San Pedro settlements

POMERENE
ST. DAVID (MACDONALD)

River

NORTH

SCALE in MILES

0   50   100 miles

LEGEND

○ Community now abandoned
  or part of a larger city

● Community (existing)

--- Mormon Trails

TUBAC

Mexico

COLONIA SAN JOSE, COLONIA MORELOS
COLONIA OAXACA

MORMON SETTLEMENTS

© 1979 by the University of Oklahoma Press

ALTHOUGH THE STATE OF DESERET (Map 20) never was accepted, and its hoped-for territory was cut down by the admission of California as a state in 1850, Nevada in 1864, and Colorado in 1876, the Mormons under the leadership of Brigham Young continued to expand into adjoining territory. This expansion was essential, because most of the irrigable farmland in Utah had been put to the plow. The first Mormon settlement in Arizona was Littlefield, in the extreme northwestern corner of the territory. This agricultural community was established in 1864, wiped out by a flood in 1867, and rebuilt in 1877.

One of the most troublesome problems that faced the Mormons in Utah was the expense of wagon freight from the Missouri River. In 1864 they hoped to reduce overland carriage of supplies by using the steamers on the Colorado River to bring freight within five hundred miles of Salt Lake City. The town of Callville was planted on the north bank of the Colorado about twenty miles southeast of present-day Las Vegas, Nevada. This plan did not work out, because the new town was too far upriver for reliable navigation. By the time the Union Pacific and Central Pacific railroads were completed across northern Utah in 1869, the Callville project had been abandoned.

Another early settlement was St. Thomas at the junction of the Muddy and Virgin Rivers in the northwest corner of the territory. When most of Pah-Ute County was transferred to the new state of Nevada, the settlers were withdrawn into Utah in 1871.

The greatest period of Mormon immigration into Arizona began in 1870 with the establishment of Pipe Springs north of the Grand Canyon and Lee's Ferry at a crossing point of the Colorado in the can-

yon. From the ferry, settlements spread southeastward. A mission was established for a while at Moenkopi, a Hopi pueblo, but was abandoned when it was found that the Indians were not interested in becoming Christians. The main thrust of the move was up the valley of the Little Colorado River: Joseph City (1865), Springerville (1871), St. Johns (1880), and Show Low (1890). Some of the settlements had to be abandoned. Brigham City and Sunset were abandoned because of poor soil and uncertain irrigation. Forestdale turned out to be on Indian land.

A notable aspect of the colonization by the Mormons was the founding of joint enterprises. The Mormon Dairy was located on the west side of Mormon Lake as a joint enterprise of Sunset, Brigham City, and Joseph City.

St. David, on the San Pedro River in Cochise County, was established in 1877 as the most southerly settlement in Arizona.

The greatest Mormon concentration and development started in the Salt River Valley with the founding of Lehi in 1877 and Mesa in the following year. Mesa was laid out along the same plan as Salt Lake City, with wide, straight streets and large city blocks. The temple of the Church of Jesus Christ of Latter-day Saints for Arizona is located in Mesa.

Some of the Arizona settlements were organized under the United Order, a comprehensive, cooperative plan of the Mormon church. A branch of the United Order called the Gospel Plan was completely communal in structure. All property was held in common; the members of the settlement ate at a common table and dressed from the same bolt of cloth. The work of all was directed to the common good, and all activities were begun and ended by bugle calls.

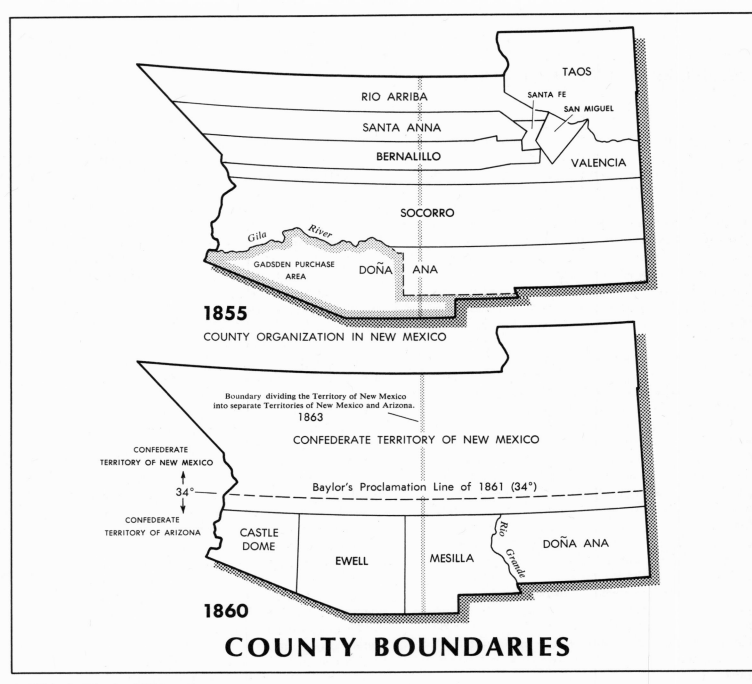

1855
COUNTY ORGANIZATION IN NEW MEXICO

TAOS

RIO ARRIBA

SANTA FE

SAN MIGUEL

SANTA ANNA

BERNALILLO

VALENCIA

SOCORRO

Gila *River*

GADSDEN PURCHASE AREA

DOÑA ANA

Boundary dividing the Territory of New Mexico into separate Territories of New Mexico and Arizona. 1863

CONFEDERATE TERRITORY OF NEW MEXICO

CONFEDERATE TERRITORY OF NEW MEXICO

34°

CONFEDERATE TERRITORY OF ARIZONA

Baylor's Proclamation Line of 1861 (34°)

CASTLE DOME

EWELL

MESILLA

Rio Grande

DOÑA ANA

1860

COUNTY BOUNDARIES

THE POLITICAL ORGANIZATION of what was eventually to become the state of Arizona began when the territory of New Mexico extended six counties from the Río Grande Valley to the Colorado River and the eastern boundary of California. In theory, this extension meant that a citizen of Las Vegas, now in Nevada, would have to travel five hundred miles to the seat of Rio Arriba County at the town of Rio Arriba (now Alcalde) to conduct any legal business. Following the Gadsden Purchase, the newly acquired area was added to the southernmost New Mexico county—Doña Ana. John Ricord of Tucson was appointed as justice of the peace for Doña Ana County in 1859.

In response to appeals from the inhabitants of the Gadsden Purchase area, the legislature of New Mexico in 1860 organized Arizona County from that part of Doña Ana lying west of a line one mile east of the stage station in Apache Pass. The decennial census of that year gave a population of 1,674 persons; Tubac was designated as the county seat. In the following year San Juan County was formed and took over the western part of Rio Arriba County. At the same time, the seat of Arizona County was moved to Tucson. Later in the same year San Juan and Arizona counties were wiped out and their lands returned to the original counties from which they had been detached. Much of the lawlessness in Arizona before 1863 can be laid to the lack of local government, with its courts and law officers.

During all this shuffling of county organization, the citizens of the southern part of New Mexico Territory decided to form a government without congressional approval. In April, 1860, a convention met in Tucson and drafted a provisional constitution that was to be effective until Congress should act. The provisional state covered all of New Mexico and Arizona south of 33° 40′ north. Four counties were included in it: Doña Ana, Mesilla, Ewell, and Castle Dome. A full slate of officers was elected or appointed, and provisions were made for a bicameral legislature, judicial districts, and a militia.

County officials were elected in May. A motion was introduced into Congress to legalize the judicial proceedings of this government, but it failed. Altogether, five bills were introduced in 1860, but all failed, largely over the issue of the extension of slavery into the territories.

Secession sentiment boiled up in November, 1860. The Texans of the Mesilla Valley called a convention which voted unanimously to join the Confederacy. At first only the fire-eaters approved, but when the Butterfield Mail was moved to the central route and the troops were withdrawn from Forts Buchanan and Breckinridge, some moderates began to feel neglected, and the southern cause gained adherents.

On August 1, 1861, Lieutenant Colonel John R. Baylor of Texas took formal possession of the "Territory of Arizona" for the Confederacy. The new territory comprised all of New Mexico and Arizona south of the 34° parallel. President Jefferson Davis formally accepted Arizona into the Confederacy on January 18, 1862. When the California Volunteers forced the Confederates out of Arizona, General James H. Carleton proclaimed the federal territory of Arizona, with boundaries set by military occupation.

The establishment of the Confederate territory finally spurred Congress to action, and on February 24, 1863, President Abraham Lincoln signed the bill creating Arizona Territory. This bill differed from the unsuccessful ones in that the boundary between Arizona and New Mexico was a north-south line starting at "the point where the southwest corner of Colorado joins the northern boundary of the Territory of New Mexico...," roughly the 109° meridian. During the debate in Congress several names for the new territory were advanced: Montezuma, Arizuma, Arizonia, Pimeria, and Gadsonia. On December 29, 1863, at Navajo Springs, Governor John N. Goodwin officially proclaimed the establishment of Arizona Territory.

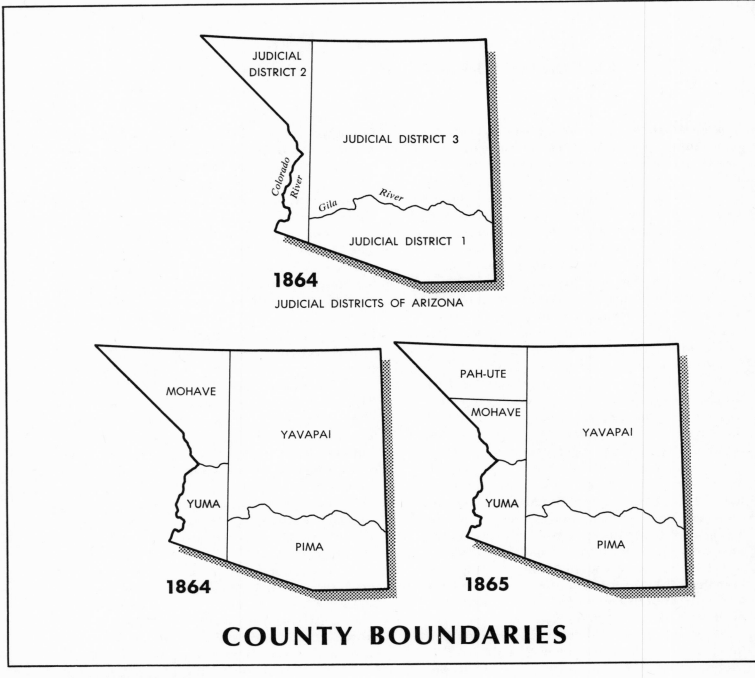

JUDICIAL DISTRICT 2

JUDICIAL DISTRICT 3

Colorado River

Gila River

JUDICIAL DISTRICT 1

1864

JUDICIAL DISTRICTS OF ARIZONA

MOHAVE

YAVAPAI

YUMA

PIMA

1864

PAH-UTE

MOHAVE

YAVAPAI

YUMA

PIMA

1865

COUNTY BOUNDARIES

WHEN THE OFFICIALS of the newly created Arizona Territory arrived in late December, 1863, the seat of government was set "at or near Fort Whipple." This new army post was located some twenty miles north of present-day Prescott to protect the new mining camps in the area. Prescott had been established only a few weeks before the arrival of the officials. In May, 1864, the fort was moved to a new location just outside the town, and the territorial government moved with the troops.

Governor John N. Goodwin made a tour of the territory soon after his arrival. On his return to Prescott, he issued a proclamation establishing three judicial districts, the first political subdivisions of Arizona. The number of districts corresponded to the number of justices of the Territorial Supreme Court. Based on these districts, Milton B. Duffield, United States marshal, assisted by a corps of assistants and interpreters, conducted a census. The total population, excluding Indians, was 4,573. The First District, which included Tucson, the largest town in the territory, had a population of 1,568. The Second District had 1,157 people, and La Paz, with 352 inhabitants, was its metropolis. The sparsely settled Third District reported only 1,039 people clustered around the mines of the Prescott region. Based on the census, Goodwin apportioned the territorial legislature of eighteen representatives and nine council members among the judicial districts and set July 18, 1864, as election day.

The first legislature met in Prescott in September, 1864, and divided the territory into four counties, all named for local Indian tribes. The north-south line that had divided the Second Judicial District from the First and Third districts was moved forty miles to the east. The former Second District was divided into two counties: Mohave and Yuma. Only Yuma County today has the same boundaries as those set in 1864. The first county seats were La Paz for Yuma County; Tucson, Pima County; Mohave City, Mohave County; and Prescott, Yavapai County.

The Second Territorial Legislature in 1865 created Pah-Ute County from the northern portion of Mohave County. This organization was in response to the rapid growth of farming along the Virgin and Muddy rivers. Pah-Ute County had a short life. Only six months after the county was organized, on May 5, 1866, an act of Congress transferred that part of Arizona lying west of the Colorado River and 114° west longitude to the new state of Nevada. Arizonans objected to this loss, and the legislators memorialized Congress for the return of the area, all to no avail. Until 1868 the territorial legislature continued to seat representatives from Pah-Ute County. It was not until 1871 that the legislature revoked the bill creating the county and restored what was left of Arizona's "Lost County" to Mohave County.

Of the four original counties, Mohave had the most restless county seat. Mohave City had been founded on the military reservation of Fort Mojave and had to be abandoned in 1867. The county seat moved to nearby Hardyville until 1873; during that year Cerbat held the seat. In 1877 there was another move, this time to Mineral Park. Eventually, in 1887, the legislature authorized an election to determine the permanent location of the county seat. The railroad town of Kingman won out.

In 1867 the territorial capital was moved to Tucson.

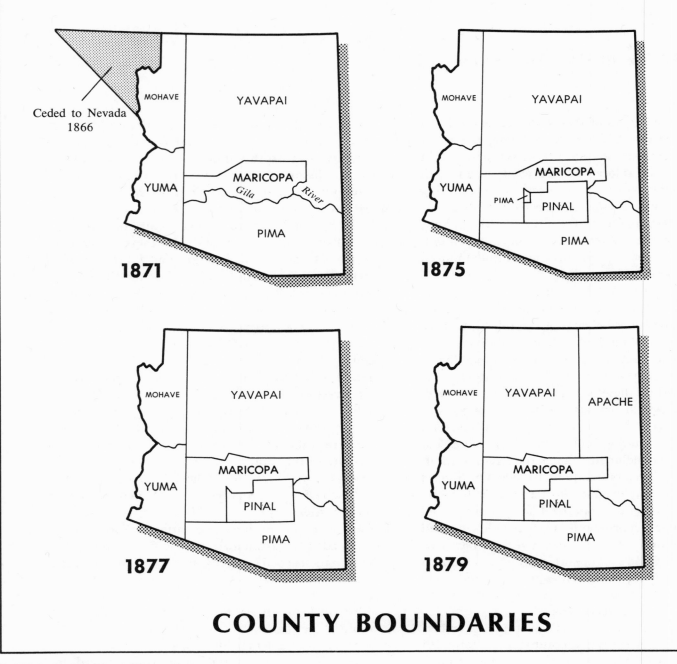

COUNTY BOUNDARIES

31. COUNTY BOUNDARIES, 1871, 1875, 1877, 1879

BY 1871 THERE HAD BEEN a number of significant changes in population in Arizona. The placer gold fields that had drawn people to La Paz had soon played out, and a flood of the Colorado River in 1869 had changed the river channel and left the town high and dry, ruining it as a river port. Most of the town's business moved downstream about three miles to Ehrenberg. As a result, the territorial legislature, in 1871, moved the seat of Yuma County to Arizona City. Two years later the Seventh Legislature changed the name of the town to Yuma.

Because of the growth of population in the Salt River valley and the distance to the county seat at Prescott, a matter of about a hundred miles on horseback or by stage, the legislature set up Maricopa County from the southwestern portion of Yavapai County in 1871. Based on a popular referendum, the county seat was set in Phoenix. Two years later a section of the northwestern part of Pima County was transferred to Maricopa County, thus placing the whole valley of the Gila River westward to the Yuma County line under Maricopa's control.

By 1875, farming was an important activity along the Gila and lower San Pedro rivers west of the Galliuro and Mazatzal mountains. The Eighth Legislature bowed to complaints of "the great distance from . . . our respective county seats" by organizing Pinal County out of parts of Pima and Maricopa counties. The county seat was placed in Florence. A fine two-story brick courthouse was built in 1881.

The Ninth Legislature, in 1877, had to make a small adjustment at the northwestern corner of Pinal County. Through oversight when the boundaries of Pinal County were laid down, an area with sides of about ten miles had been left as part of Pima County, completely isolated from the rest of the county. Also, another slice of southwestern Yavapai County was added to Maricopa County. The same legislature incorporated the city of Tucson and, under pressure from the representatives of the northern counties, moved the territorial capital back to Prescott.

The settlers in the farming communities along the Little Colorado River and miners in the recently opened mines around Clifton found themselves facing a 180-mile trip to the seat of Yavapai County at Prescott to conduct legal business. The Tenth Legislature, meeting in 1879, created Apache County from all that part of Yavapai County lying east of 119° 45′ west longitude and a very small piece of eastern Maricopa County. The legislature placed the county seat initially at Snowflake (named for two early Mormon settlers, Erastus Snow and William J. Flake). However, there was provision for a local election, and the voters chose St. John's as the county seat. In the following year the seat was moved once more, this time to Springerville.

1881

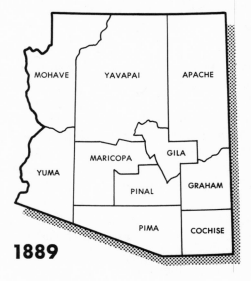

1889

1891

1895

1899

1909

COUNTY BOUNDARIES

THE ELEVENTH LEGISLATURE, meeting in 1881, moved the county seat of Apache County back to St. John's from Springerville. Following the discovery of silver in 1877, Tombstone had grown rapidly, becoming the largest town in Arizona. Local pride and the distance to Tucson led to the establishment of Cochise County, cut from eastern Pima County with the county seat at Tombstone. All early bills and court records misspelled the name "Cachise." This was the only Arizona county named for an individual Indian.

In the mountains east of Phoenix, Globe City had become a distribution center for the nearby mines. The middle Gila valley boomed with the founding of the San Carlos Indian agency. The legislature, in 1881, formed Gila County from parts of Apache, Maricopa, and Pinal counties. The county seat was at Globe.

Along the eastern border of the territory the Eleventh Legislature cut Graham County from Pima and Apache Counties. The county seat was at Safford until 1883, when it was moved to Solomonville. The naming of this county was the first break with the tradition of naming counties for native Indians.

The Twelfth Legislature in 1883 amended the county lines in the northwest. That part of Yavapai County lying north of the Colorado River and west of Kanab Wash was transferred to Mohave County. The area between the Colorado River and the Utah and Nevada state lines is commonly referred to as the "Arizona Strip."

As early as 1887 the citizens of the northwestern part of Yavapai County had sought to have Frisco County erected, with the seat at Flagstaff. In 1891 they succeeded, and Coconino County was formed from the northern two-thirds of Yavapai. Flagstaff, the county seat, has become an important railroad town and the center of a logging industry. Four years later, in 1895, Apache County was divided down the middle, and the western part became Navajo County, with its seat at Holbrook. This division ended a long struggle between Holbrook and St. John's over the seat of Apache County. Now each could be a county seat.

The legislature, in 1889, lopped off the southwest corner of Yavapai County and added it to Gila County. A quarter century of pulling and hauling between the northern and southern parts of the state ended when the Fifteenth Legislature moved the territorial capital to Phoenix.

The growth of Nogales as a border crossing and railroad town led to the erection of the smallest county in Arizona—Santa Cruz County—in 1899. It was cut from Pima County, and the seat was placed in Nogales. The original bill had included much of southern Pima County, including the Papago Indian reservation.

In 1909 the legislature formed the fourteenth, and last, county. Taken from the eastern part of Graham County, Greenlee was the second smallest county and the only one to be named for an Anglo pioneer, Mason Greenlee, an early prospector in the area, though the first name proposed was Lincoln.

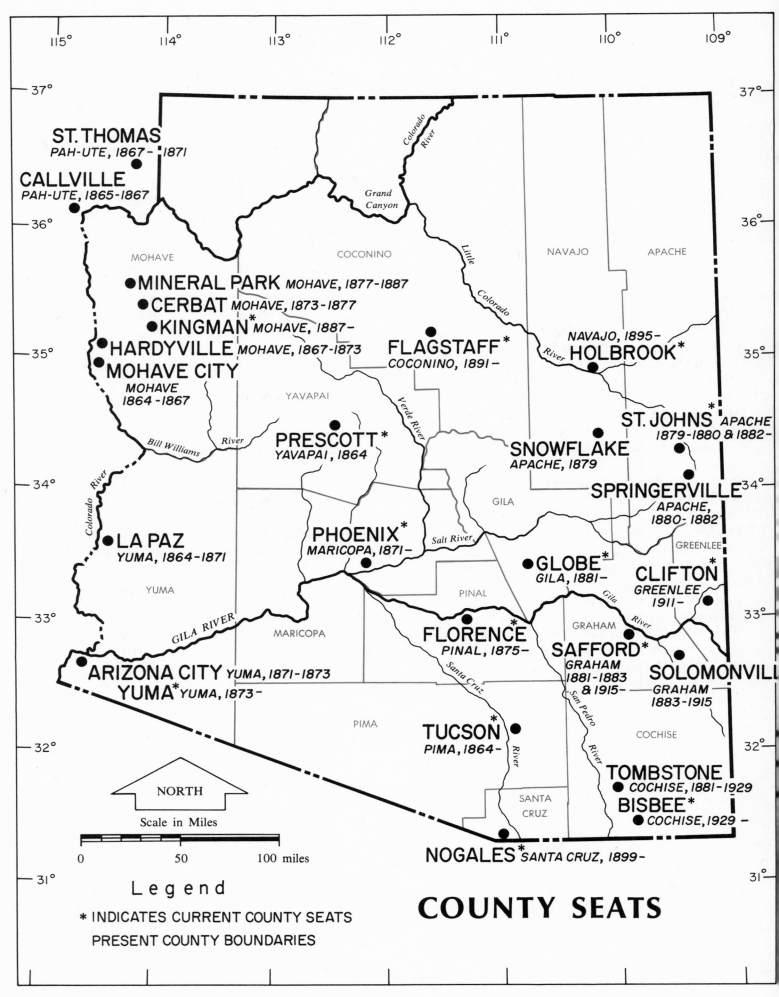

ST. THOMAS
PAH-UTE, 1867–1871

CALLVILLE
PAH-UTE, 1865-1867

MOHAVE

COCONINO

Colorado River

Grand Canyon

NAVAJO

APACHE

MINERAL PARK MOHAVE, 1877-1887

CERBAT MOHAVE, 1873-1877

KINGMAN* MOHAVE, 1887–

HARDYVILLE MOHAVE, 1867-1873

MOHAVE CITY
MOHAVE
1864-1867

Little Colorado

NAVAJO, 1895–

HOLBROOK*

FLAGSTAFF*
COCONINO, 1891–

YAVAPAI

Verde River

SNOWFLAKE
APACHE, 1879

ST. JOHNS* APACHE
1879-1880 & 1882–

Bill Williams   River

PRESCOTT*
YAVAPAI, 1864

SPRINGERVILLE
APACHE,
1880-1882

GILA

GREENLEE

Colorado River

LA PAZ
YUMA, 1864-1871

PHOENIX*
MARICOPA, 1871–

Salt River

YUMA

GLOBE*
GILA, 1881–

Gila River

CLIFTON*
GREENLEE
1911–

PINAL

GILA RIVER

MARICOPA

FLORENCE*
PINAL, 1875–

GRAHAM

SAFFORD*
GRAHAM
1881-1883
& 1915–

SOLOMONVILL

GRAHAM
1883-1915

ARIZONA CITY YUMA, 1871-1873
YUMA* YUMA, 1873–

Santa Cruz

San Pedro River

COCHISE

PIMA

TUCSON*
PIMA, 1864–

River

TOMBSTONE
COCHISE, 1881-1929

BISBEE*
COCHISE, 1929 –

NORTH

Scale in Miles

0   50   100 miles

SANTA
CRUZ

NOGALES* SANTA CRUZ, 1899–

L e g e n d

* INDICATES CURRENT COUNTY SEATS

PRESENT COUNTY BOUNDARIES

COUNTY SEATS

33. COUNTY SEATS

THERE HAVE BEEN NO CHANGES in the number of counties—fourteen—since Arizona achieved statehood in 1912, nor have there been any changes in their boundaries. However, there have been a number of minor changes in organization of the counties. In 1929 the county seat of Cochise County was moved from the moribund silver mining town of Tombstone to the booming copper center of Bisbee. Also, Safford was established as the seat of Graham County in place of Solomonville.

There were many attempts to alter the county lines. In 1881 Maricopa County tried to annex the town of Maricopa in Pinal County, and Pima County tried to extend north to the Aravaipa River. The territorial legislature considered a bill to move the county seat of Pima County from Tucson to Tombstone and another bill to move it to Tubac. Pinal County sought to extend south to include the Old Hat and Canyon del Oro mining districts on the grounds that they were twenty miles closer to Florence, the Pinal County seat, than to Tucson.

There were attempts to cut bits from Yavapai County and add them to Maricopa County or to Gila County. Still another bill was designed to move the county seat of Apache County back to St. Johns from Springerville.

Practically all attempts to change the shape or organization of the counties had economic roots. Changes in county lines were designed to enrich the county by adding high-tax property. The location of the county seat in one town or another meant more business for the local merchants, landlords, and saloon keepers.

In size and population, Arizona's counties vary greatly. Coconino, the largest, is slightly smaller than the combined areas of the states of New Hampshire and Vermont and is the second largest county in the contiguous United States. Santa Cruz County, the smallest, is larger in area than the state of Rhode Island. The extent of the counties is very deceptive, because large tracts in all counties are under the control of the federal government as Indian reservations, national forests, parks and monuments, and military installations (Maps 52–56).

Since the depression of 1929 there have been a number of moves to consolidate certain counties in order to reduce the expense of local government.

COUNTY	AREA IN ACRES*	RELATIVE STANDING	1970 POPULATION	RELATIVE STANDING
Apache	7,151,360	3	32,304	9
Cochise	4,003,840	9	61,918	4
Coconino	11,886,720	1	48,326	6
Gila	3,040,000	11	29,255	10
Graham	2,950,400	12	16,578	12
Greenlee	1,199,360	13	10,330	14
Maricopa	5,904,640	7	969,425	1
Mohave	8,486,400	2	25,857	11
Navajo	6,343,040	5	47,559	7
Pima	5,914,240	6	351,667	2
Pinal	3,441,920	10	68,579	3
Santa Cruz	797,240	14	13,966	13
Yavapai	5,179,240	8	36,837	8
Yuma	6,390,400	4	60,827	5
	72,688,800		1,773,428	

*Acreage rounded to nearest ten acres.

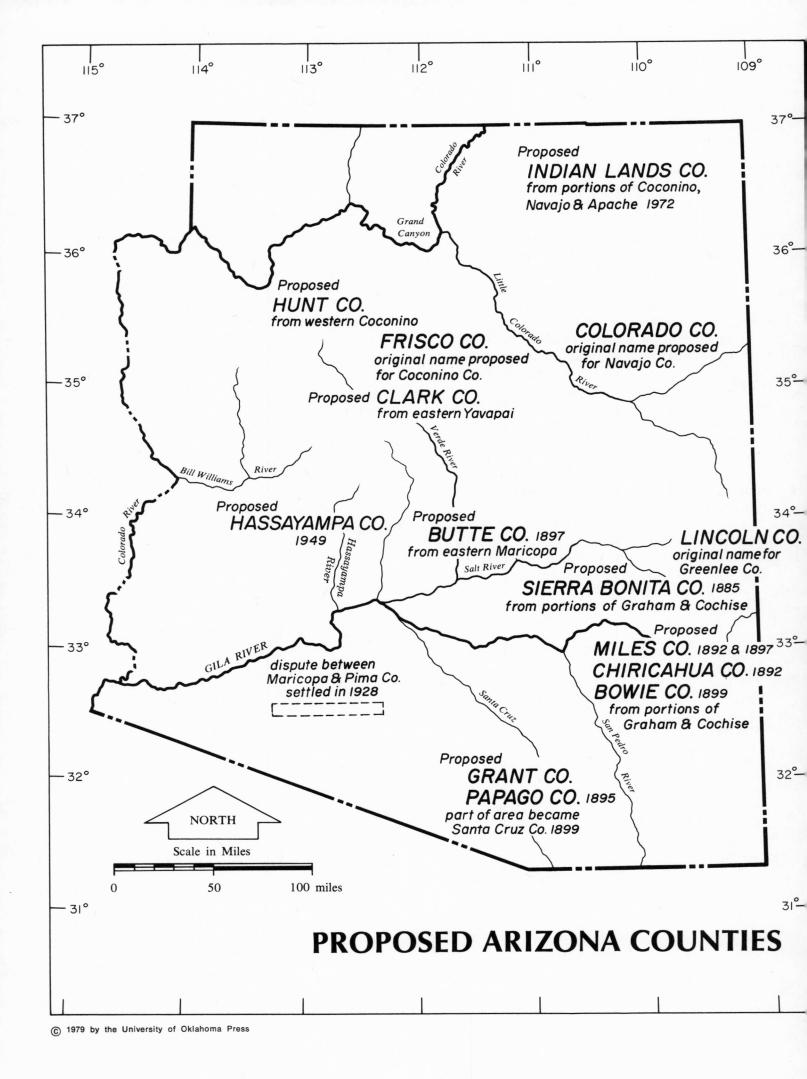

Proposed
INDIAN LANDS CO.
from portions of Coconino,
Navajo & Apache 1972

Proposed
HUNT CO.
from western Coconino

FRISCO CO.
original name proposed
for Coconino Co.

COLORADO CO.
original name proposed
for Navajo Co.

Proposed **CLARK CO.**
from eastern Yavapai

Proposed
HASSAYAMPA CO.
1949

Proposed
BUTTE CO. 1897
from eastern Maricopa

LINCOLN CO.
original name for
Greenlee Co.

Proposed
SIERRA BONITA CO. 1885
from portions of Graham & Cochise

Proposed
MILES CO. 1892 & 1897
CHIRICAHUA CO. 1892
BOWIE CO. 1899
from portions of
Graham & Cochise

dispute between
Maricopa & Pima Co.
settled in 1928

Proposed
GRANT CO.
PAPAGO CO. 1895
part of area became
Santa Cruz Co. 1899

Colorado River
Grand Canyon
Little Colorado River
Verde River
Bill Williams River
Colorado River
Hassayampa River
Salt River
GILA RIVER
Santa Cruz
San Pedro River

NORTH

Scale in Miles

0   50   100 miles

PROPOSED ARIZONA COUNTIES

UNHAPPINESS OVER various aspects of local government from time to time led prominent local citizens to support drives for the formation of new counties. From 1885 to 1899 attempts were made to erect from parts of Cochise and Graham counties a new unit to be called Sierra Bonita County, with its seat at Willcox. The name came from that of the ranch of Henry Clay Hooker, chief proponent of the plan.

Reaction to this sort of move was largely a matter of whose ox was being gored. In 1887 a mass meeting in Tombstone voiced opposition to the new county. The proposal was considered to be nothing but a drive to enhance the value of town lots in Willcox. On the other hand, just one month later it was reported that a bill had been introduced to the territorial legislature to annex the town of Nogales to Cochise County.

Charles T. Hayden, a leading citizen of Tempe, in 1897 supported a drive to have Butte County organized from the eastern half of Maricopa County. This drive was not successful.

Around the turn of the century the inhabitants of the Verde district of Yavapai County, which included the bustling copper camp of Jerome, discovered that they were paying a large share of the county taxes and were receiving less than their proportional share of county services. A move was started, heartily supported by the *Jerome Mining News*, to organize a new county. The name selected was Clark, in honor of William A. Clark, owner of the very rich United Verde mine. Clark gave weak endorsement to the idea of an additional county, but took no steps to implement the action. The idea was dropped for a time but was renewed several times in later years.

There was an attempt, pressed by the city of Williams, to create Hunt County (named for the first governor of the state of Arizona) out of the western portion of Coconino County. Of course, Williams was to be the county seat.

Because of an error in survey, a strip of land about fifty miles long, east and west, and about six miles wide, north and south, had long been in dispute between Maricopa and Pima counties. This boundary dispute was not settled until 1928, in favor of Maricopa County.

In the late 1930's a dispute over the paving of a road in northern Cochise County spurred a move to set up a new county in the northern part of Cochise County. The county seat was to be located in the city of Tombstone. Still another county was proposed in the western end of Maricopa County in 1949 to be named Hassayampa County.

As recently as 1972 the state legislature considered a bill to create a new county embracing the Hopi and Navajo Indian reservations, to be called Indian Lands County.

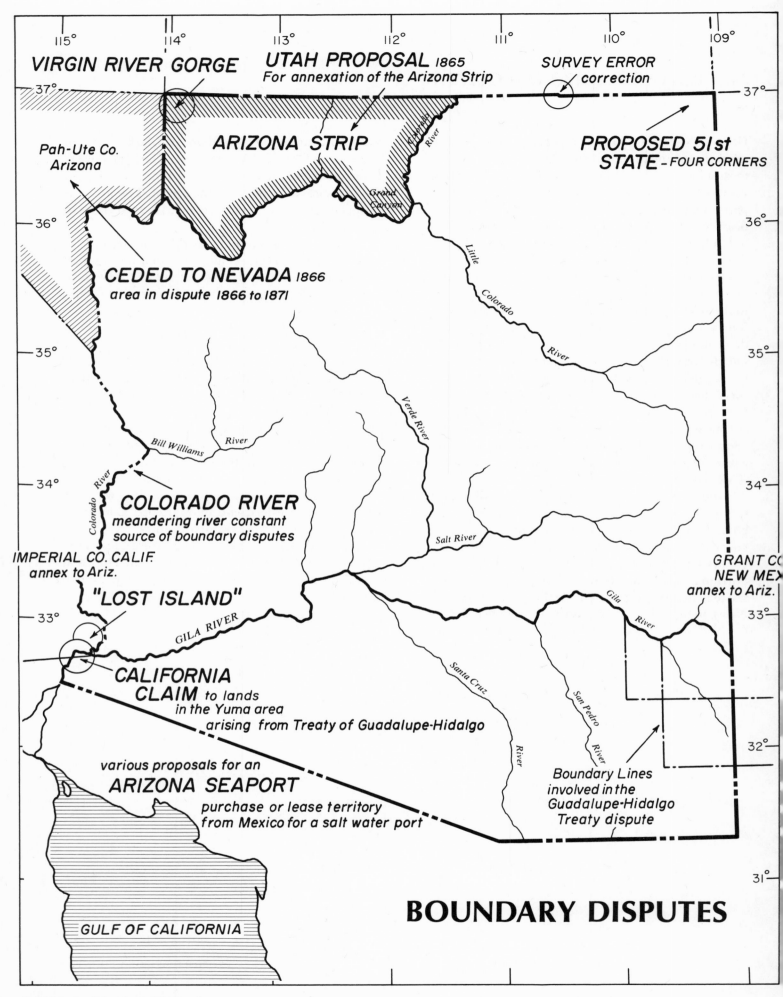

VIRGIN RIVER GORGE

UTAH PROPOSAL 1865
For annexation of the Arizona Strip

SURVEY ERROR
correction

115° 114° 113° 112° 111° 110° 109°

37° 37°

ARIZONA STRIP

PROPOSED 51st
STATE - FOUR CORNERS

Pah-Ute Co.
Arizona

Little

Colorado

36° 36°

River

CEDED TO NEVADA 1866
area in dispute 1866 to 1871

River

35° 35°

Verde River

Bill Williams *River*

COLORADO RIVER
meandering river constant
source of boundary disputes

Colorado River

Salt River

34° 34°

IMPERIAL CO. CALIF.
annex to Ariz.

GRANT CO
NEW MEX
annex to Ariz.

"LOST ISLAND"

Gila

River

33° 33°

GILA RIVER

CALIFORNIA
CLAIM to lands
in the Yuma area
arising from Treaty of Guadalupe-Hidalgo

Santa Cruz

San Pedro River

32°

various proposals for an
ARIZONA SEAPORT
purchase or lease territory
from Mexico for a salt water port

River

Boundary Lines
involved in the
Guadalupe-Hidalgo
Treaty dispute

31°

GULF OF CALIFORNIA

BOUNDARY DISPUTES

35. BOUNDARY DISPUTES

LAND GRABBING in one form or another was typical of the American West. Arizona suffered its first loss when most of Pah-Ute County was transferred to Nevada by act of Congress in 1866. By 1871 nearly all the Mormon settlers in that area, estimated to number some twelve hundred, had left Pah-Ute County for Utah.

Furthermore, the lack of a deep-water port on the Gulf of California was a political issue in Arizona for a long time. The Thirteenth Territorial Legislature in 1885 memorialized Congress to purchase from Mexico that part of Sonora lying west of 111° west longitude and north of 30° north latitude in order to procure a seaport. In 1919 the state legislature urged Congress to purchase enough land from Mexico to obtain such a port. In 1937 the request shifted to a long-term lease of a port site to be under American jurisdiction.

As stated in the Treaty of Guadalupe Hidalgo, the line between California and Baja California was to run in a straight line from the Pacific Coast to the junction of the Gila and Colorado rivers. Just below the junction the Colorado flows for about five miles in a northwesterly direction. When the boundary was finally staked out, a small sliver of the left bank of the river lay north of the line, or theoretically in California. Both Arizona and California claimed this land, because it contained the ferry buildings and other taxable property in Yuma.

The Second Territorial Legislature asked for a survey of territorial boundaries in hopes of settling the Yuma matter and possibly acquiring the Mormon settlements of Santa Clara and St. George on the Virgin River. These towns had a population estimated at two thousand persons and were thought to lie south of the thirty-seventh parallel. At the same time, the territorial delegate from Utah introduced in Congress memorials seeking to obtain a tract in northern Arizona and another in Colorado. As late as 1897 a senator from Utah sought the assistance of Arizona delegate Marcus A. Smith in acquiring, for Utah, that part of Arizona lying north and west of the Colorado River.

In the mid-1870's the inhabitants of Grant County, New Mexico, became unhappy over the lack of a public school system in their territory. In 1876 a "Declaration of Independence" was issued in Silver City suggesting annexation to Arizona. Next year the territorial legislature of Arizona memorialized Congress asking for the transfer of Grant County. The request was promptly buried in congressional files.

The most radical proposal came in 1881, when it was suggested in the territorial legislature that all of Arizona except Mohave, Yavapai, and Apache counties be attached to southern California to form a new state.

A minor adjustment in the northern boundary of the state had to be made at about 110° 30' west longitude when a survey error of 2,178 feet was discovered. This correction makes a noticeable jog in the state line.

In the 1920's, Imperial County, California, was agitating for annexation to Arizona. In conjunction with the construction of the interstate highways, Arizona briefly considered ceding the area around the Virgin River gorge and the town of Littlefield to Utah. Proposals were advanced in 1972 to form a new state, predominantly Indian, in the Four Corners area by taking parts of Arizona, New Mexico, Colorado, and Utah.

The shifting channel of the Colorado River has caused numerous disputes between Arizona and California. The largest of these was over "Lost Island" near Yuma. A large ox-bow bulged into California and the Yuma Indian Reservation. This area was good agricultural land, and both states claimed it. The Bureau of Indian affairs and the Bureau of Land Management were also involved. In the 1950's the two states compromised the problem and settled other problems caused by the river.

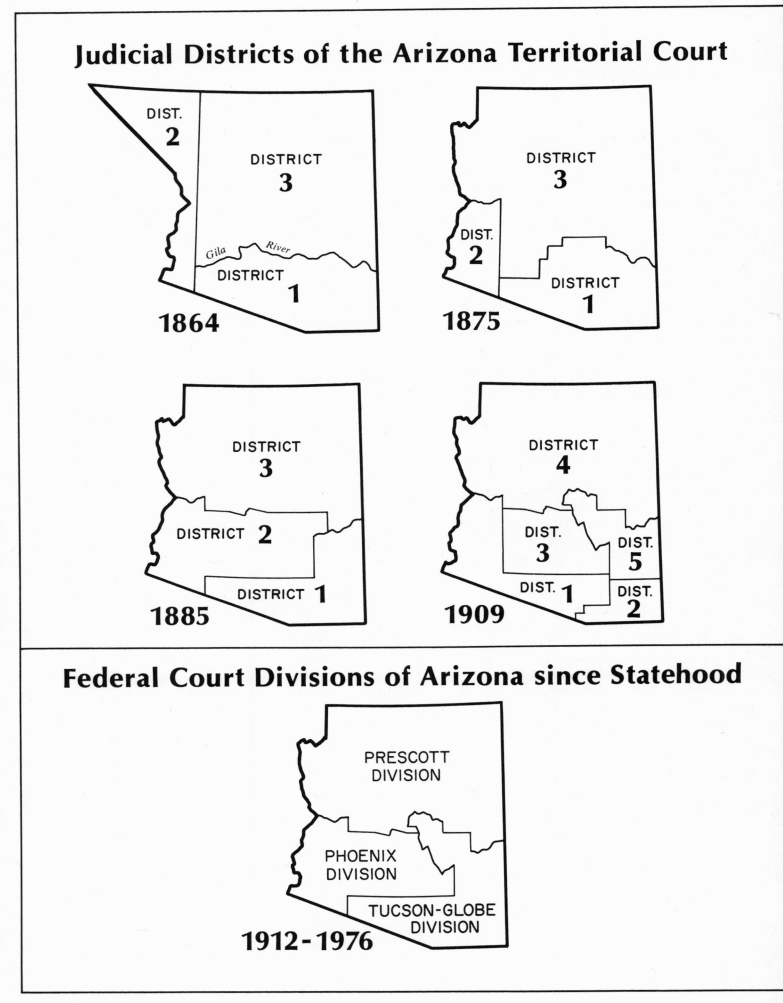

Judicial Districts of the Arizona Territorial Court

DIST. 2

DISTRICT 3

Gila River

DISTRICT 1

1864

DISTRICT 3

DIST. 2

DISTRICT 1

1875

DISTRICT 3

DISTRICT 2

DISTRICT 1

1885

DISTRICT 4

DIST. 3

DIST. 5

DIST. 1

DIST. 2

1909

Federal Court Divisions of Arizona since Statehood

PRESCOTT DIVISION

PHOENIX DIVISION

TUCSON-GLOBE DIVISION

1912-1976

As INDICATED EARLIER (Map 30), Governor John N. Goodwin divided Arizona Territory into three judicial districts to conform to the number of federally appointed judges. Each judge presided over the district court of his area, and together the three justices composed the Arizona Territorial Supreme Court. Thus, any of the judges might sit in judgment on an appeal from the district court where he had rendered a decision.

This duality of roles caused a great deal of discontent among Arizonans. In 1883 Governor F. A. Tritle asked Congress to provide a fourth federal judge so that the supreme court could be made up of three judges, none of whom had sat on the case being appealed. The request was ignored. The Thirteenth Territorial Legislature in 1885 provided that a judge could not hear an appeal of a case heard by him in a lower court. This law effectively reduced the supreme court to two justices.

Shifts in population led to a number of reorganizations of the judicial districts. In 1875 the loss of Pah-Ute County to Nevada and other minor changes led to a redistricting. The First Judicial Distrct comprised Pima and Pinal counties. District Two covered only Yuma County. District Three was made up of Maricopa, Mohave, and Yavapai counties.

There was another reorganization in 1885. District One was arranged to include Cochise, Graham, and Pima counties. District Two was expanded to cover Gila, Maricopa, Pinal, and Yuma counties. District Three comprised Apache, Mohave, and Yavapai counties.

Not until 1909 was the number of federal judges increased to five because of the work load imposed on the courts by the rapid growth of population. The First Judicial District was extended to cover Pima and Yuma counties. District Two comprised Cochise and Santa Cruz counties. District Three consisted of Maricopa and Pinal counties. District Four was made up of Apache, Coconino, Mohave, Navajo, and Yavapai counties. District Five covered Graham, Greenlee, and Gila counties.

With the coming of statehood in 1912, a great deal of legal business was transferred from federal to state jurisdiction, and the federal court system was again reorganized. Three divisions were established. The Tucson-Globe Division embraced Cochise, Gila, Graham, Greenlee, Pima, and Santa Cruz counties. The Phoenix Division covered Maricopa, Pinal, and Yuma counties. The Prescott Division included the rest of the state. This organization of the federal courts is still in effect.

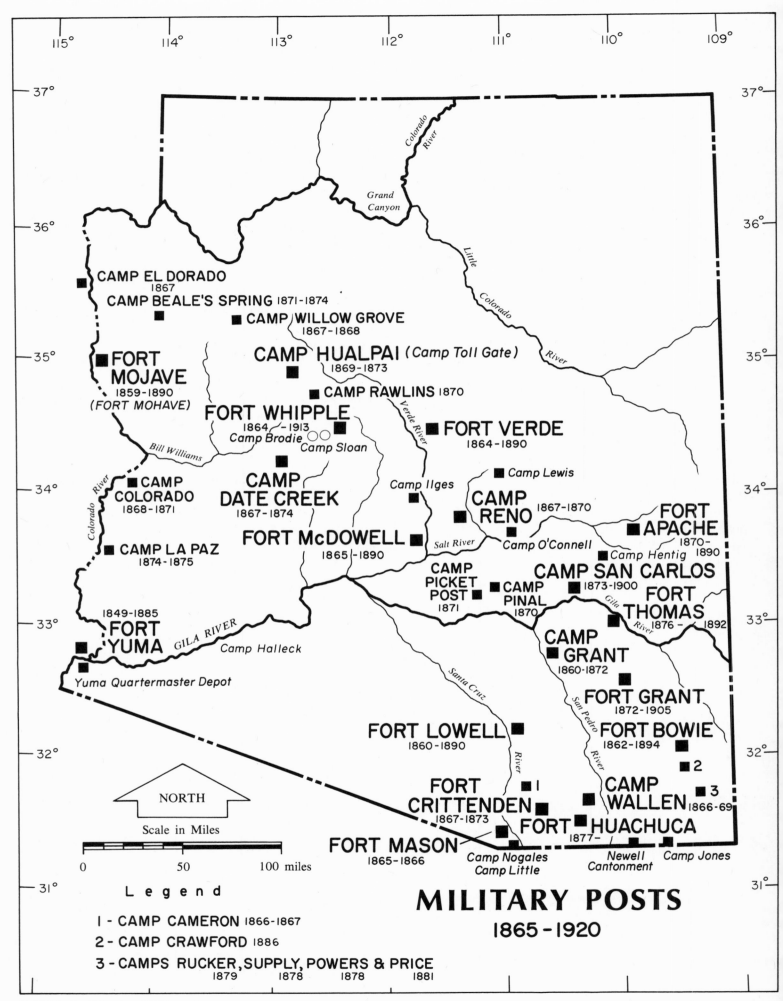

CAMP EL DORADO 1867

CAMP BEALE'S SPRING 1871-1874

CAMP WILLOW GROVE 1867-1868

CAMP HUALPAI *(Camp Toll Gate)* 1869-1873

CAMP RAWLINS 1870

FORT MOJAVE 1859-1890 *(FORT MOHAVE)*

FORT WHIPPLE 1864 – -1913 Camp Brodie Camp Sloan

FORT VERDE 1864-1890

Camp Lewis

CAMP COLORADO 1868-1871

CAMP DATE CREEK 1867-1874

Camp Ilges

CAMP RENO 1867-1870

FORT APACHE 1870- -1890

Camp O'Connell

Camp Hentig

CAMP LA PAZ 1874-1875

FORT McDOWELL 1865-1890

Salt River

CAMP PICKET POST 1871

CAMP PINAL 1870

CAMP SAN CARLOS 1873-1900

FORT THOMAS 1876- -1892

1849-1885 FORT YUMA

GILA RIVER

Camp Halleck

CAMP GRANT 1860-1872

Yuma Quartermaster Depot

FORT GRANT 1872-1905

FORT LOWELL 1860-1890

FORT BOWIE 1862-1894

2

FORT CRITTENDEN 1867-1873

1

CAMP WALLEN 1866-69

3

FORT HUACHUCA 1877-

FORT MASON 1865-1866

Camp Nogales Camp Little

Newell Cantonment

Camp Jones

NORTH

Scale in Miles

0   50   100 miles

L e g e n d

1 - CAMP CAMERON 1866-1867

2 - CAMP CRAWFORD 1886

3 - CAMPS RUCKER, SUPPLY, POWERS & PRICE
1879   1878   1878   1881

MILITARY POSTS
1865-1920

A NUMBER OF THE POSTS established before or during the Civil War were reoccupied after the war by regular army troops. The regulars returned to Camp (later Fort Mohave) Mojave in 1866. (The designation of many stations was changed from "camp" to "fort" in 1879 in compliance with General Orders 79, dated November 8, 1878.) The fort was turned over to the Indian service in 1890.

The site of Fort Breckinridge was reoccupied in 1865 as Camp on San Pedro River, but soon it was called Fort Grant. In 1867 the name was changed to Camp Grant. Five years later the post was moved to the foot of Mount Graham and named New Camp Grant. The old site was abandoned in 1873, and the new site became Camp Grant until 1879. The post was abandoned in 1905, and in 1912 the buildings were given to the state for a reform school.

Fort Bowie was changed to a camp in 1867 and back to a fort in 1879. During the Geronimo campaign, Generals Crook and Miles made it their headquarters. The site was sold at auction in 1911, but now it is a national historic site.

Camp Lowell was established in 1866 at the former Tucson Supply Depot, but was moved to a new site in 1873 and called a fort. It was abandoned in 1891, and part of it is now a park maintained by the Arizona Historical Society.

Whipple Barracks, long the military headquarters of Arizona, remained in use until 1898. It was rebuilt in 1904 only to be vacated again in 1913, and it is now a veterans' hospital.

During the Apache Wars a number of new posts were opened. In July, 1870, Camp Ord was founded in Navajo County. The next month the name was changed to Camp Mogollon and in September to Camp Thomas. Six months later it became Camp Apache and in 1879 Fort Apache.

Fort McDowell, first called Camp Verde, was established in 1865. Camp Verde soon became Camp McDowell and then Fort McDowell. It was vacated in 1891.

Camp San Carlos was set up in 1873 to serve as the headquarters for the San Carlos Indian Agency. At times a subpost of Fort Grant or Fort Apache, the camp was closed in 1900.

When Camp Goodwin was abandoned in 1871 because of malaria, it was replaced in 1876 by the "New Post on the Gila," located seven miles upriver. Within a month the name was changed to Fort Thomas. Located in a dry, desolate region, though threatened by malaria, Thomas was often referred to as the worst post in the country. It was closed in 1892.

One of several camps called Lincoln was opened by New Mexico Volunteers in 1866 on the Verde River. Two years later it was renamed Camp Verde, and in 1879, Fort Verde. Abandoned in 1890, part of the post is now a state park.

Temporary posts were established to protect the roads to Prescott: Beale's Spring, Date Creek, Hualpai (originally Camp Toll Gate), Rawlins, and Willow Grove. Another group of temporary camps was set up during the Apache Wars: Cameron, Crawford, Ilges, Lewis, O'Connell, Pinal (later called Camp Picket Post), Price, Reno, Wallen, and John A. Rucker.

Three camps were opened on the Mexican border. Camp Nogales opened in 1910 and was renamed Camp Stephen D. Little in honor of a soldier killed in action during the troubles. Camp Harry T. Jones at Douglas and Newell Cantonment at Naco resulted from Pancho Villa's raid on Columbus, New Mexico, in 1916.

Another Camp Colorado was opened near La Paz because of trouble with the local Indians. Camp La Paz was a supply depot for forwarding supplies to the interior of the state.

By 1920 Fort Huachuca was the only active regular army post in Arizona. Camps Brodie and Sloan were training areas for the Arizona National Guard.

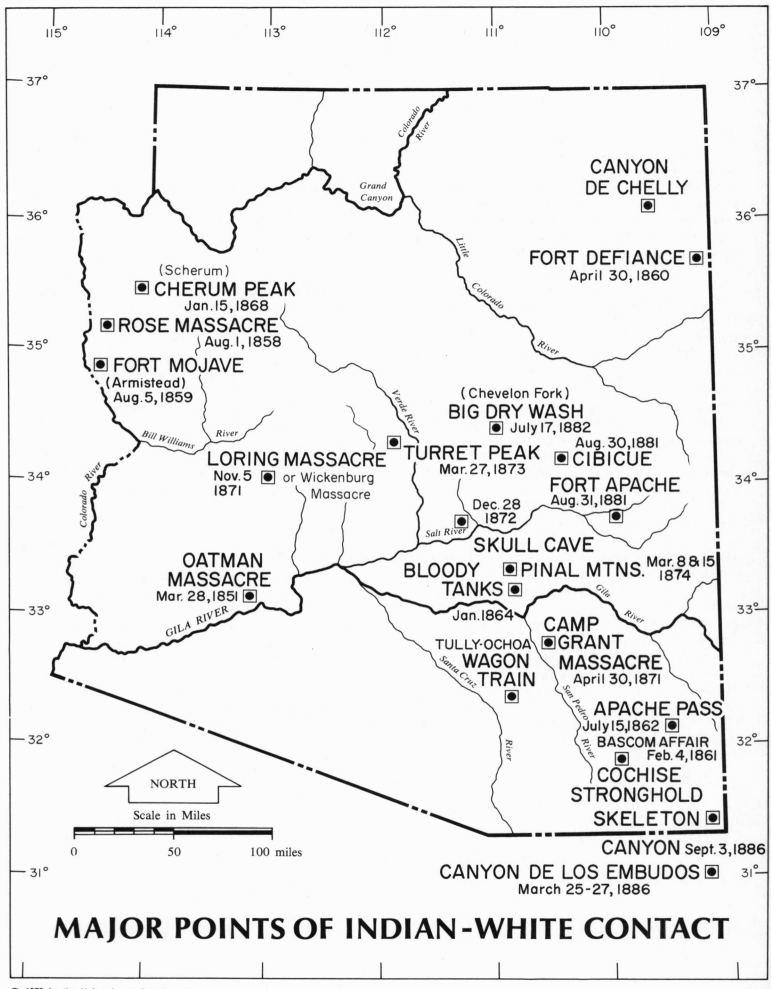

38. MAJOR POINTS OF INDIAN-WHITE CONTACT

NOT ALL POINTS OF CONTACT, peaceful and violent, can be shown. Between 1866 and 1875 an average of twenty-one skirmishes occurred each year. Only those considered most important are shown.

Cherum (Sherum) Peak. Here occurred a skirmish between detachments of the First and Eighth Cavalry regiments and Cherum's band of Walapais, who were at war because a chief had been killed by a freighter.

Skull (Salt River) Cave. Three companies of the Fifth Cavalry and 130 Indian scouts located a band of hostiles in a cave in the canyon wall. Thirty-seven Indians were killed, and 20 were taken prisoner.

Turret Peak. Detachments of the Fifth Cavalry, Twenty-third Infantry, and scouts surprised a camp atop the peak. This engagement practically ended the 1873 campaign against the Apaches.

Cibicue Creek. In an attempt to arrest Nock-ay-del-klinne, a medicine man who had started a revival, fighting broke out. This is the only recorded battle in which Apache scouts mutinied.

Big Dry Wash (Chevelon Fork). Six troops of the Third and Sixth Cavalry regiments were trailing a band of fifty-eight Apaches. The Indians laid an ambush for the leading troop, but while concentrating on their target they were outflanked by the other troops.

Oatman Massacre. On March 28, 1851, a family of emigrants who had left the Pima Villages alone were attacked by Indians. The father, mother and two children were killed. A son, Lorenzo, left for dead, escaped. Olive, age sixteen, and Mary, ten, were taken prisoner. Mary died in captivity, but Olive was ransomed after six years.

Camp Grant Massacre. A party of 148 Anglos, Mexicans, and Papagos from Tucson attacked an Indian village on the Camp Grant Reservation. About eighty Indians, mostly women and children, were killed, and twenty-eight children were seized. The warriors were absent.

Cochise Stronghold. General O. O. Howard met the Chiricahua chief here and drew up a treaty giving the Indians a huge reservation and assuring several years of peace with this band.

Skeleton Canyon. This canyon was the site of Geronimo's final surrender to General Nelson A. Miles, ending the Apache wars.

Apache Pass. This is the site of Lieutenant George N. Bascom's attempt to arrest Cochise and of a battle between California Volunteers and Apaches. The pass later became the site of Fort Bowie.

Loring (Wickenburg) Massacre. A stage was attacked by Indians, probably from the Date Creek Reservation, at this location. Among those killed was Frederick W. Loring, a well-known eastern writer.

Fort Defiance. This fort was the first army post in Arizona. In 1860 an estimated 1,000 Navajos seized some buildings before the garrison could drive off the attackers.

Fort Apache. While most of the troops were at Cibicue Creek, Apaches fired into this post from long range and cut the telegraph wire.

Canyon de Chelly. This stronghold of the Navajos was penetrated by New Mexico Volunteers under Colonel Kit Carson in 1864.

Fort Mohave. Detachments of the Sixth Infantry, under Captain Lewis A. Armistead, fought the only battle with the Mojaves about ten miles south of this fort.

Rose Massacre. Fort Mohave was built after the advance party of an emigrant train was attacked by Mojaves. Nine persons were killed and sixteen wounded.

Bloody Tanks (Pinole Treaty). Settlers and friendly Indians, under King S. Woolsey, invited some Apaches into camp and then killed them. The alternate name derives from the tale that the Apaches were fed poisoned *pinole* (corn mush).

Canyon de los Embudos. This was the site of a meeting between Geronimo and General George Crook.

Tully & Ochoa Wagon Train. This attack was an unusual affair, because there were thirty well-armed men with the train. One driver was killed, two were wounded, and the loss was set at $100,000.

Pinal Mountains. Detachments of the Fifth Cavalry had several clashes with Apaches in this area during Crook's 1873 campaign.

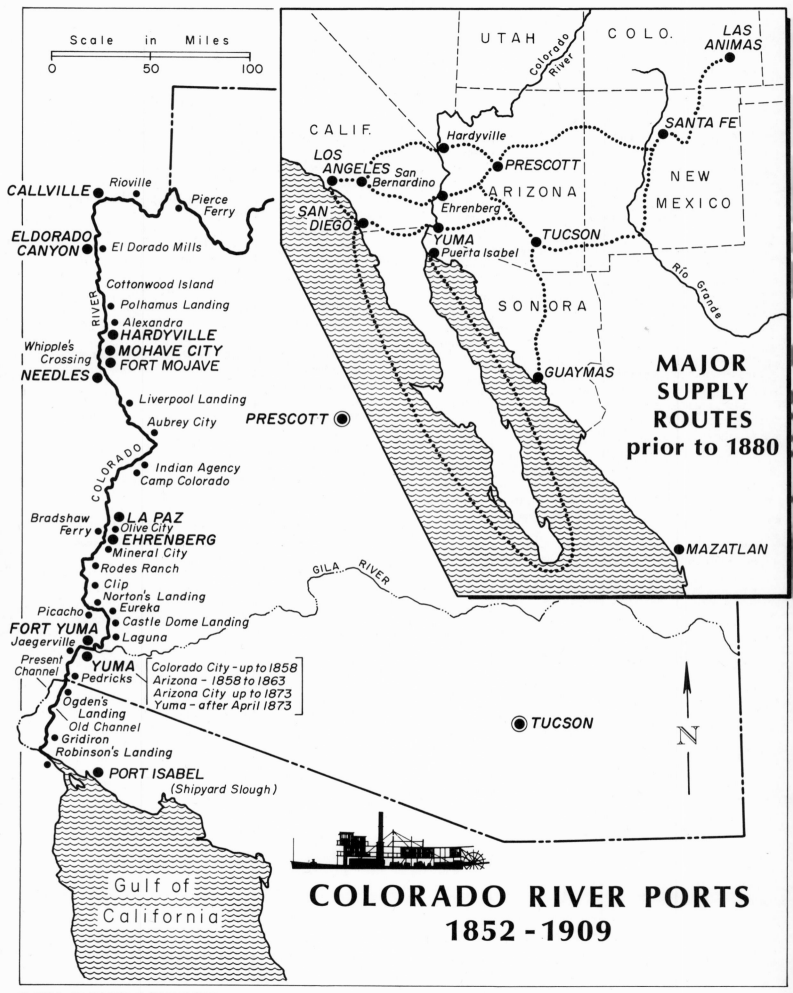

Scale in Miles

0   50   100

CALLVILLE
Rioville
Pierce Ferry

ELDORADO CANYON
El Dorado Mills

RIVER

Cottonwood Island
Polhamus Landing
Alexandra
HARDYVILLE
MOHAVE CITY
FORT MOJAVE
Whipple's Crossing
NEEDLES

Liverpool Landing
Aubrey City

COLORADO

Indian Agency
Camp Colorado

PRESCOTT ◉

Bradshaw Ferry
LA PAZ
Olive City
EHRENBERG
Mineral City
Rodes Ranch
Clip
Norton's Landing
Picacho
Eureka
Castle Dome Landing
FORT YUMA
Laguna
Jaegerville
Present Channel
YUMA
Pedricks
Ogden's Landing
Old Channel
Gridiron
Robinson's Landing
PORT ISABEL
(Shipyard Slough)

Colorado City – up to 1858
Arizona – 1858 to 1863
Arizona City up to 1873
Yuma – after April 1873

Gulf of California

UTAH   COLO.
                            LAS ANIMAS
Colorado River

CALIF.
                    Hardyville   SANTA FE
LOS ANGELES   San Bernardino   PRESCOTT
SAN DIEGO   NEW MEXICO
              Ehrenberg   ARIZONA
              YUMA   TUCSON
              Puerta Isabel
                         Río Grande
                    SONORA

MAJOR SUPPLY ROUTES prior to 1880

GUAYMAS

MAZATLAN

GILA RIVER

◉ TUCSON

N

COLORADO RIVER PORTS 1852-1909

ARIZONA WAS FORTUNATE in that before the arrival of the Southern Pacific Railroad in 1877 it had several routes over which supplies and machinery could be brought in by wagon or river steamer.

By far the most important line of supply was the Colorado River. Under the Treaty of Guadalupe Hidalgo, American vessels could ply the river without interference by Mexican authorities. Thus, goods imported via the river avoided the ruinously high Mexican import duties. Goods were brought to the mouth of the river in ocean-going ships and were transferred to shallow-draft river steamers. These steamers varied from the *Uncle Sam*, with a capacity of thirty-five tons, to the *Mohave II* at over one hundred tons. The steamers often towed one-hundred-ton barges. In the 1870's six steamers and five barges were in operation. Repair shops and a dry dock were built at Port Isabel at the mouth of the river.

The practical head of navigation was at Hardyville. In seasons of high water, steamers reached Callville, at the mouth of the Vegas Wash, or even Rioville, near the mouth of the Virgin.

Yuma was the chief port from which supplies were hauled by wagon to all of Arizona south of the Gila and Salt rivers. Although it was only 80 air-line miles from the river's mouth, the meandering of the stream made the distance some 170 miles by steamer. About seventy miles north of Yuma, La Paz was the port for central Arizona. In 1869 a shift of the river channel left La Paz high and dry, and Ehrenberg, about three miles to the south, took its place. Hardyville, some three hundred miles upstream from Yuma, was the distribution point for the mines of the northwest and was connected to Prescott by a toll road.

In addition, there were numerous landing places on both banks of the river that served single mines or groups of mines, some as far back as twenty miles from the river. Throughout most of the territorial period the legislature memorialized Congress for money for the improvement of navigation on the Colorado River.

From the east a small trickle of supplies came from the Texas coast as early as 1856, when Charles D. Poston imported mining machinery and supplies for the mines near Tubac. Other merchandise came from the Missouri Valley over the Santa Fe Trail. These routes both involved distances of over one thousand miles. As the railroads pushed west after the Civil War, goods were brought by wagon from successive railheads, and crudely smelted copper and lead were shipped east.

A natural road led northward from the port of Guaymas, Sonora, on the Gulf of California. Before the Civil War the Tubac mines were given permission to ship their silver through Guaymas duty free, but political strife in northwestern Mexico discouraged much use of this route. During the Civil War arrangements were made with Governor Ignacio Pesqueira of Sonora to move government supplies from Guaymas to Tucson without payment of import duties. Until 1877 civilian goods came in over the same route at only 5 per cent of the usual Mexican duties. When the central government took full control of the Guaymas customs house, the red tape involved in getting permits from Mexico City discouraged use of this route.

There were also routes leading from the Pacific Coast. The citizens of San Diego County, which reached east to the Colorado River, raised several thousand dollars to improve the road to Yuma. Another wagon route ran from San Bernardino to either Ehrenberg or Fort Mohave. The great drawback of these routes was that about one-half of the weight capacity of the teams had to be devoted to carrying water and forage for the animals while crossing the California desert.

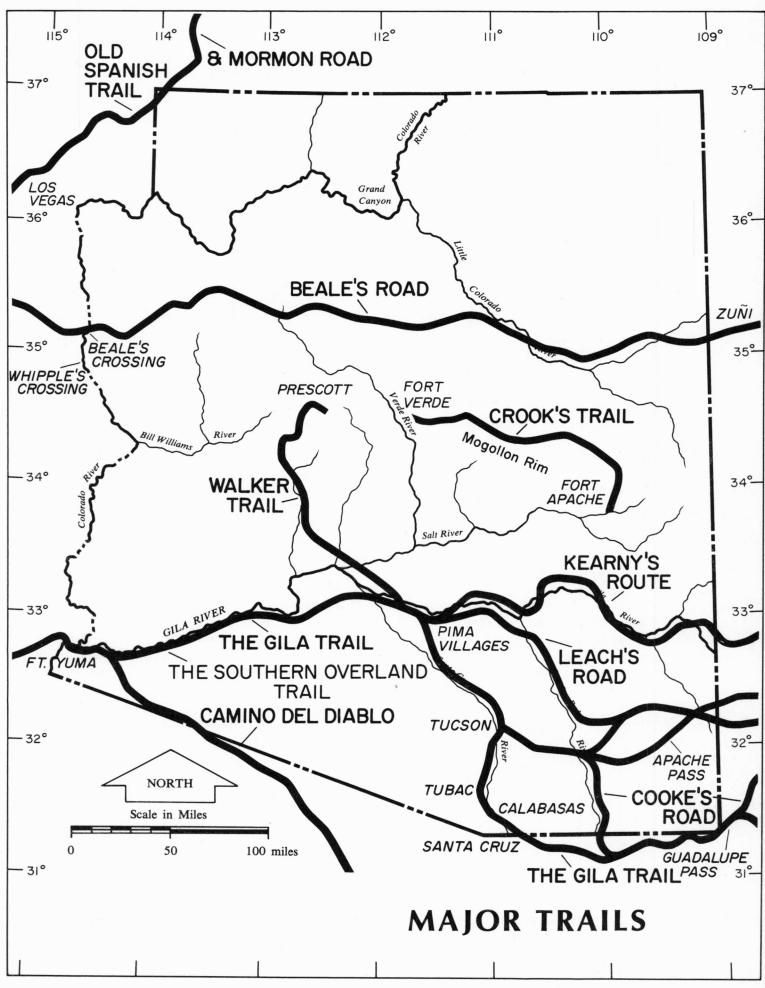

OLD
SPANISH
TRAIL

& MORMON ROAD

LOS
VEGAS

BEALE'S ROAD

ZUÑI

BEALE'S
CROSSING

WHIPPLE'S
CROSSING

Colorado River

Bill Williams   River

PRESCOTT

FORT
VERDE

Verde River

CROOK'S TRAIL

Mogollon Rim

FORT
APACHE

WALKER
TRAIL

Salt River

KEARNY'S
ROUTE

GILA RIVER

THE GILA TRAIL

PIMA
VILLAGES

LEACH'S
ROAD

FT. YUMA

THE SOUTHERN OVERLAND
TRAIL

CAMINO DEL DIABLO

TUCSON

APACHE
PASS

NORTH

TUBAC

COOKE'S
ROAD

Scale in Miles

CALABASAS

0   50   100 miles

SANTA CRUZ

GUADALUPE
PASS

THE GILA TRAIL

MAJOR TRAILS

THROUGHOUT THE HISTORY of the westward movement in the United States the lines of travel followed, for the most part, trails already established by the Indians. West of the one hundredth meridian these trails followed rivers such as the Platte or marched from one water hole to the next.

The Southern Overland Trail, with its many variants, was one of those that ran between reliable sources of water. Portions of this trail were known to the Spaniards as early as the 1700's, when Apache Pass was known as Puerto del Dado, the Gate of the Die, undoubtedly reflecting the gamble one took in passing through this stronghold of the Chiricahua Apaches.

During the Mexican War, Colonel Stephen W. Kearny led the Army of the West over a trail, well known to the mountain men (Map 17), along the Gila River all the way across Arizona. This trail was known to be unsuited for wagons, so Brevet Lieutenant Colonel Philip St. George Cooke, who had orders to build a wagon road from the Río Grande to California, blazed a new trail farther to the south (Map 18).

During the Gold Rush of 1849 many parties of emigrants used various branches of the southern trail—through Janos and Fronteras in northern Mexico or through Apache Pass, as well as Cooke's Wagon Road.

To make travel easier, the federal government appropriated money for the surveying, marking, and improvement of wagon roads. In 1857–59 James B. Leach supervised the work on the El Paso and Fort Yuma Wagon Road—generally referred to as Leach's Wagon Road. This road followed the line of Parke's railroad survey (Map 23), with one notable exception. On reaching the San Pedro River from the east, the road turned north, striking the Gila River about fifteen miles below the junction of the San Pedro and the Gila. While this line saved some thirty miles, it bypassed Tucson, much to the disgust of the residents. Local newspapers commented that many of the water tanks on the road were so constructed that water could not possibly flow into them. This section of the road was little used by travelers, who preferred to stop in Tucson.

Another thought behind the wagon roads was that the route of a wagon road might be converted into a railroad line. Edward F. Beale was sent out to build a road generally along the line surveyed by Captain Amiel W. Whipple in 1853–54 (Map 23). As Beale approached the Colorado River he deviated from Whipple's line by holding directly west instead of swinging south and west along Bill Williams River. This road was followed by a few California-bound parties, most notably the Rose party (Map 38).

A north-south trail was pioneered by James R. Walker and his party of prospectors in 1863. Leaving the Pima Villages, the trail struck out northwesterly to the Hassayampa River, followed that stream to its headwaters, and crossed the Bradshaw Mountains to Prescott. This trail was followed by freighters and stagecoaches.

To shorten the line of communications between Fort Apache and Fort Verde (Map 37), General George Crook had a rough wagon road cut up and along the Mogollon Rim in 1874. This trail, rough as it was, reduced the distance between the two posts by about 50 per cent.

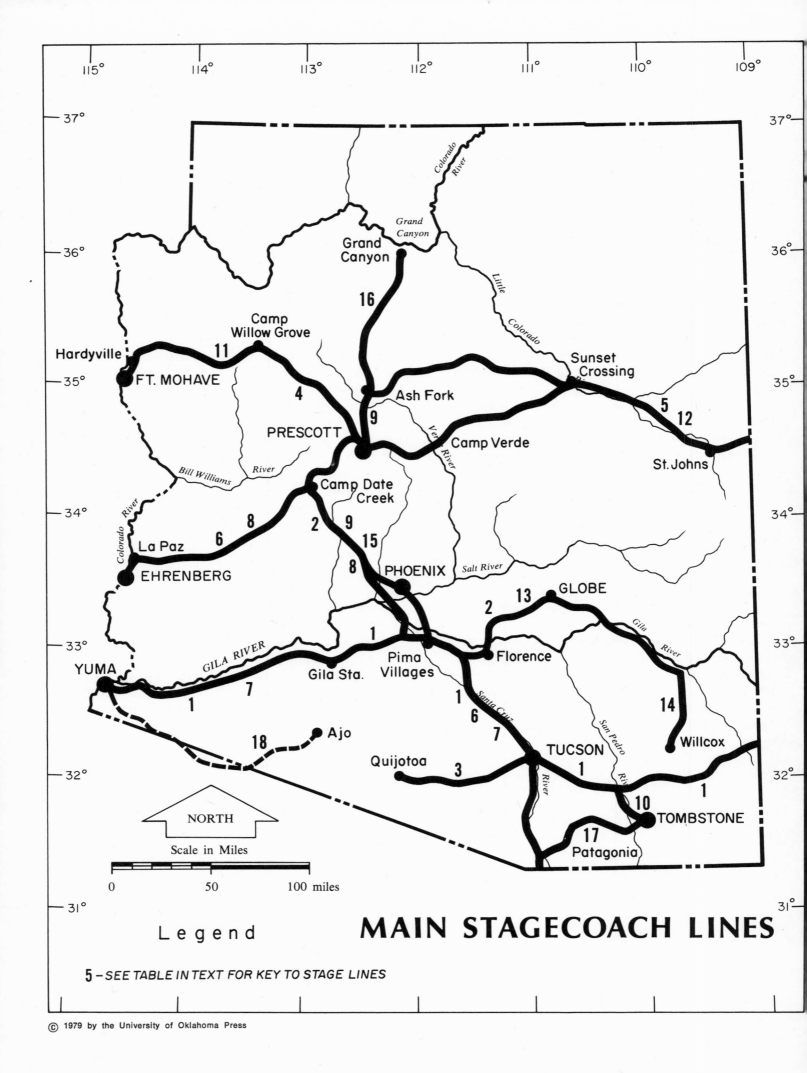

MAIN STAGECOACH LINES

Legend

5 — SEE TABLE IN TEXT FOR KEY TO STAGE LINES

NORTH

Scale in Miles

0   50   100 miles

In 1853 TUCSON and the area southward along the Santa Cruz River were isolated from California by some 350 miles and from New Mexico by at least 250 miles. Under these conditions, communications were vital to the development of the territory. The first line with the outer world was the San Antonio & San Diego Mail Line, which began operating a semimonthly service in mid-1857. The line has been described as running from nowhere, through nothing, to no place, and it was nicknamed "the Jackass Mail."

The Butterfield Overland Mail began semiweekly service from Missouri via El Paso, Tucson, and Los Angeles to San Francisco in 1858. Operation continued until March, 1861, when the equipment was transferred to the route through Nebraska, Wyoming, and Utah.

Until 1864 Arizona had to rely on military couriers for mail service. In that year Dukes & Company started a line from Prescott to Fort Mohave connecting with their line to Los Angeles. The Santa Fe Stage Company provided service, in 1866, from Prescott to Denver and Kansas City and connections between Prescott and Tucson. The Arizona Stage Company in 1868 ran from Prescott and Tucson and connected at La Paz with the Noble & Winters line to San Francisco.

Stage companies went out of business or changed names with exasperating frequency. A very important element in the financial health of a stage line was the contract to carry the United States mail. The loss of this contract, or a successful bid that was too low, might ruin a company. Carrying the Wells-Fargo treasure box was an additional source of income, if somewhat risky.

The Tucson, Arizona City [Yuma] & San Diego Stage Company started operations in 1870 with triweekly service. The business was sold to James A. Moore and L. W. Carr in February, 1872. Connections to the east were offered by J. F. Bennett & Company running from Tucson to Mesilla, where the connections were made. In 1872 the Tucson, Prescott & San Bernardino Line left Tucson weekly for Wickenberg, where connections were made with the semiweekly stage from Prescott to San Bernardino.

The fare from Prescott to San Bernardino was about forty dollars.

Kerens & Mitchell, proprietors of the Southern Pacific Mail Stage Lines, offering triweekly service from San Diego to Mesilla in 1874, claimed to have the longest stage line in the country. After April, 1877, daily service was offered, and the fare from Phoenix to San Francisco was quoted at ninety-three dollars.

In 1878 Gilmer, Salisbury & Co's Stage Lines took over the two-year-old California & Arizona Stage Company and later offered service from Prescott to Ash Fork on the Atlantic and Pacific Railroad and from Dos Palmas, California, on the Southern Pacific to Prescott. Early the next year the Tucson & Tombstone Stage Line offered four trips per week, but increased this schedule to daily service later in the year. The fare was ten dollars, and the running time was seventeen hours.

With the completion of the two major railroads across the territory in 1881 and 1883, short lines proliferated, connecting the larger settlements with the rails and to each other. As the railroads developed branch lines, the stages disappeared.

NUMBER ON MAP	MAJOR STAGE LINES
1.	San Antonio and San Diego Mail Line, 1857–58
	Butterfield Overland Mail, 1858–61
	Texas and California Stage Line, 1878
	Southern Pacific Mail Line, 1874–78
	National Mail & Transportation Co., 1878
2.	Southern Pacific Mail
3.	Pedro Aguirre & Co.
4.	Duke's Express, 1864
5.	Santa Fe Stage Co., 1866
6.	Arizona Stage Co., 1868
7.	Tucson, Arizona City & San Diego Stage Co., 1870
8.	California & Arizona Stage Co., 1875
9.	Gilmer, Salisbury & Co. Stage Lines, 1878
10.	Tucson & Tombstone Stage Lines, 1879
11.	Hugh White & Co., 1879
12.	Prescott–Santa Fe Stage Line
13.	Arizona Stage Co., 1881
14.	Norton & Stewart, 1881
15.	Prescott & Phoenix, 1886
16.	Grand Canyon Stage Line, 1895
17.	Tombstone & Patagonia Express, 1880
18.	Jaeggers Pack Trail, 1854

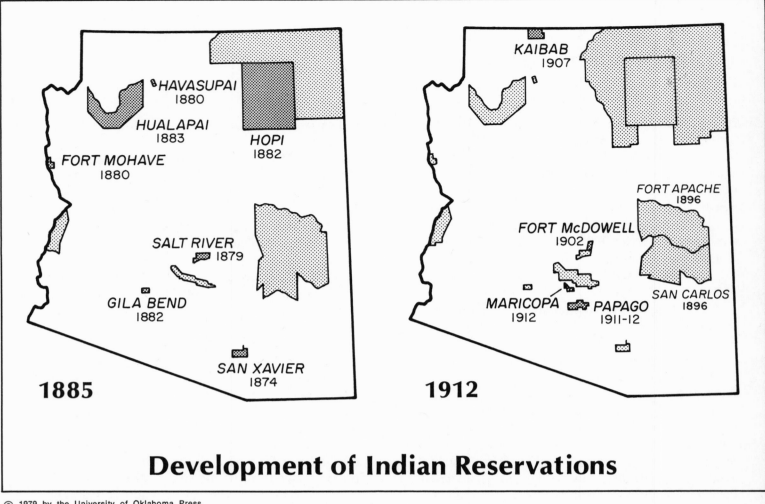

1885

HAVASUPAI
1880

HUALAPAI
1883

HOPI
1882

FORT MOHAVE
1880

SALT RIVER
1879

GILA BEND
1882

SAN XAVIER
1874

1912

KAIBAB
1907

FORT APACHE
1896

FORT McDOWELL
1902

MARICOPA
1912

PAPAGO
1911-12

SAN CARLOS
1896

Development of Indian Reservations

THE ESTABLISHMENT AND MODIFICATION of Indian reservations were accomplished by treaty, act of Congress, or Executive Order of the President of the United States. In 1919 Congress forbade the formation of new reservations by Executive Order, and in 1927 Congress took complete control of changing the boundaries of all reservations.

The first reservation in Arizona was established by act of Congress in 1859 for the Pima and Maricopa Indians on their ancestral lands on the Gila River. An area "not to exceed one hundred square miles" was set aside on both banks of the river. This was the only reservation set up before the Civil War. In 1869 the reserve was increased by 81,000 acres, bringing the total to 145,000 acres.

Because of the lack of detailed survey data, the boundaries of many of the reservations were very vaguely stated. For example, the description of the Chiricahua reservation, as set forth in the Executive Order of December 4, 1872, was the following: "Beginning at Dragoon Springs, near Dragoon Pass, and running thence northeasterly along the north base of the Chiricahua Mountains to a point on the summit of Peloncillo Mountains or Stevens Peak range; then running southeasterly along said range through Stevens Peak to the boundary of New Mexico; thence running westerly along said boundary 55 miles; thence running northerly following substantially the western base of the Dragoon Mountains, to the place of beginning."

As the land began to fill with miners, farmers, and ranchers, surveying became more detailed and the reservation boundaries were set forth more accurately. Also, there was a growing demand that the Indians be restricted in their wanderings. The First Territorial Legislature in 1864 asked Congress for $150,000 to be used to place the various tribes of the Colorado River Valley, plus the Hualapais and Yavapais of the central part of the territory, on a reservation. As a result, the Colorado River Reservation was established in March, 1865. In addition, some 75,000 acres surrounding Fort Mohave were set aside. Only a few Chemehuevis from Nevada and California and about half of the Mojaves settled on these reserves. The Hualapais and Yavapais left the reservations several times and were forced back by the army only to leave again. Eventually the Hualapais were given a reservation of their own, while the Yavapais split up among several Apache reservations.

Between 1866 and 1872 temporary reservations were set up for some bands of Apaches on the military reservations at Camps Goodwin, Grant, McDowell, Beale Springs, and Date Creek. These reserves were more in the nature of feeding stations. Most were closed when more permanent reservations were founded.

The Navajos of northeastern Arizona had been rounded up in 1864 and placed on an unhealthy reservation on the Pecos River in New Mexico. In 1868 they were allowed by treaty to return to a reservation in northwestern New Mexico and northeastern Arizona. The Navajo Agency was established in 1870 at Fort Defiance, just inside the Arizona line.

On the recommendation of the War Department, in 1870 a reservation was set up for the Apaches in the White Mountains. Two years later Vincent Colyer of the Board of Indian Peace Commissioners recommended the establishment of the San Carlos Division of the White Mountain Reservation. This organization placed two agencies on the same reservation—one at Camp Apache and the other at San Carlos. The Executive Order which made this division increased the size of the reservation over that the army had recommended. It also abolished the Chiricahua and Camp Grant reservations and restored the lands to the public domain.

Old Camp Grant on Aravaipa Creek was the site of the notorious Camp Grant Massacre in 1871. A band of Apaches were being fed at the camp. The citizens of Tucson blamed them for depredations in the area, and a party of Anglos, Mexican-Americans, and Papago Indians struck the Indian camp, killed about eighty, mostly oldsters and women, and took twenty-eight children prisoners. This action caused a nation-wide sensation. The leaders were brought to trial and were acquitted. Most of the children just disappeared.

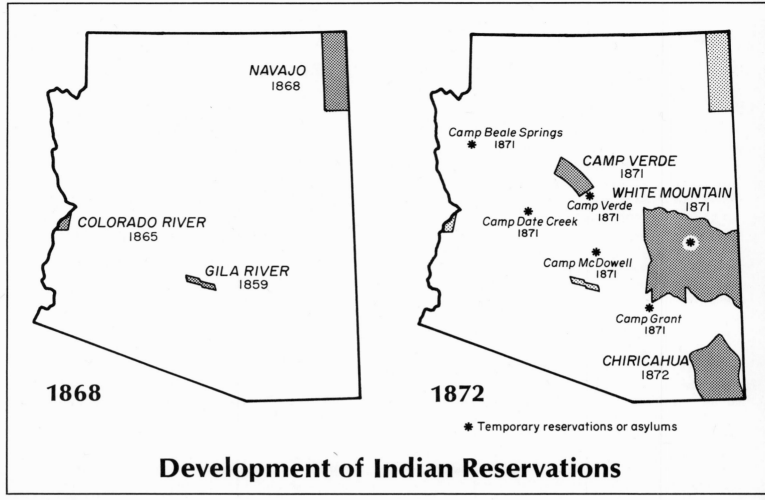

NAVAJO
1868

COLORADO RIVER
1865

GILA RIVER
1859

1868

Camp Beale Springs
1871

CAMP VERDE
1871

WHITE MOUNTAIN
1871

Camp Date Creek
1871

Camp Verde
1871

Camp McDowell
1871

Camp Grant
1871

CHIRICAHUA
1872

1872

✳ Temporary reservations or asylums

Development of Indian Reservations

43. DEVELOPMENT OF INDIAN RESERVATIONS, 1873–1912

THE MID-1870'S WERE MARKED by a policy of concentrating the Indians on a few reservations. In March, 1875, some fourteen hundred Indians, mostly Yavapais, were transferred from Camps Date Creek and Verde to the White Mountain Reservation, despite the fact that they had started farming. Some months later about 1,800 Indians arrived from Fort Apache, and in June, 1876, a party of 325 Chiricahua Apaches arrived from their recently abolished reservation. The Warm Springs Apaches were moved from their reservation in New Mexico in 1877. This policy soon proved to be shortsighted because many of these bands were traditionally hostile to each other.

The Colorado River Reservation was increased in 1873 by adding bottom lands along the river to the south. In the following year another small extension was made on the south, and lands on the California shore were added.

A reserve was set aside for the Papagos in the valley of the Santa Cruz River in 1874. The area encompassed the famous Spanish mission of San Xavier del Bac.

Beginning in 1869, a period of drought set in, and some twelve hundred Pimas left the reservation along the Gila River and settled on the Salt River, starting farms among the white settlers. In 1877 the Ninth Territorial Legislature requested that these Pimas be forced back onto their reservation. Two years later an area along the Salt River was set aside for the Pimas by Executive Order. The Tenth Legislature in 1879 appropriated two thousand dollars to send two agents to Washington to seek withdrawal of the order. The order was canceled, and instead a new area was set aside in the Verde River valley south of Fort McDowell. By 1887 white farmers upstream of the Gila River reservation had pre-empted most of the water needed for irrigation of the Indians' farms.

The Havasupais were given a reservation in 1880. Located in twenty-five-hundred-foot-deep Cataract Canyon, a branch of the Grand Canyon, the reserve was twelve miles long, north and south, and five miles wide. Of this land, only the strip in the bottom of the canyon was arable. The following year saw the establishment of a reserve of some three thousand square miles for the Hualapais on the south rim of the Grand Canyon.

The Gila River Reservation of the Pimas and Maricopas was extended in 1882 and 1883, with the exception of any land to which title had passed from the federal government or on which any valid homestead or preemption claims had previously been located.

A tract of land was set aside for the Yuma (Quechan) Indians on the Arizona side of the Colorado River and north of the mouth of the Gila River. The Executive Order setting up that reservation was canceled in the following year, and a new reservation was established on the California side of the river.

Indan reservations were under constant pressure from the white settlers for various reasons. The Twelfth Territorial Legislature in 1883 memorialized Congress "that the costly system of Arizona Reservations with its attendant temptations to peculation, may be terminated and that the lands, included in the reservations may be relegated to the uses of the citizens of the United States." Two years later, the legislature asked that the Apaches on the San Carlos and White Mountain reserves be removed from Arizona and that the land be restored to the public domain.

In 1878 the Southern Pacific Railroad had been granted a right-of-way across the original Pima-Maricopa Reservation. Eleven years later the projected Arizona and California Railway was granted a right-of-way across the Colorado River Reservation. This line was never built.

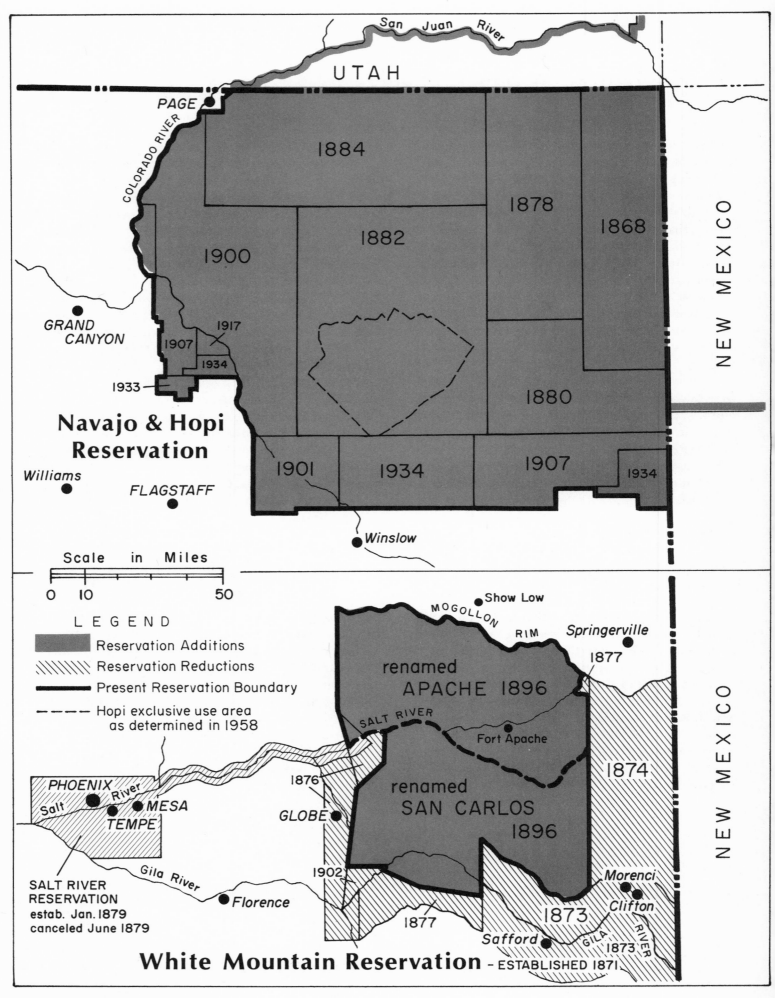

San Juan River

UTAH

PAGE

1884

1878

1868

COLORADO RIVER

1882

1900

NEW MEXICO

GRAND
CANYON

1917

1907

1934

1880

1933

**Navajo & Hopi
Reservation**

Williams

FLAGSTAFF

1901

1934

1907

1934

Winslow

Scale   in   Miles

0   10   50

Show Low

MOGOLLON

Springerville

L E G E N D

RIM

1877

Reservation Additions

Reservation Reductions

renamed
APACHE 1896

Present Reservation Boundary

SALT RIVER

NEW MEXICO

Hopi exclusive use area
as determined in 1958

Fort Apache

1874

PHOENIX

River

1876

renamed
SAN CARLOS

Salt

MESA

GLOBE

1896

TEMPE

SALT RIVER
RESERVATION
estab. Jan. 1879
canceled June 1879

Gila River

Morenci

1902

Clifton

Florence

1873

1877

GILA RIVER

Safford

1873

White Mountain Reservation – ESTABLISHED 1871

44. INDIAN RESERVATIONS: APACHE, HOPI, AND NAVAJO

WHILE MOST Indian reservations underwent changes in the years following their establishment, none experienced as radical changes as the Apache, Hopi, and Navajo reservations.

The Navajo Reservation was established in 1868 when that tribe was allowed to return to its ancestral lands after five years' internment on the Bosque Redondo Reservation in eastern New Mexico. The new reservation covered a large tract of land in northwestern New Mexico and northeastern Arizona. In the next twelve years the Arizona portion more than doubled in size. In 1882 a reservation was set up for the Hopis, but the Navajo reservation continued to expand until it entirely surrounded the Hopis' lands. Both tribes were basically pastoral and needed large tracts of the poor rangeland for their herds of cattle, goats, and sheep.

The original executive order that set up the Hopi Reservation of some three thousand square miles stated that it was for the Hopis and other Indians at the discretion of the secretary of the interior. Over the years the Navajos ranged their herds over much of the Hopi Reservation. In the 1930's and 1940's the two reservations were divided into more than twenty grazing distrcts for range management. District Six, some 300,000 acres, was inhabited by Hopis, while the other districts were inhabited by Navajos. The Hopis sought clarification of their rights to the land, and in 1958 a federal court ordered that District Six be set aside for the exclusive use of the Hopis and that the balance of the three-thousand-square-mile reservation be divided equally between the two tribes. This decision was upheld by the United States Supreme Court in 1962. Because the Navajos practically monopolize the joint-use area, the Hopis have sent bills to the Navajos for grazing fees and taxes on trading posts. The Navajos have refused to honor the bills. Recently, the Hopis have taken to impounding Navajo cattle found in District Six, and this activity has bred bad feelings between the two tribes.

While the Navajo Reservation expanded steadily, the Apache reservations, founded as the White Mountain Reservation in 1871, have been under constant pressure and have been cut down numerous times. The first major cut came in 1873 on the grounds that farmers had settled on the land before the reservation was laid out and had started an irrigation project. In the following year the development of rich copper deposits in the Clifton-Morenci area brought another cut. The opening of rich silver and copper mines around Globe led to further reductions in 1876 and 1877. The western boundary was redefined in 1893, resulting in the loss of land along the south bank of the Salt River.

In 1896 it was recognized that, because of the rugged nature of the land and the size of the reservation, the White Mountain Reservation had to be divided. The northern one-third was made into the Fort Apache Reservation, and the balance became the San Carlos Reservation.

There was a further reduction in 1896, when the area around the Deer Creek Coal Fields was returned to the public domain, with the profits going to the Apaches. This so-called San Carlos Mineral Strip, some 232,320 acres, was restored to the reservation in 1963 and 1969.

The Salt River Reservation was an excellent example of attempts to run everything from Washington. By Executive Order of President Rutherford B. Hayes a reservation was laid out that covered Phoenix, Tempe, and Mesa and extended up the Salt River to the western boundary of the San Carlos and Fort Apache reservations. Needless to say, the order was annulled in less than six months.

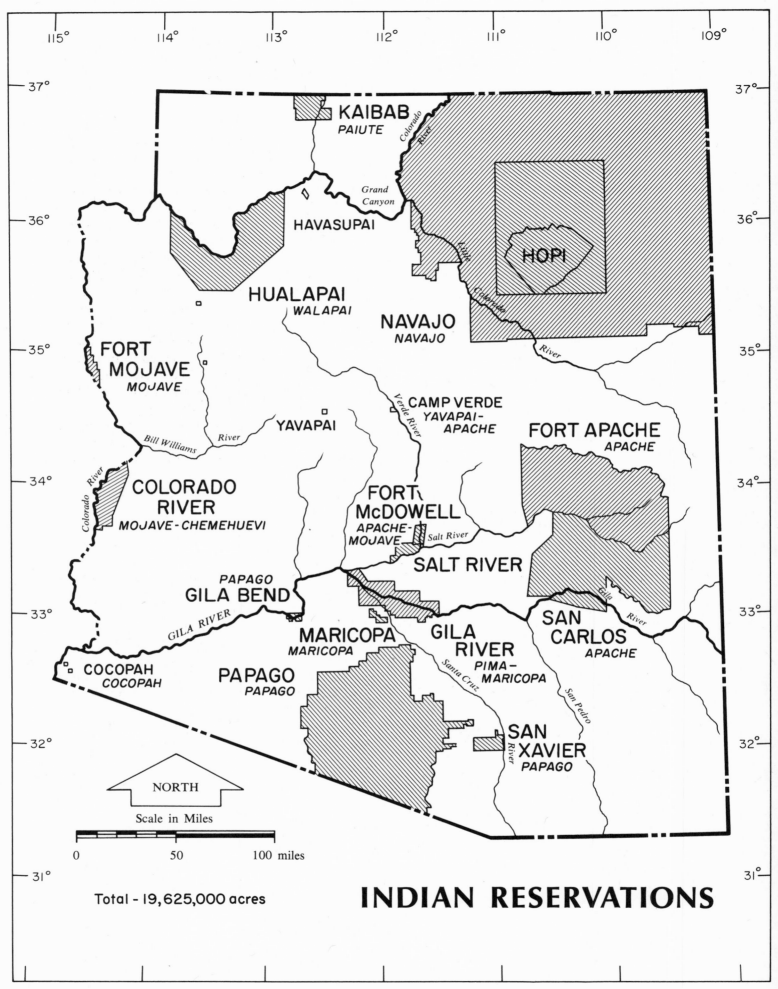

KAIBAB
PAIUTE

Colorado River

Grand Canyon

HAVASUPAI

HOPI

HUALAPAI
WALAPAI

NAVAJO
NAVAJO

River

FORT
MOJAVE
MOJAVE

Bill Williams   *River*

YAVAPAI

CAMP VERDE
*YAVAPAI-
APACHE*

Verde River

FORT APACHE
APACHE

Colorado   River

COLORADO
RIVER
MOJAVE-CHEMEHUEVI

FORT
McDOWELL
*APACHE-
MOJAVE*

Salt River

SALT RIVER

Gila   River

PAPAGO
GILA BEND

GILA RIVER

MARICOPA
MARICOPA

GILA
RIVER
*PIMA-
MARICOPA*

SAN
CARLOS
APACHE

Gila   River

COCOPAH
COCOPAH

PAPAGO
PAPAGO

Santa Cruz

San Pedro   River

SAN
XAVIER
PAPAGO

NORTH

Scale in Miles

0   50   100 miles

Total - 19,625,000 acres

INDIAN RESERVATIONS

45. INDIAN RESERVATIONS

IN 1911 THE Gila River Reservation was made available for the use of "such other Indians as the Secretary of the Interior may see fit to settle thereon." From 1911 through 1915 several minor changes were made in the limits of the reservation.

The Navajo Reservation was again extended on the west in 1900 to accommodate a growing population and its increasing herds of sheep, goats, and cattle. As the range was of poor quality, large areas were needed to support the flocks and herds. In 1947 tracts of land on the Colorado River Reservation were offered to the Hopis to ease pressure on the Hopi Reservation. The extensions of the Navajo Reservation had covered areas claimed by the Hopis as part of their ancestral range. Some Navajos also moved to the river. However, this emigration ended when the Mojave leaders feared that the newcomers might soon outnumber the original inhabitants.

The old abandoned military reservation of Fort McDowell was set aside in 1903 for the use of such "Mohave-Apache Indians" as were living on or near the military reservation. Exempted from this change were the immediate site of the old post, the post garden and farm, the old government irrigation ditch, and the post target ranges.

In 1907, north of the Grand Canyon and adjoining the Utah line, 120,500 acres were reserved for the use of the Southern Ute Indians. South of Yuma a small reservation was set aside for the Cocopah Indians in 1917.

In 1908 the Arizona and California Railway Company was granted an additional forty acres of the Colorado River Reservation for station grounds and terminal facilities. This railroad was never built. The Colorado River Reservation came under fire again in 1912 when the First State Legislature requested that the eastern boundary be moved to exclude the potential mineral area of the mountains lying to the east of the bottom lands along the river.

At present Arizona has twenty Indian reservations which cover some 19.6 million acres, or approximately 27 per cent of the state's land surface. On these reservations live about 110,640 Indians.

DATE OF ESTABLISHMENT	NAME	AREA IN ACRES*	1970 POPULATION
1859	Gila River	372,000	7,992
1865	Colorado River	226,000†	1,730
1868	Navajo	8,969,500†	71,400
1871‡	Fort Apache	1,665,000	6,230
1871‡	San Carlos	1,827,500	4,709
1914	Camp Verde	500	690
1874	San Xavier	71,000	574
1879	Salt River	46,500	2,345
1880	Havasupai	3,000	370
1880	Fort Mohave	23,500†	336
1882	Hopi	2,472,500§	6,144
1882	Gila Bend	10,500	244
1883	Hualapai	993,000	1,033
1902	Fort McDowell	25,000	335
1907	Kaibab	120,500	138
1911	Papago	2,774,500	4,688
1912	Ak-Chin (Maricopa)	22,000	248
1914	Yavapai	1,500	90
1917	Cocopah	500	101
	TOTAL	19,624,500	109,397

*Acreage rounded to nearest 500 acres.
†Arizona Acreage only.
‡The White Mountain Reservation was formed in 1871 but was divided into the Fort Apache and San Carlos Reservations in 1896.
§Hopi Reservation—650,500. Hopi-Navajo joint use area—1,822,000.

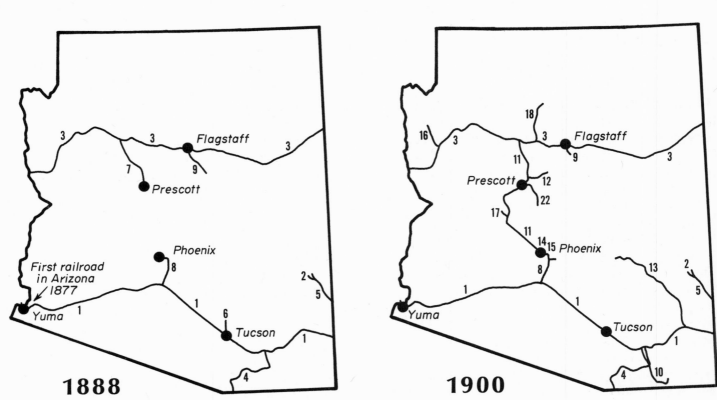

1888

1900

Refer to numbered table for key to maps

1888,1900 & 1920 maps show existence of railroads by their initial corporate names. The 1972 map indicates current operating company.

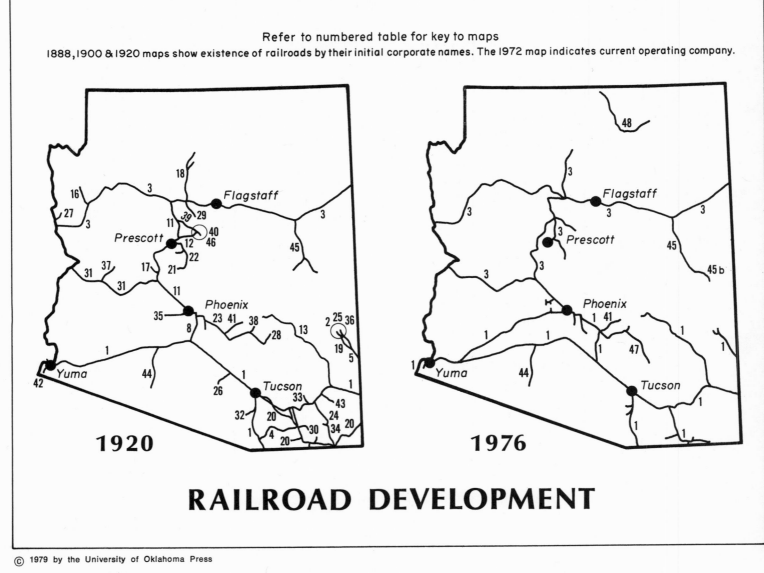

1920

1976

RAILROAD DEVELOPMENT

46. RAILROAD DEVELOPMENT

MUCH OF THE EARLY exploration and mapping of Arizona was done in anticipation of building a railroad from the Mississippi River to California (Map 23). However, it was not until 1877 that the Southern Pacific Railroad reached the western border at Yuma and four years later that it connected with the Texas Pacific east of El Paso. The second line to cross the territory was the Atlantic & Pacific (later the Atchison, Topeka & Santa Fe), which built west from Albuquerque in 1880 and reached the Colorado in 1883.

The four decades between 1880 and 1920 was a period of great activity in railroad building. Lines were projected, and some were built to provide north-south links between the two major lines, but most of the new roads were designed to serve the mining industry.

NUMBER ON MAP	COMPANY NAME	YEAR OF FIRST SERVICE TO ANY PART OF ARIZONA
1	Southern Pacific	1877
2	Coronado	1879–80
3	Atlantic & Pacific	1881–83
	3a Santa Fe Pacific	1897
	3b Atchison, Topeka & Santa Fe	1902
4	New Mexico & Arizona	1881–82
5	Arizona and New Mexico	1883–84
	5a Clifton & Southern Pacific (New Mexico)	
	5b Clifton & Lordsburg (Arizona)	
6	Arizona Narrow Gauge	1886
	6a Tucson, Globe & Northern	
7	Prescott & Arizona Central	1886
8	Maricopa & Phoenix	1887
9	Arizona Mineral Belt	1887
	9a Central Arizona	
10	Arizona Southeastern	1888–89
11	Santa Fe, Prescott & Phoenix	1893
12	United Verde & Pacific	1894
13	Gila Valley, Globe & Northern	1894–98
14	Maricopa and Phoenix and Salt River Valley	1895
15	Phoenix, Tempe and Mesa	1895
16	Arizona and Utah	1899
17	Congress Consolidated	1899
18	Santa Fe & Grand Canyon	1901
	18a Grand Canyon Railway	
19	Morenci Southern	1901
20	El Paso & Southwestern	1901
21	Bradshaw Mountain	1902–1904
22	Prescott & Eastern	1898
23	Phoenix and Eastern	1903
24	Arizona & Colorado	1903–1909
25	Clifton & Northern Railroad	1903
26	Arizona Southern	1904
27	Mohave & Milltown	1904
28	Arizona Eastern	1910
29	Saginaw Southern	1904
30	Tombstone & Southern	1905
31	Arizona & California	1905
32	Twin Buttes	1906
33	Johnson, Dragoon & Northern	1908
34	Mexico & Colorado	1909
35	Phoenix and Buckeye	1910
36	Shannon-Arizona	1909
37	Arizona & Swansea	1910
38	Ray & Gila Valley	1900, 1910
39	Verde Valley	1913
40	Verde Tunnel & Smelter	1914
41	Magma Arizona	1915
42	Yuma Valley	1914
43	Mascot & Western	1915
44	Tucson Cornelia & Gila Bend	1916
45	Apache Railway	1918–1919
	45a Southwest Forest Industries	
	45b White Mountain Scenic (operated on lumber railroad connecting with the Apache Railway)	
46	Arizona Extension	1918
47	San Manuel & Arizona	1955
48	Black Mesa & Lake Powell	1971–72

NOTE: The complete story of railroads in Arizona is quite complex. The purpose of this listing is to provide a chronology of railroads based on their original corporate names. The date given is for the year of first service in Arizona. No attempt has been made to indicate acquisition and consolidation of the initial lines into the larger roads, nor has any attempt been made to provide dates of abandonment for those routes no longer in existence.

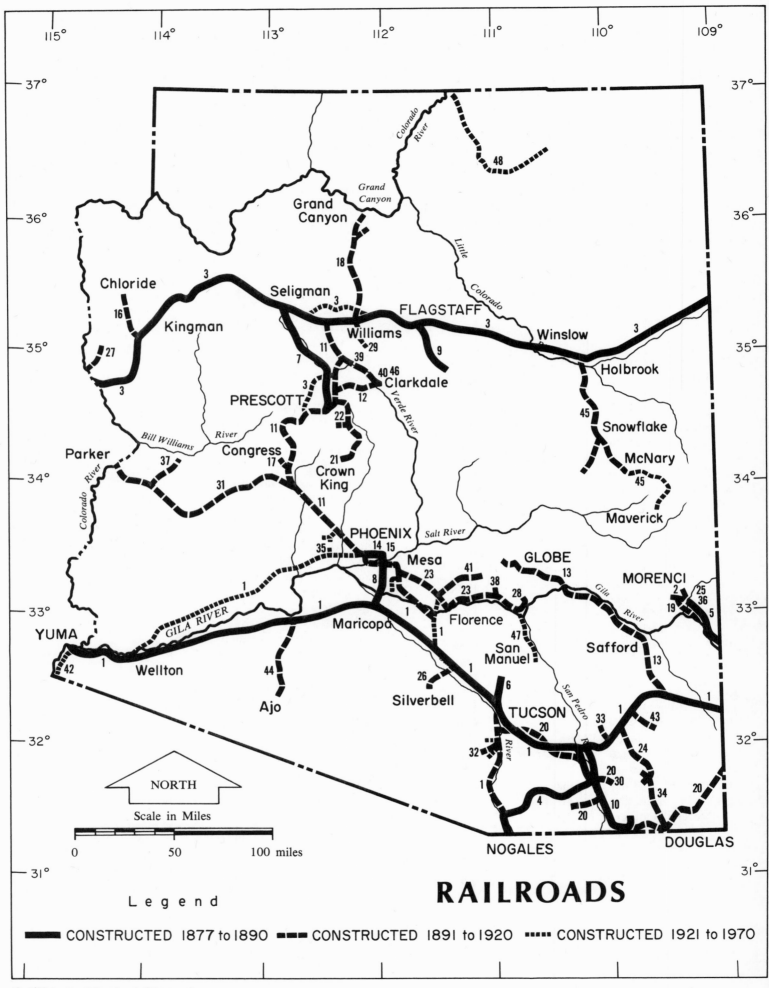

RAILROADS

NORTH

Scale in Miles

0   50   100 miles

L e g e n d

CONSTRUCTED 1877 to 1890   CONSTRUCTED 1891 to 1920   CONSTRUCTED 1921 to 1970

47. RAILROADS

FOLLOWING THE COMPLETION of the two transcontinental railroads, several connecting links were built by local businessmen. The Maricopa & Phoenix was built in 1887 to connect Phoenix to the Southern Pacific. In the preceding year Prescott was tied in to the Atlantic & Pacific at Seligman by the Prescott & Arizona Central Railway.

An attempt was made to connect Flagstaff on the Atlantic & Pacific with the mineral district around Globe. The Arizona Mineral Belt laid about thirty-six miles of track and started a tunnel through the Mogollon Rim, but then funds ran out. Another attempt to reach Globe was the Arizona Narrow Gauge, which laid about ten miles of track out of Tucson before the company went bankrupt. Changing the name to the Tucson, Globe & Northern Railroad did not help.

Possibly the most interesting railroad in Arizona was the Coronado, a twenty-inch narrow-gauge line built in 1879 from the Longfellow Mine to the smelter at Clifton. The empty cars were hauled up to the mine by mules and were run down to the smelter by gravity with the mules riding on platforms on the cars. Then a steam locomotive was built in Baltimore, shipped by rail to Las Animas, Colorado, and thence by ox-wagon to Clifton. A second locomotive made the trip around the Horn to San Francisco, thence in another ship to the mouth of the Colorado River, up to Yuma by river steamer, and finally to Clifton by wagon.

Most of the trackage in the complexes east of Prescott, east of Phoenix, and southeast of Tucson was laid to provide cheap transportation for the big mining districts. In fact, the real development of Arizona's mining industry had to await the arrival of the railroads.

There were some exceptions. The Apache Railroad was designed primarily to haul lumber out of the forests of the Mogollon Rim country. The Santa Fe & Grand Canyon provided transportation for tourists visiting the Grand Canyon. The newest line in the state is the Black Mesa & Lake Powell, which carries coal from the Black Mesa coal fields to an electric power generated plant.

In 1881–82 the Atchison, Topeka & Santa Fe built the New Mexico & Arizona from Benson to Nogales, connecting with the Sonora Railway to Guaymas on the Gulf of California.

The Southern Pacific laid a new line from Wellton to Phoenix in 1926, thus finally putting the state capitol on a main line. A few short spurs have been built in recent years to provide access to new mines such as the Twin Buttes Mine some twenty-five miles south of Tucson.

When Arizona became a state in 1912 it had 1,678 miles of railroad track, and by 1930 the total had grown to 2,524 miles. Since then there has been a steady decline as a result of the development of the automobile and truck as well as the closing of a number of mines because the ore had been mined out. A number of short-line railroads have been closed down as common carriers but continue to operate as "factory facilities" to move ore from mine to concentrator or smelter.

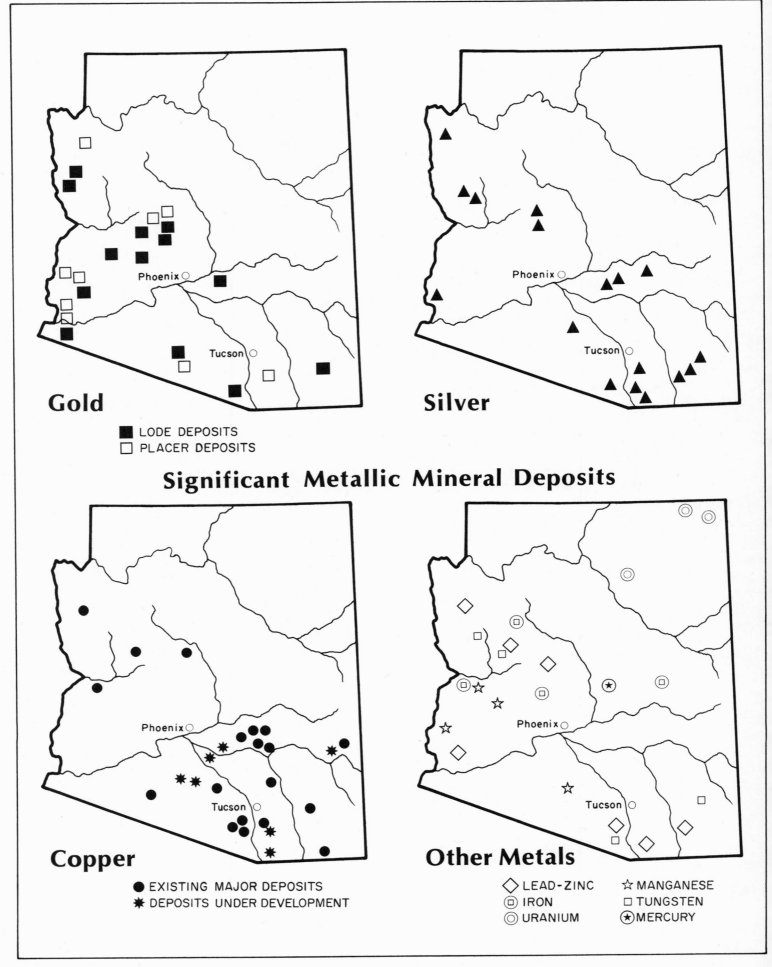

Gold

◼ LODE DEPOSITS
◻ PLACER DEPOSITS

Silver

Significant Metallic Mineral Deposits

Copper

● EXISTING MAJOR DEPOSITS
✳ DEPOSITS UNDER DEVELOPMENT

Other Metals

◇ LEAD-ZINC   ☆ MANGANESE
⊡ IRON   □ TUNGSTEN
◎ URANIUM   ⊛ MERCURY

48. MINING

Mining in Arizona was a backwash from the California Gold Rush of 1849. By the mid-1850's most of the easily worked placer deposits in California had been cleaned out, and hard-rock mining required expensive machinery. As a result, many fortune seekers crossed the Sierra Nevada and worked their way eastward.

A placer deposit was a point where native gold, weathered out of nearby rock, had been concentrated by stream action. Such deposits could be easily worked, were limited in area, and so were cleaned out quickly. Arizona's first gold strike was a small placer deposit near the confluence of Sacramento Wash and the Colorado River. The discovery was made in 1857. Once the placers were gone, attention turned to the rock from which the gold came. Machinery was imported, and miners were hired to do the work. Between 1890 and 1917 a new gold boom struck in central Arizona because of improved processes. Overall, probably more money was invested in hard-rock mines than was ever taken out in gold.

The search for precious metals was one of the drives behind the northward expansion of New Spain. In 1736 the Bolas de Plata or Planchas de Plata find was made near the Papago ranchería of Arizonac, just west of Nogales. Between 1790 and 1820 mines were opened around Tubac, Patagonia, Ajo, and Arivaca. It was stories of these mines that brought Anglo-Americans into the area following the Gadsden Purchase. In 1856 the Sonora Exploring and Mining Company set up its headquarters in the ruins of Tubac presidio and reopened several old mines.

Weathering of the rock, over eons of time, often produced secondary enrichment. The metal was dissolved near the surface and redeposited deeper in the rock. This action produced pockets of very rich ore which did not extend very deeply, and the unenriched rock often was not worth working. Such may have been the case in Tombstone.

Most of the gold and silver production now is a by-product of the treatment of copper ore. Copper mining in the early days suffered from two serious drawbacks: the high cost of transportation and limited knowledge of the treatment of the ore. Although the Spaniards knew of the deposits near Ajo as early as 1750, it was not until 1853 that active work started. The deposits had been secondarily enriched, and only that ore could pay for transportation by pack to Yuma and by ship to Swansea, Wales, the site of a great copper smelter. Full development of copper mining had to wait for cheaper transportation, improved metallurgical processes, and the suppression of the Apaches. By 1900 copper production had grown to three times the value of gold and silver combined.

In addition to gold, silver, and copper, a number of other metals are mined in small quantities. From 1951 to 1955, manganese, an alloying component in some steels, was mined for wartime stockpiling. The price paid for it was about twice the world price. Tungsten, another alloying metal, was first mined in 1898. Over the years some two hundred small mines were opened.

Mercury was sought by the Spaniards because of its ability to amalgamate with gold and silver. There are early reports of Indians using cinnabar, a mercury ore mineral, as a cosmetic. Commercial mining began in 1920, but has been sporadic because of the low grade of the deposits.

Lead and zinc are common by-products of the processing of copper ore, but two mines were operated primarily for these metals. Until 1945 these mines were hampered by expensive transportation and problems of ore treatment. Valuable by-products helped pay for the operation.

The combination of vanadium and uranium has been mined, vanadium for alloying in steel and uranium for use in nuclear reactors. The peak of uranium production came in 1957, when 303,000 tons of ore were mined.

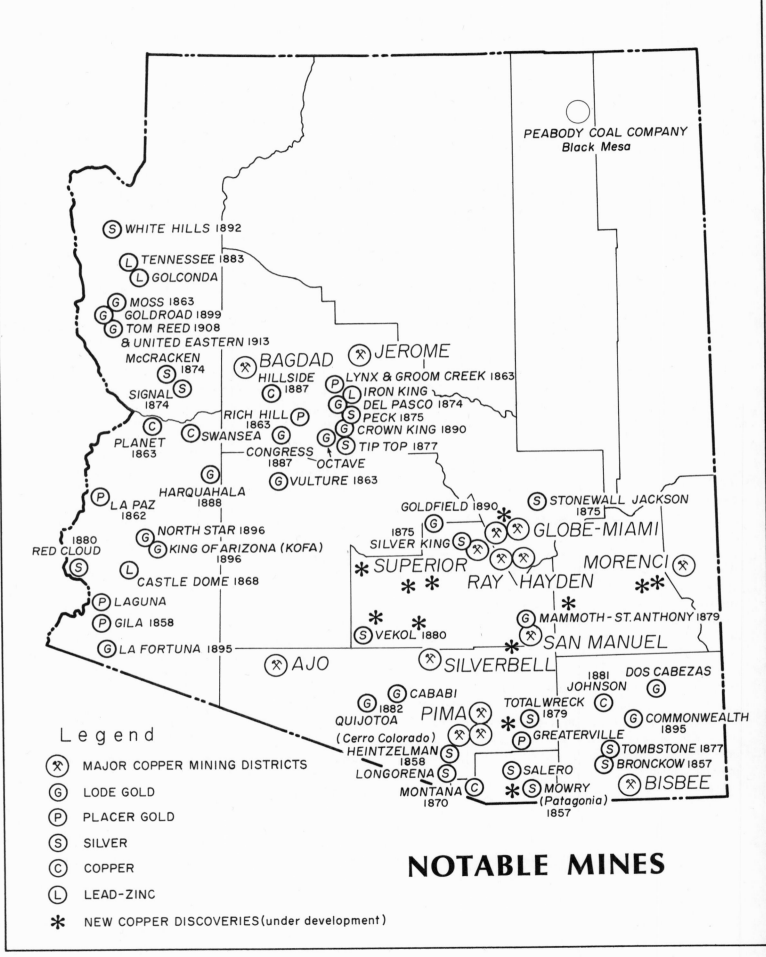

PEABODY COAL COMPANY
Black Mesa

(S) WHITE HILLS 1892

(L) TENNESSEE 1883
(L) GOLCONDA

(G) MOSS 1863
(G) GOLDROAD 1899
(G) TOM REED 1908
& UNITED EASTERN 1913
McCRACKEN
(S) 1874
SIGNAL
(S) 1874

(C) PLANET
1863

(C) SWANSEA

RICH HILL
1863 (P)

(G)

(G) HARQUAHALA
1888

(P) LA PAZ
1862

NORTH STAR 1896
(G) KING OF ARIZONA (KOFA)
(G) 1896

1880
RED CLOUD
(S)

(L) CASTLE DOME 1868

(P) LAGUNA
(P) GILA 1858

(G) LA FORTUNA 1895

(⚒) AJO

(⚒) BAGDAD
HILLSIDE
(C) 1887

(⚒) JEROME

LYNX & GROOM CREEK 1863
(P) IRON KING
(L)
(G) DEL PASCO 1874
(S) PECK 1875
(G) CROWN KING 1890
(S) TIP TOP 1877
CONGRESS
1887
OCTAVE
(G) VULTURE 1863

(S) STONEWALL JACKSON
1875

GOLDFIELD 1890
(G) ✱
1875 ⚒ ⚒ GLOBE-MIAMI
SILVER KING (S) ⚒
✱ SUPERIOR ⚒ ⚒ MORENCI ⚒
RAY HAYDEN ✱ ✱
✱ ✱ ✱
✱ ✱ ✱
(G) MAMMOTH - ST. ANTHONY 1879
(S) VEKOL 1880 ⚒ SAN MANUEL
✱
⚒ SILVERBELL

1881 DOS CABEZAS
JOHNSON
(G) CABABI TOTALWRECK (C) (G)
(G) 1882 ⚒ (S) 1879 (G) COMMONWEALTH
QUIJOTOA PIMA ✱ GREATERVILLE 1895
(Cerro Colorado) ⚒ (P) (S) TOMBSTONE 1877
HEINTZELMAN ⚒ ⚒ (S) BRONCKOW 1857
1858 (S)
LONGORENA (S) (S) SALERO
MONTANA (C) ✱ (S) MOWRY ⚒ BISBEE
1870 (Patagonia)
1857

Legend

(⚒)	MAJOR COPPER MINING DISTRICTS
(G)	LODE GOLD
(P)	PLACER GOLD
(S)	SILVER
(C)	COPPER
(L)	LEAD-ZINC
✱	NEW COPPER DISCOVERIES (under development)

NOTABLE MINES

49. NOTABLE MINES

THERE WERE, AND ARE, too many notable mines in Arizona to allow for discussion of them all. More than 400,000 mining claims were filed, and it has been estimated that over 4,000 mining companies were incorporated. While the records, especially for the early years, are incomplete, more than 200 mines have been listed as having produced over $100,000 in metals. Of these, a mere handful produced over $1 million. The stories of the discovery and operation of many mines read like romances of literature, and some of the stories are pure romance.

One of the richest, and strangest, placer deposits was discovered in 1863. On the top of a mesa about twenty miles northeast of present-day Wickenburg gold nuggets were found in the surface dirt that could be stirred up with a knife. It is said that one acre yielded more than $500,000 in gold. The site was named Rich Hill.

This same area contained one of the richest hard-rock mines. Henry Wickenburg discovered a ledge of rich ore in 1863. Not being an experienced hard-rock miner, he sold the ore in place for $15.00 per ton. The mine is said to have yielded $2.5 million in gold during its first six years of operation. However, this figure does not account for an estimated 20 per cent to 40 per cent stolen by high-grading miners. In contrast, after Captain John Moss had taken $200,000 from the Moss Mine, the eastern interests who bought him out discovered that the mine had been a superficial pocket with no substantial ore body below.

The richest gold mines were the Tom Reed and the adjacent United Eastern in western Mohave County. These mines produced, between them, $26.7 million in the years 1908 and 1933.

While silver mining had been the earliest industry in Arizona, it was not until the country had been made safe from Indian depredations that large-scale, profitable mining began. The Silver King was located in 1875 and continued in operation until 1893, yielding an estimated $6.5 million. The greatest silver strike was made in 1877 in the hills east of Fort Huachuca. There the town of Tombstone soon rose, to be greatly overrated as a wild and woolly place. By 1879 the town was the largest town in the territory and had several satellite mill towns along the San Pedro River. Some 5.8 million ounces of silver were taken out in the single year of 1882. In the following year water was struck at the five-hundred-foot level of the Sulphuret Mine. Pumping was tried for a while, but by 1888 mining in Tombstone was at a standstill and the great period of silver mining had passed.

Small copper mines such as the Ajo and Planet were operated as early as 1856 and 1863, respectively, but the work was spasmodic. Only secondarily enriched ore could pay for the expense of transportation to distant smelters. Cheaper transportation and a better knowledge of metallurgy led to a slow but steady growth of copper mining. About 1880 the price of copper was $0.21 per pound, and by 1893 it had dropped to $0.10 per pound. Nevertheless, by 1888 copper had replaced silver as the chief metal mined in the territory. Improved methods of concentrating low-grade ores have made it possible to work huge deposits that earlier had been considered uneconomical. The best-known open-pit mine is the Lavender Pit at Bisbee. The first big producer was the Copper Queen at Bisbee, which was discovered in 1877 and developed about 1885 on the advice of Dr. James Douglas.

There were a few important producers of lead-zinc ores. In general their ores were such a complex mixture of lead, zinc, copper, silver, and gold that successful operation had to await the development of selective flotation. The Tennessee Mine in Mohave County yielded about $7.5 million. The Iron King started out as a gold-silver mine, but below the oxidized zone the precious metals turned into a complex lead-zinc ore. Careful management made this mine the largest producer of lead and zinc in the state. Early records of the Castle Dome give some interesting figures: cost of mining and sacking the ore was $12 per ton, transportation to the Colorado River, $15; and freight to San Francisco, $18.

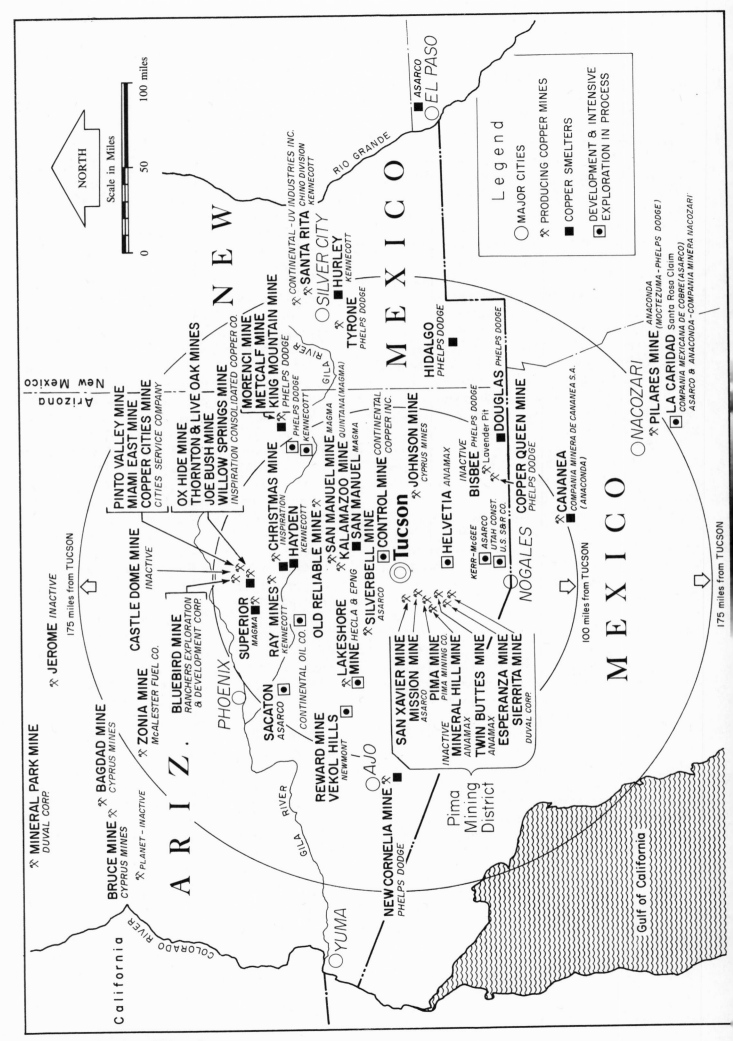

Scale in Miles
0   50   100 miles
NORTH

California

COLORADO RIVER

ARIZ.

Arizona
New Mexico

N E W

MINERAL PARK MINE
DUVAL CORP.

BRUCE MINE ⚒
CYPRUS MINES
⚒ PLANET - INACTIVE

⚒ **BAGDAD MINE**
CYPRUS MINES

⚒ **ZONIA MINE**
McALESTER FUEL CO.

CASTLE DOME MINE
INACTIVE

BLUEBIRD MINE
RANCHERS EXPLORATION
& DEVELOPMENT CORP.

⚒ **JEROME** INACTIVE

175 miles from TUCSON

PHOENIX

GILA
RIVER

REWARD MINE
NEWMONT

VEKOL HILLS

○ **AJO**
NEW CORNELIA MINE ⚒
PHELPS DODGE

○ **YUMA**

SUPERIOR ⚒
MAGMA

SACATON ⦿
ASARCO

RAY MINES ⚒
KENNECOTT

⦿ CONTINENTAL OIL CO.
OLD RELIABLE MINE ⚒

LAKESHORE ⚒
MINE HECLA & EPNG ⦿

SILVERBELL MINE ⚒
ASARCO

SAN XAVIER MINE ⚒
MISSION MINE ⦿
ASARCO

PIMA MINE ⦿
Pima Mining Co.
INACTIVE
MINERAL HILL MINE
ANAMAX

TWIN BUTTES ⦿
ANAMAX
ESPERANZA MINE ⦿
SIERRITA MINE ⦿
DUVAL CORP.

Pima
Mining
District

PINTO VALLEY MINE
MIAMI EAST MINE
COPPER CITIES MINE
CITIES SERVICE COMPANY

OX HIDE MINE
THORNTON & LIVE OAK MINES
JOE BUSH MINE
WILLOW SPRINGS MINE
INSPIRATION CONSOLIDATED COPPER CO.

⚒ ⚒
■ ■

CHRISTMAS MINE ⚒
INSPIRATION
HAYDEN ■
KENNECOTT

SAN MANUEL MINE QUINTANA (MAGMA)
KALAMAZOO MINE ⚒ MAGMA
SAN MANUEL MAGMA

CONTROL MINE CONTINENTAL
COPPER INC.

○ **TUCSON**

⦿ **HELVETIA** ANAMAX

KERR-McGEE ⦿
ASARCO ⦿
UTAH CONST. ⦿
U.S. S&R CO. ⦿

MORENCI MINE
METCALF MINE
KING MOUNTAIN MINE
⚒ PHELPS DODGE
■ PHELPS DODGE
⦿ KENNECOTT

GILA
RIVER

JOHNSON MINE ⚒
CYPRUS MINES

⚒ **SANTA RITA** ⚒ CONTINENTAL - UV INDUSTRIES INC.
CHINO DIVISION
KENNECOTT

○ **SILVER CITY**

⚒ **TYRONE**
PHELPS DODGE

HURLEY ■
KENNECOTT

M E X I C O

HIDALGO ■
PHELPS DODGE

BISBEE PHELPS DODGE
INACTIVE
⚒ Lavender Pit
DOUGLAS ■ PHELPS DODGE

COPPER QUEEN MINE ⚒
PHELPS DODGE

⚒ **CANANEA**
COMPANIA MINERA DE CANANEA S.A.
(ANACONDA)

○ **NOGALES**

100 miles from TUCSON

M E X I C O

○ **NACOZARI**

⚒ **PILARES MINE** ANACONDA
(MOCTEZUMA - PHELPS DODGE)
⦿ **LA CARIDAD** Santa Rosa Claim
COMPANIA MEXICANA DE COBRE (ASARCO)
ASARCO & ANACONDA - COMPANIA MINERA NACOZARI

175 miles from TUCSON

○ **EL PASO**
ASARCO ■

RIO GRANDE

Gulf of California

Legend

○ MAJOR CITIES
⚒ PRODUCING COPPER MINES
■ COPPER SMELTERS
⦿ DEVELOPMENT & INTENSIVE
    EXPLORATION IN PROCESS

50. MAJOR COPPER MINES

HISTORICALLY, MINING HAS BEEN the lodestar that drew men to Arizona. First it was gold in the placers of Rich Hill and Lynx Creek and the hard-rock Vulture Mine; then came the great silver bonanzas such as the Silver King Mine and the Tombstone district; finally, copper became the most important mineral.

The United States meets approximately 22 per cent, or 1,717,900 tons, of the world's demand for copper. Southern Arizona and immediately adjacent areas are unique in copper production. Within 100 miles of Tucson, over half of the country's copper mining, concentration, and smelting takes place. Within 175 miles of Tucson, an area covering southwestern New Mexico and northern Sonora, nearly half of the world's copper is produced.

In recent years the copper industry has faced a serious problem. Supporters of the ecology movement have attacked the mines for their admittedly unsightly dumps of waste rock. Some companies now spend considerable amounts of money planting native growth on the slopes of the dumps. More serious has been the criticism of air pollution by the smelters. Although there probably has been no increase in emissions from smelters in fifty years, they have become a whipping boy of the pure air enthusiasts.

Another, and possibly even more serious, problem is the matter of water supply. The concentrators require large amounts of water, only half of which can be recycled, the rest being lost through evaporation from the tailings (waste) settling ponds. With ore running less than one-half of 1 per cent copper, the concentration must be done near the mine. Most of the concentrators in the Tucson area pump water from underground, a finite supply.

While mining and its allied businesses are a very important part of Arizona's economy, the industry occupies only 0.14 per cent of the land area of the state.

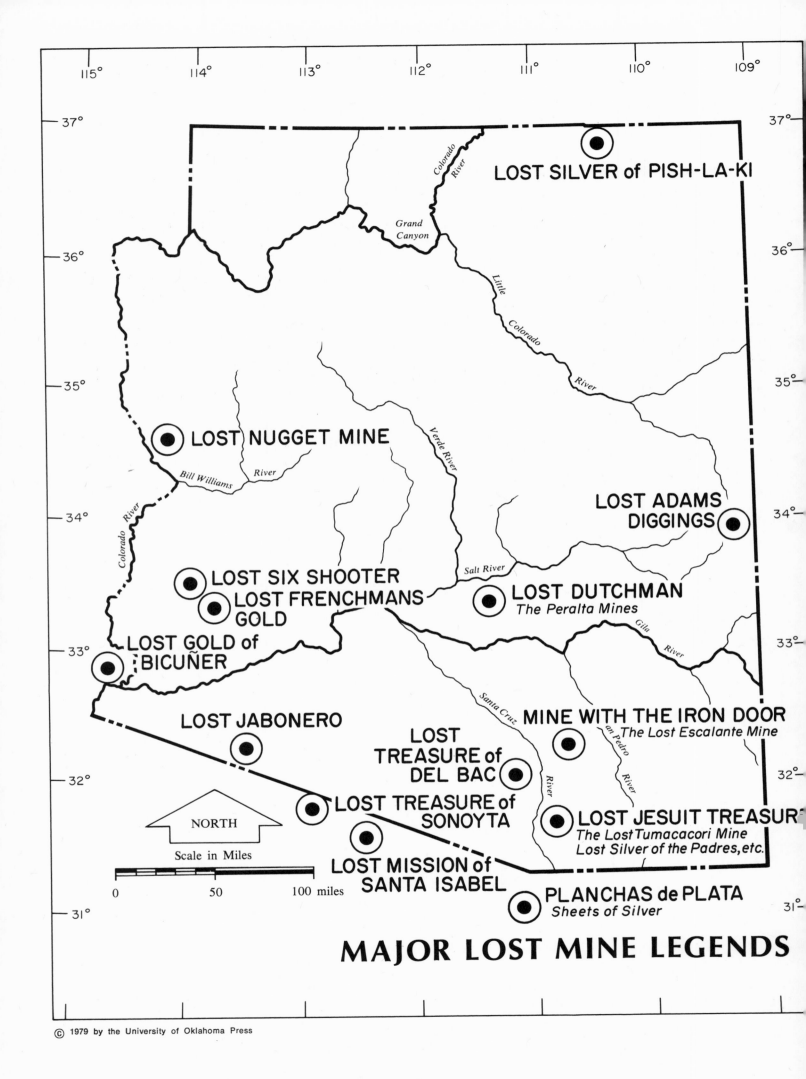

LOST SILVER of PISH-LA-KI

LOST NUGGET MINE

LOST ADAMS DIGGINGS

LOST SIX SHOOTER
LOST FRENCHMANS GOLD

LOST DUTCHMAN
The Peralta Mines

LOST GOLD of BICUÑER

MINE WITH THE IRON DOOR
The Lost Escalante Mine

LOST JABONERO

LOST TREASURE of DEL BAC

LOST TREASURE of SONOYTA

LOST JESUIT TREASURE
The Lost Tumacacori Mine
Lost Silver of the Padres, etc.

LOST MISSION of SANTA ISABEL

PLANCHAS de PLATA
Sheets of Silver

NORTH

Scale in Miles

0   50   100 miles

MAJOR LOST MINE LEGENDS

51. MAJOR LOST MINE LEGENDS

ONE OF THE MOST important and difficult tasks facing the historian of the American Southwest is to "demythologize" the history of the area—to separate fact from fiction and to indicate which is which.

The literature of Arizona is full of legends and fairy tales of lost mines and buried treasure. Many are purest fiction, but some are based on historic fact. The Planchas de Plata is an example of the latter category. About 1736, Spaniards were drawn to northwestern Sonora by reports of the discovery of masses of native silver lying about on the ground. Disposition of this wealth was the subject of litigation for at least two years, and eventually most of it wound up in the royal treasury.

Some of the legends spring from known Indian uprisings. The Lost Treasure of Sonoyta was said to have been buried during the second Pima uprising in 1751. The Lost Gold of Bicuñer disappeared at the time of the Yuma revolt of 1781.

By far the greatest number of yarns stem from the expulsion of the Jesuits from New Spain in 1767. The missionaries were supposed to have buried the wealth of their missions and to have covered their mines before the soldiers marched them away. It seems to have been stories about the fantastically rich mines operated by the padres in the general area of Tumacacori and San Xavier that brought many of the first Americans to southern Arizona in hopes of reopening the mines.

Not all the lost mines went astray two hundred years ago. A number of them were lost during the early prospecting rush to Arizona in the 1860's. Some have disappeared in the early years of the twentieth century.

Possibly the most highly publicized lost mine is the Lost Dutchman. Its legend seems to have started with a few newspaper items reporting the death of one Jacob Walz, who claimed to have discovered a rich gold mine in the Superstition Mountains. Fiction writers picked up these scraps and successively embroidered the story, making it more fantastic with each retelling. From time to time, within recent years, Arizona newspapers have carried reports that the Lost Dutchman Mine has been rediscovered. Such rumors soon fade from sight. The best explanation seems to be that Walz got hold of some gold that had been stolen by miners in real mines.

It is interesting to note that the legends often spell out the details of the discovery of a very rich deposit, but the discoverer dies before he can pass on the information. The story of the Lost Six Shooter is such a case.

An unfortunate aspect of these legends is the fact that many people who cannot tell fact from fancy have dug for the "treasure" around or in old buildings, thus hastening the complete disappearance of structures of historic significance. The story of the Lost Bells of Guevavi hastened the disappearance of what was left of the adobe walls of that old mission. Small artifacts are often removed by "pot hunters" who have no knowledge of their historical significance. Very often the spot where an artifact was found and its surroundings can tell a trained archaeologist more than the item itself. The uninitiated digger has no understanding of this factor.

The most mobile site of a legend is the Lost Mission of Santa Isabel. It is reported all the way from a point about fifty miles west of Nogales to the west coast of Baja California.

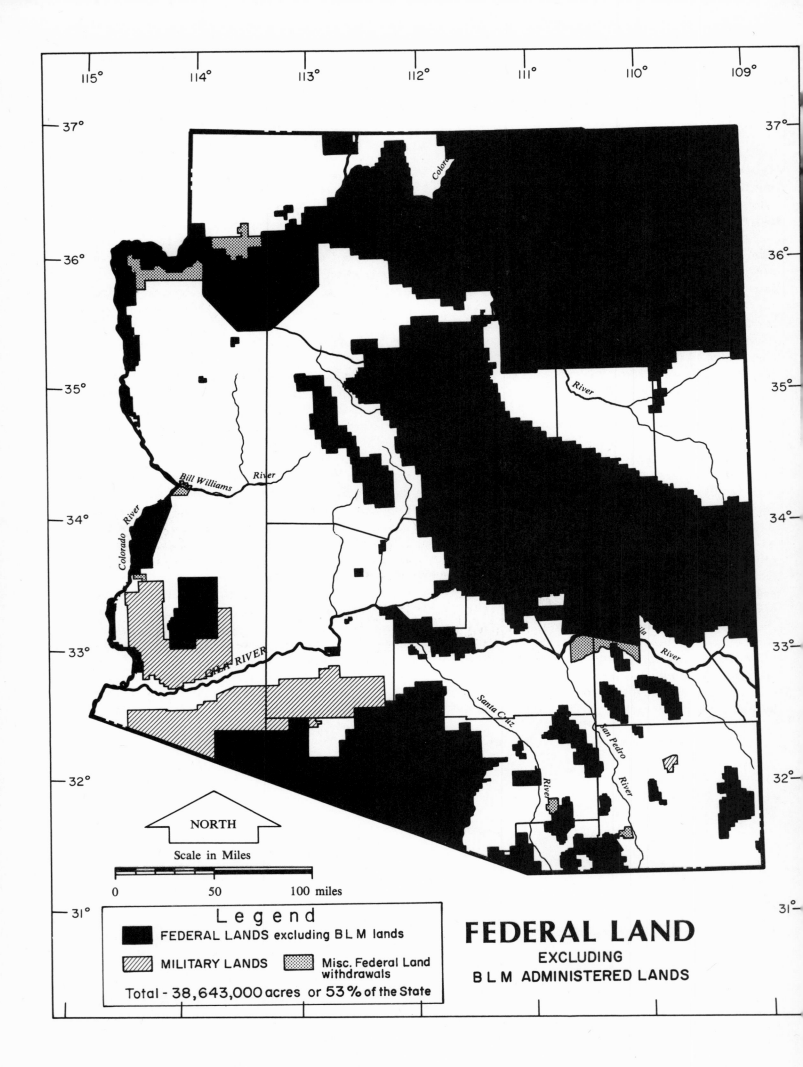

NORTH

Scale in Miles

0   50   100 miles

Legend

FEDERAL LANDS excluding B L M lands

MILITARY LANDS

Misc. Federal Land withdrawals

Total - 38,643,000 acres or 53% of the State

FEDERAL LAND
EXCLUDING
B L M ADMINISTERED LANDS

By 1803 all of the original states of the Union had ceded to the federal government the trans-Appalachian lands extending to the Mississippi River, which they had claimed under British grants. This land became the public domain, which was to be disposed of for the benefit of the people of the United States.

At the time Arizona became a United States territory, the whole area was in the public domain. Under the Treaty of Guadalupe Hidalgo and the Gadsden Purchase treaty the United States agreed to recognize the land grants made by the Mexican government if the claimants could establish the legality of the grants. (Map 15). Early Anglo settlers soon started taking up homesteads on the more desirable land.

The federal government began setting aside land for its own use with the establishment of Fort Buchanan in 1856. Three years later came the first large withdrawal in the opening of the Gila River Indian Reservation for the Pima and Maricopa Indians. Since then there have been many other withdrawals by the federal government. For example, the first forest reserve was set aside on the Kaibab Plateau in 1893.

The general status of land ownership in Arizona is shown in the following table:

Ownership or Jurisdiction	Area (acres)	Percentage of Total Area of Arizona	Refer to Map No.
Federal Lands	51,393,000	70.70	52, 53
Indian reservations	19,625,000	27.00	45
U.S. forests	11,392,000	15.67	54
Bureau of Land Management (BLM) *	12,750,000	17.54	53
National parks and monuments	2,490,000	3.42	55
Department of Defense*	3,640,000	5.01	56
All other federal lands—misc. depts.	1,496,000	2.06	52
State Lands	9,637,000	13.26	57
Arizona Land Department	9,594,000	13.20	57
Arizona Fish and Game	20,000	0.03	57
Arizona state parks	23,000	0.03	55
Private Lands	11,658,000	16.04	58
Cropland (irrigated agriculture) †	1,424,000	1.96	59
Total Land Area of Arizona	72,688,000	100.00	

Source: *Ownership and Administration of Public Lands in Arizona*. Phoenix: Planning Division, Arizona Dept. of Economic Planning and Development, 1971.

* For these jurisdictions there are areas of shared or joint responsibilities.

† *Arizona Statistical Review*, Valley National Bank, Phoenix, 1973

Measures of land ownership and jurisdictional responsibility vary from year to year as well as from month to month. Surveys, summaries and land classification and measures are in progress continually. Additionally, lands are constantly being transferred between governmental agencies. The state of Arizona continues to exercise rights of selection from certain federal lands. The state also occasionally sells lands to the private sector (auctions and the like). The table reflects the status as of the date noted in the source reference, and the acreage figures have been rounded to the nearest thousand acres.

Of the eleven Western states, Arizona ranks first in total land area owned or controlled by federal or local government (61,030,000 acres) and second in the percentage of its total surface that is controlled by government (83.96 per cent). Among these same states, Arizona ranks tenth in total land held in private or organizational hands.

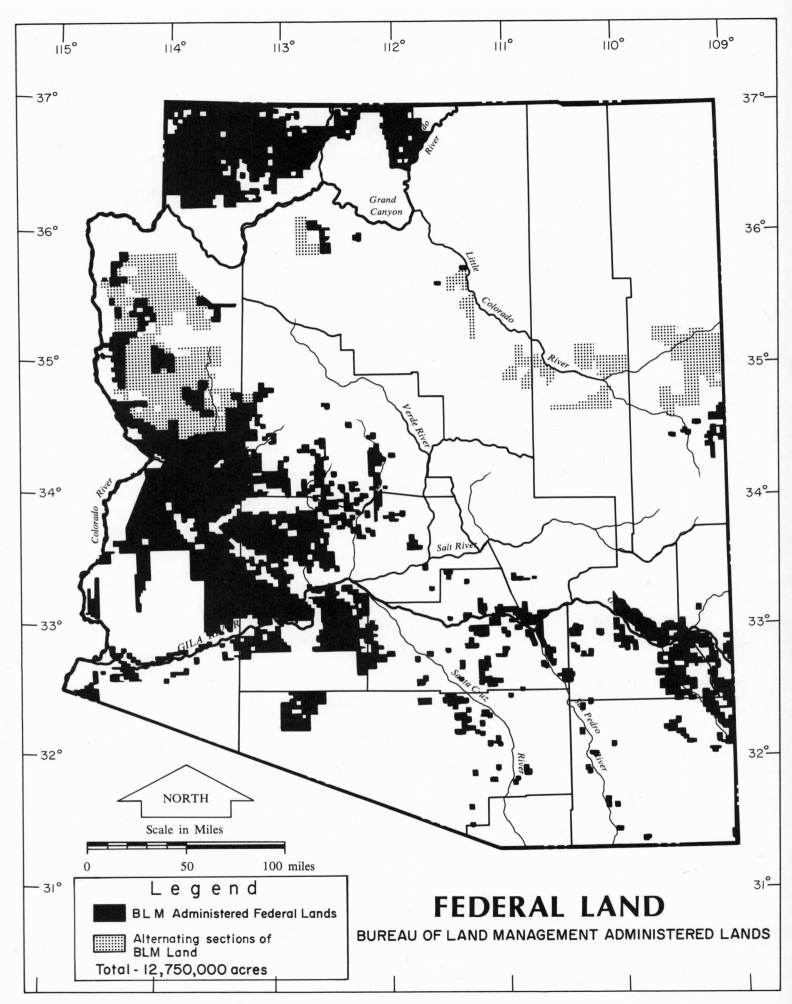

NORTH

Scale in Miles

0   50   100 miles

L e g e n d

■ BLM Administered Federal Lands

▨ Alternating sections of BLM Land

Total - 12,750,000 acres

FEDERAL LAND

BUREAU OF LAND MANAGEMENT ADMINISTERED LANDS

53. FEDERAL LAND: BUREAU OF LAND MANAGEMENT LAND

In 1812 Congress established the General Land Office, whose mission was to sell off the vast areas of the public domain, essentially to pay off the debts incurred during the Revolutionary War. Many laws were subsequently passed to expedite the process of getting rid of the public domain: the Homestead Act (1862), the Morrill Act (1862), the Timber Culture Act (1873), the Desert Land Act (1877), and the Timber and Stone Act (1878). Throughout most of its existence the General Land Office was a plum of the political spoils system, noted for indifference if not corruption.

Under the Taylor Grazing Act of 1934, a Division of Grazing, later called the Grazing Service, was established to control grazing on the remains of the public domain, amounting at that time to 165,695,-000 acres. Grazing districts were established, and the grazing fees were divided between the federal and the state governments. The districts were to be administered cooperatively by the Grazing Service and the local state governments. The Taylor act was designed to be a temporary expedient pending congressional decision on final disposal of the public lands.

Finally, in 1946, President Harry S. Truman instituted a reorganization plan which consolidated the General Land Office and the Grazing Service in the new Bureau of Land Management (BLM) as part of the Department of the Interior.

BLM lands in Arizona are controlled under the "multiple use" doctrine similar to the Forest Service doctrine. However, most of the land is usable only for cattle grazing on a limited scale because the natural forage is so sparse. Cattle raisers are charged a fee for permission to run cattle on the range. The fee was computed on the variable basis of the amount of land needed to sustain one adult cow for one month and the market price of cattle. By 1963 the fee had reached sixty cents per animal month. When Secretary of the Interior Stewart L. Udall of Arizona announced an increase in grazing fees in 1963, he was strongly opposed by the state's cattlemen on the basis that they had spent a large sum of money in improvements on the public range.

At present the Bureau of Land Management controls some 12,750,000 acres, or 17.54 per cent of the land surface of the state.

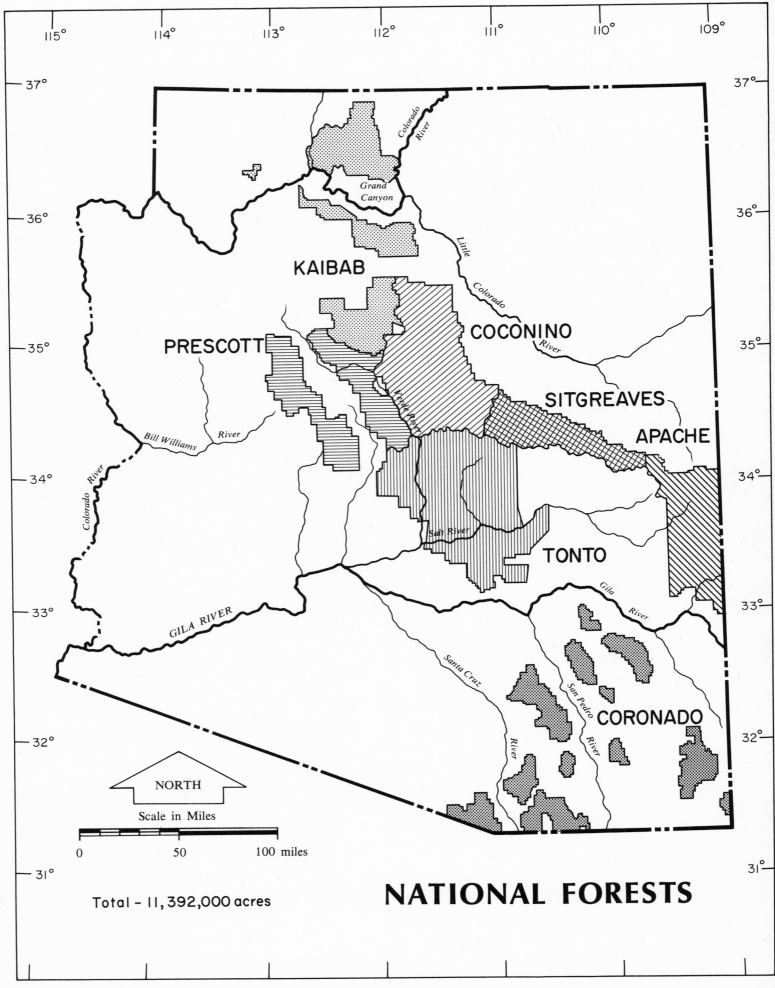

KAIBAB

PRESCOTT

COCONINO

SITGREAVES

APACHE

TONTO

CORONADO

Colorado River

Little

Colorado River

Grand Canyon

Verde River

Bill Williams River

Colorado River

Salt River

GILA RIVER

Gila River

Santa Cruz

San Pedro River

River

NORTH

Scale in Miles

0   50   100 miles

Total – 11,392,000 acres

NATIONAL FORESTS

54. NATIONAL FORESTS

As early as 1873 the American Association for the Advancement of Science called attention to the serious depletion of the nation's forests. However, it was not until 1891 that Congress passed the Forest Reserve Act, which authorized the President to set aside timberland from the public domain. Presidents Harrison, Cleveland, McKinley, and Theodore Roosevelt set aside some 195 million acres and withdrew from public entry another 85 million pending study of their mineral and water power resources.

The first Arizona reserve was the Kaibab Forest Reserve (1893) on the north rim of the Grand Canyon. Later the Kaibab Forest was expanded to include a large area south of Grand Canyon National Park. For the sake of forestry control, several parts of Indian reservations were transferred from control of the Bureau of Indian Affairs to the Forest Service. These lands were restored to the reservations in 1912. By 1964 seven different national forests contained approximately three-fourths of the state's timber. Many recreational areas and sites for summer homes have been developed under the multiple use concept.

The presence of the national forests has been a constant source of irritation to many citizens. In 1899 the Twentieth Territorial Legislature objected to control of grazing by forestry officials. They wanted completely uncontrolled grazing. In 1917 the Third State Legislature complained about a proposal by the Secretary of Agriculture to double the grazing fee. Six years later the legislature asked for two years' free pasturage in the forests as an aid to the depressed condition of the cattle industry. The Eighth and Ninth State Legislatures requested the federal government to build roads through national forests and Indian reservations to connect various parts of the state highway network.

Under the Wilderness Bill of 1964, tracts of national forest land were closed to all forms of exploitation, mining, lumbering, grazing, and so on, in hopes that they would revert to the condition of virgin forest. This action reduced the amount of grazing land available.

Some valuable timberland in the central part of the state was already claimed as part of the land grant of the Atlantic & Pacific Railroad. In order to consolidate its holdings, the Department of Agriculture has been gradually exchanging forest land held by the New Mexico and Arizona Land Company, formerly the Aztec Land & Cattle Company, for areas that are not timberland.

Originally, many small forest reserves were established. For example, the Coronado National Forest was formed from five forest reserves in the southern part of the state. In 1911 the Garces National Forest, comprising three forest reserves, was consolidated with the Coronado National Forest, and in 1917 the Chiricahua National Forest was added. Again, in 1953 nearly half a million acres were transferred from Crook National Forest to Coronado National Forest.

National Forest	Acreage
Apache	1,192,000
Coconino	1,815,000
Coronado	1,720,000
Kaibab	1,720,000
Prescott	1,248,000
Sitgreaves	813,000
Tonto	2,884,000
Total	11,392,000

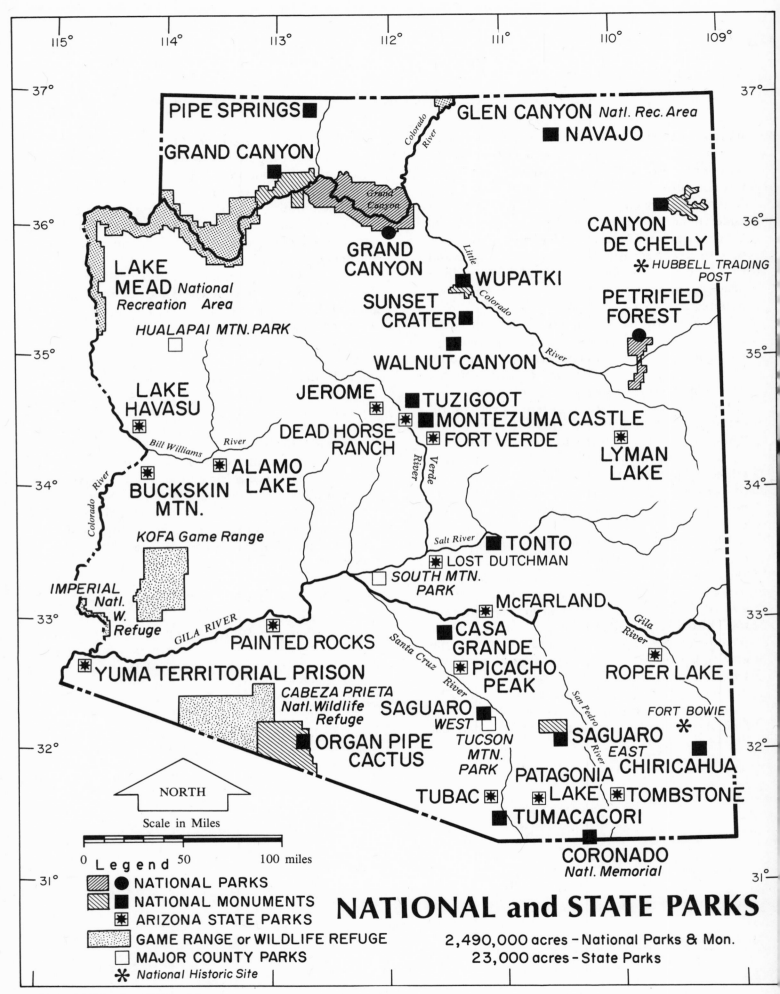

NATIONAL and STATE PARKS

PIPE SPRINGS

GLEN CANYON *Natl. Rec. Area*

NAVAJO

GRAND CANYON

Grand Canyon

CANYON DE CHELLY

✳ HUBBELL TRADING POST

LAKE MEAD *National Recreation Area*

GRAND CANYON

WUPATKI

PETRIFIED FOREST

Little

Colorado

SUNSET CRATER

HUALAPAI MTN. PARK

WALNUT CANYON

River

LAKE HAVASU

JEROME

TUZIGOOT

✳

MONTEZUMA CASTLE

✳ FORT VERDE

LYMAN LAKE

DEAD HORSE RANCH

Bill Williams   *River*

✳ ALAMO LAKE

✳ BUCKSKIN MTN.

Verde

River

Colorado River

KOFA Game Range

Salt River   TONTO

✳ LOST DUTCHMAN

☐ SOUTH MTN. PARK

Gila

River

IMPERIAL Natl. W. Refuge

✳ McFARLAND

GILA RIVER

✳ PAINTED ROCKS

CASA GRANDE

✳ PICACHO PEAK

ROPER LAKE ✳

Santa Cruz

✳ YUMA TERRITORIAL PRISON

CABEZA PRIETA Natl. Wildlife Refuge

SAGUARO *WEST*

River

San Pedro

FORT BOWIE ✳

SAGUARO *EAST*

ORGAN PIPE CACTUS

☐ *TUCSON MTN. PARK*

River

CHIRICAHUA

PATAGONIA ✳ LAKE

✳ TOMBSTONE

NORTH

TUBAC ✳

TUMACACORI

Scale in Miles

0   Legend   50   100 miles

CORONADO *Natl. Memorial*

Legend

▨ ●	NATIONAL PARKS
▨ ■	NATIONAL MONUMENTS
✳	ARIZONA STATE PARKS
▨	GAME RANGE or WILDLIFE REFUGE
☐	MAJOR COUNTY PARKS
✳	National Historic Site

2,490,000 acres – National Parks & Mon.
23,000 acres – State Parks

55. NATIONAL AND STATE PARKS

NATIONAL PARKS MUST BE ESTABLISHED by act of Congress. They are relatively large areas with two or more unique and important scenic or scientific attributes. On the other hand, national monuments may be established by act of Congress or by presidential proclamation and need only one prehistoric, historic, or scientific asset. In some cases units of the national park system have been carved from national forest land. For example, the Saguaro National Monument was set up in part of the Coronado National Forest. In such cases, the National Park Service exercises administrative jurisdiction of the monuments.

In 1872 the first national park was established by act of Congress to preserve the scenic and scientific wonders of the Yellowstone area of Wyoming. Exploitation by timber interests and railroads threatened to ruin the natural wonders. Arizona's first and largest national park was established by act of Congress at the Grand Canyon in 1919 from parts of Kaibab and Tusuyan National Forests. The Grand Canyon Game Preserve covers the same area. The other national park in Arizona is Petrified Forest, established initially as a national monument in 1906. In 1938 the state legislature requested that the monument be redesignated as a national park in hopes that the change in classification would draw more visitors. This step was taken in 1962.

Arizona has many national monuments, which range in size from the Organ Pipe Cactus National Monument, covering some five hundred square miles, to the forty-acre Pipe Spring National Monument. Most of the monuments in the state are set up for the preservation of more recent structures such as the Spanish-built Tumacacori Mission or the Mormon-built pioneer fort at Pipe Spring. The Organ Pipe Cactus and Saguaro monuments were established to preserve striking and unusual forms of cactus.

The federal government has also established wildlife and fish preserves, some of which are designated as national recreation areas. These preserves occupy some 1,527,000 acres.

In addition, the state of Arizona has established a parks system and has set up a number of state parks, such as the former Cochise County Courthouse at Tombstone and the preservation of the ruins of the Spanish Presidio at Tubac.

Not all local reaction was in opposition to the development of the national and state park systems. The Twenty-third Territorial Legislature in 1905 memorialized Congress for ten thousand dollars to be used for the protection and preservation of San Xavier Mission. Two years later the sum was reduced to five thousand dollars, and in 1909 the request was repeated. The Second State Legislature pointed out in 1915 that the Tumacacori Mission had been set aside as a national monument, but no provision had been made for restoring the "partially decayed walls." They requested an appropriation of ten thousand dollars "or as much as may be necessary, to restore and preserve the historical mission of San José de Tumacacori."

National Park Service holdings amount to approximately 1,591,000 acres.

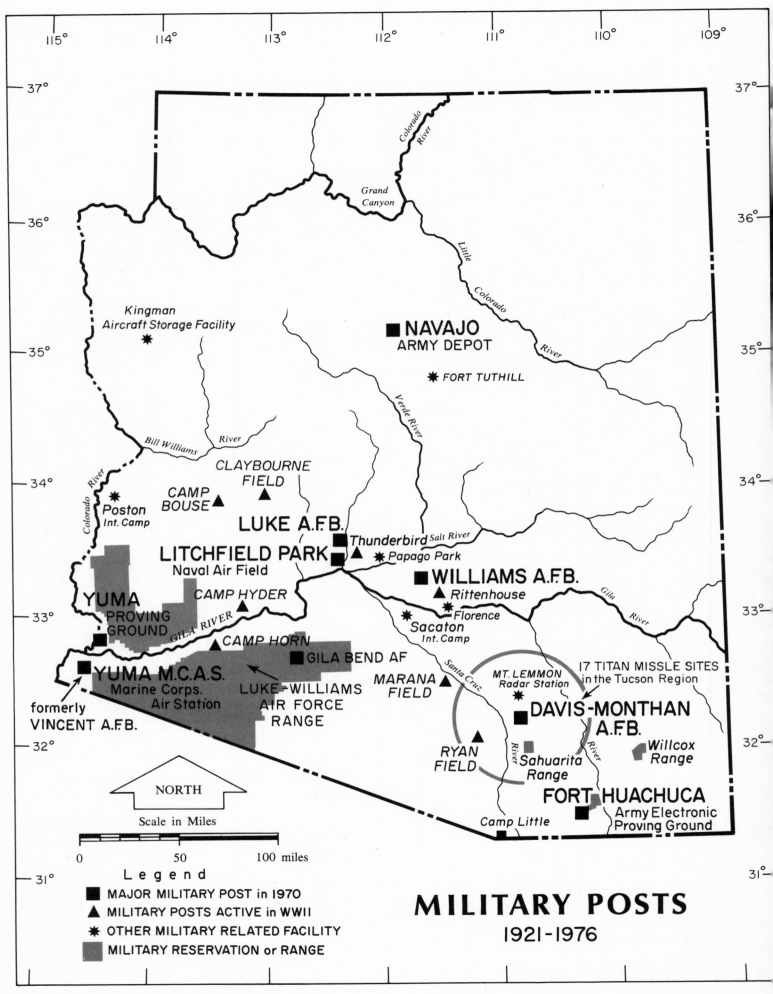

MILITARY POSTS

1921-1976

Legend

■ MAJOR MILITARY POST in 1970
▲ MILITARY POSTS ACTIVE in WWII
✳ OTHER MILITARY RELATED FACILITY
▨ MILITARY RESERVATION or RANGE

NORTH

Scale in Miles

0   50   100 miles

Kingman
Aircraft Storage Facility

NAVAJO
ARMY DEPOT

✳ FORT TUTHILL

Poston
Int. Camp

CLAYBOURNE
FIELD

CAMP
BOUSE

LUKE A.F.B.

Thunderbird

LITCHFIELD PARK
Naval Air Field

Papago Park

WILLIAMS A.F.B.

YUMA
PROVING
GROUND

CAMP HYDER

Rittenhouse

Florence

GILA RIVER

CAMP HORN

Sacaton
Int. Camp

YUMA M.C.A.S.
Marine Corps.
Air Station

GILA BEND AF

MARANA
FIELD

MT. LEMMON
Radar Station

17 TITAN MISSLE SITES
in the Tucson Region

LUKE - WILLIAMS
AIR FORCE
RANGE

formerly
VINCENT A.F.B.

DAVIS - MONTHAN
A.F.B.

RYAN
FIELD

Sahuarita
Range

Willcox
Range

FORT HUACHUCA
Army Electronic
Proving Ground

Camp Little

Colorado River
Grand Canyon
Little Colorado River
Verde River
Bill Williams River
Salt River
Gila River
Santa Cruz River

56. MILITARY POSTS, 1921–76

AFTER WORLD WAR I all posts and camps in Arizona were closed except Fort Huachuca. However, with the outbreak of World War II a number of large military installations were opened.

In January, 1943, the Yuma Test Branch of the Engineer Board of Fort Belvoir, Virginia, was opened to test pontoon bridges. The facility was closed in December, 1949. Because of the increased range of artillery weapons and the expense of extending existing reservations in the east, the Yuma Proving Ground of some 990,000 acres was opened in April, 1951, and is still in use. Camps Bouse, Horn, and Hyder were established as parts of the Arizona-California Desert Maneuver Area.

In the southeastern part of the state, Fort Huachuca, after serving as a World War II training area, was turned over to the state of Arizona for use by the National Guard. For a short time it was abandoned, and plans were drawn up to make it a retirement community. Pressures of the Korean War brought about its reopening. Now the fort serves as an electronic proving ground and the site of the Army Intelligence School. In the north-central area, near Flagstaff, the Navajo Ordinance Depot has been established within the Kaibab National Forest.

Arizona's weather is particularly important for the United States Air Force. During World War II, Claybourne Flying Field was used for training glider pilots. A number of fields were opened for preliminary flight training. Among them were Ryan, Marana, Thunderbird No. 1, and Kingman fields.

At Tucson, Davis-Monthan Air Force Base was opened in 1927 as a training base. However, in recent years the dry climate has made it an excellent site for a storage and salvage operation. Some special training is still conducted at the base. The Willcox Dry Lake and Sahuarita Bombing Ranges have been abandoned.

Outside Phoenix are Luke and Williams Air Force Bases, both of which are used for advanced training. In addition, both fields have a number of auxiliary fields in the area. Luke Air Force Base is also responsible for the Luke Air Force Bombing and Gunnery Range, which extends for 140 miles east and west between U.S. Interstate 8 and the Mexican border.

Two internment camps, Sacaton and Poston, were set up during World War II for citizens of Japanese ancestry who had been moved from California. There were also two prisoner of war camps, one at Florence for Italian POW's taken in North Africa and the other at Papago Park, near Phoenix, for German naval prisoners. Within twenty-five miles of Tucson, seventeen Titan II missile sites have been built and manned.

At present, military installations cover about 5.01 per cent of the state's area, or some 3,640,000 acres.

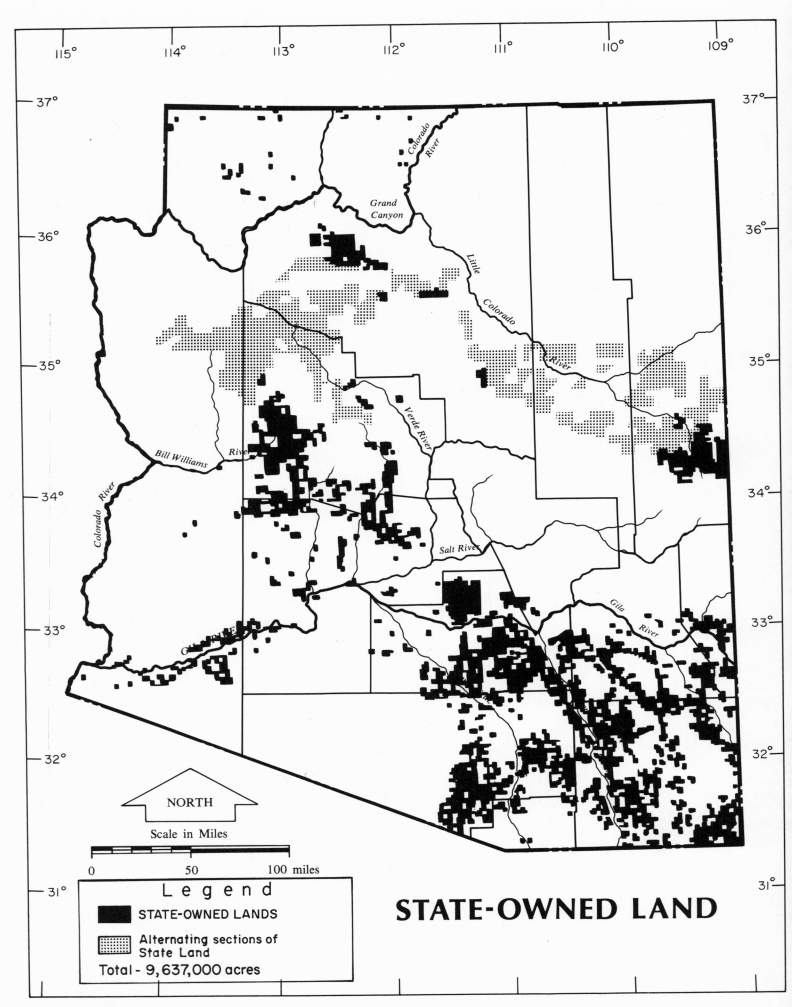

115°   114°   113°   112°   111°   110°   109°

37°   37°

Colorado River

Grand Canyon

Little

36°   36°

Colorado

River

35°   35°

Verde River

Bill Williams   *River*

34°   34°

Colorado River

Salt River

Gila

33°   33°

River

32°   32°

NORTH

Scale in Miles

0   50   100 miles

31°   31°

L e g e n d

■ STATE-OWNED LANDS

▦ Alternating sections of State Land

Total – 9,637,000 acres

STATE-OWNED LAND

57. STATE-OWNED LAND

STATE-OWNED LAND accounts for 9,637,000 acres, or 13.2 per cent of the area of the state. This land is mostly from the public domain granted to the state by the federal government. At the time of statehood, Arizona received 8,333,837 acres for the benefit of the common schools. This acreage consisted of sections 2, 16, 32, and 36 of each township or equal acreage in other sections. In 1881 the Forty-sixth Congress set aside 46,086 acres for the benefit of Arizona's universities at such time as Arizona should become a state. As of June 30, 1964, some 687,000 acres of the original grant had not been selected by the state.

Both the amount and distribution of state-owned land is constantly changing. As communities spread or other developments make particular parcels of land in the public domain more valuable, the state may select these parcels for transfer to state ownership. The state may then retain the land for itself or sell it to private parties, thus enhancing the state's income and increasing the tax base. This activity goes on almost daily and affects the size of the holdings of federal and state government and private ownership.

Among the counties, Cochise County has the largest amount of state land, 1,363,000 acres, and Gila County has the smallest amount, 30,000 acres. On the basis of percentage of the area of the counties, the state owns 35.6 per cent of Pinal County, the highest percentage among the fourteen counties. Gila County has the smallest percentage, 0.9 per cent.

Another complicating factor in the presentation of statistics of land ownership is the fact that from time to time the state will exchange land with other governmental agencies or with the private sector on the basis of dollar value instead of acreage. Thus, the state may pick up one acre of high-value land in exchange for three acres of less desirable land, or vice versa.

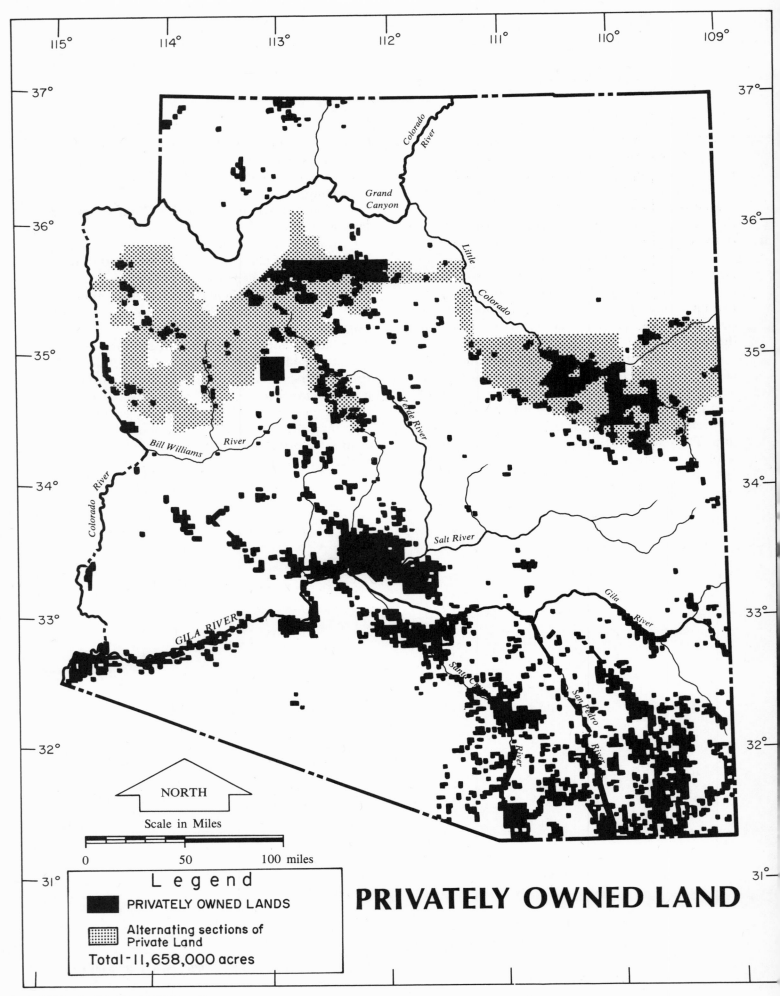

PRIVATELY OWNED LAND

Legend

■ PRIVATELY OWNED LANDS

▦ Alternating sections of Private Land

Total – 11,658,000 acres

NORTH

Scale in Miles

0   50   100 miles

© 1979 by the University of Oklahoma Press

58. PRIVATELY OWNED LAND

As INDICATED by the previous four maps, only a small portion, about 16 per cent or 11,658,000 acres, of the land area of the state is in private hands, thus severely limiting the tax base for state and local revenue. In general, the privately owned land is the best and most valuable land in the state, with the possible exception of forest lands. The early settlers homesteaded or bought lands along the rivers, where water could be had for irrigation, or on the grasslands, which provided good grazing for cattle.

As well drilling and water pumping techniques improved, lands with underground water supplies were taken up by individuals. Lands in the public domain were taken up under several federal statutes; the Homestead Act of 1862 and the Desert Land Act of 1877 were the most important. In 1934 President Franklin D. Roosevelt withdrew what was left of the public domain from homestead entry.

Under the multiple use concept of operation of the national forests, private citizens may be granted permission to build summer homes within the forests. For example, there are a number of such homes on Mt. Lemmon in the Coronado National Forest. The home owners pay to the United States Forest Service a fee for rental of the land. Improvements built on the land are assessed and taxed by the appropriate county. Thus, there is some revenue to local government from some of the federally owned land.

Of all the counties in Arizona, Mohave County has the greatest amount of land held by private individuals, some 1,782,000 acres. On the other hand, Greenlee County has the smallest amount, 68,000 acres. The amount of acreage in private hands varies almost from day to day as the state sells off some of its land, forecloses for delinquent taxes, or exchanges one parcel for another.

By far the largest single land operation in the private sector was the land grant originally given to the Atlantic & Pacific Railroad by federal charter in 1866 and finally earned by the Atchison, Topeka & Santa Fe Railroad. Under the grant the railroad received forty sections of 640 acres each, in a checkerboard pattern of alternate sections, for every mile of track built. Much of this land was sold to the Aztec Land and Cattle Company, commonly called the "Hashknife." The United States Forest Service, as part of its program to consolidate its holdings, is still exchanging land with both the railroad and the cattle company.

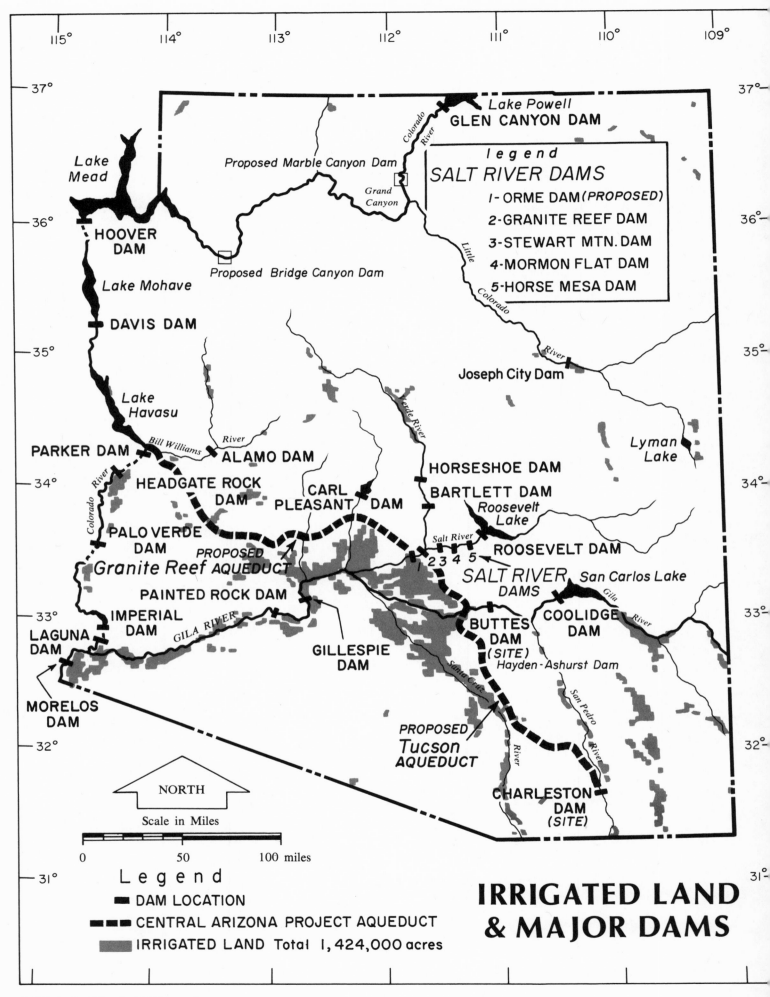

Lake Powell
GLEN CANYON DAM

Proposed Marble Canyon Dam

Lake Mead

Grand Canyon

legend
SALT RIVER DAMS
1- ORME DAM *(PROPOSED)*
2- GRANITE REEF DAM
3- STEWART MTN. DAM
4- MORMON FLAT DAM
5- HORSE MESA DAM

HOOVER DAM

Lake Mohave

Proposed Bridge Canyon Dam

Colorado River

Little Colorado

DAVIS DAM

Lake Havasu

River

Joseph City Dam

Verde River

Lyman Lake

PARKER DAM

Bill Williams River

ALAMO DAM

HORSESHOE DAM
BARTLETT DAM

HEADGATE ROCK DAM

CARL PLEASANT DAM

Roosevelt Lake

Colorado River

PALO VERDE DAM

PROPOSED
Granite Reef AQUEDUCT

Salt River

2 3 4 5
SALT RIVER DAMS

ROOSEVELT DAM

San Carlos Lake

Gila River

PAINTED ROCK DAM

IMPERIAL DAM

GILA RIVER

BUTTES DAM (SITE)

COOLIDGE DAM

LAGUNA DAM

GILLESPIE DAM

Hayden-Ashurst Dam

Santa Cruz

San Pedro River

MORELOS DAM

PROPOSED
Tucson AQUEDUCT

River

River

NORTH

Scale in Miles

0   50   100 miles

CHARLESTON DAM (SITE)

Legend

━ DAM LOCATION

▬▬ CENTRAL ARIZONA PROJECT AQUEDUCT

▨ IRRIGATED LAND Total 1,424,000 acres

IRRIGATED LAND & MAJOR DAMS

THE IRRIGATION OF LAND for agricultural purposes has been carried on since prehistoric times. The network of early canals in the vicinity of Phoenix was very extensive. Some of the canals were as much as eighteen miles long, twenty-five feet wide at the top, fifteen feet wide at the bottom, and ten feet deep below their banks. Traces of impounding ponds have been found in the hills along the river. When Father Kino reached the Gila River in 1694, he found that the Pima Indians were irrigating small fields south of present-day Phoenix. They were growing cotton, maize, beans, and melons.

The first American-built canal was started by Jack Swilling in 1867. He started to reopen a prehistoric canal, which later became the Grand Canal (1878), about four miles upstream from eastern Phoenix. But he soon hit bedrock, dropped downstream a short distance, and opened the Salt River Valley Canal, also called the Swilling Ditch. This start was followed in 1887 by the Arizona Canal and in 1888 by the Highland Canal. Floods in the river repeatedly washed out the diversion dams and left the head gates high and dry, making it difficult to maintain these early systems.

An important milestone in the matter of legal rights to water for irrigation came in 1892. Judge Joseph C. Kibby of the Territorial Supreme Court ruled that the canal companies did not own the water but were simply distributors; they could not sell water rights apart from the land to which they pertained. This ruling annulled the English common-law principle of riparian rights, which gave a landowner rights to all the water flowing through his land.

The fact that precipitation came in two short seasons soon indicated the need for reservoirs to store the surplus floodwaters. Mormon farmers on the Little Colorado River raised $200,000 and built Slough Dam in 1886. The dam was washed out by floods in 1903 and again in 1915. Clearly, private enterprise could not raise sufficient funds to build storage dams stout enough to stand up to maximum floods.

In 1902 Congress passed the Newlands Act, which set up the Bureau of Reclamation, and a year later a project was authorized for the Salt River. Roosevelt Dam was started in 1905 and completed in 1911 at a cost of $5,560,000, or $49.50 per acre for the 245,940 acres for which it stored water. The Salt River Valley Water Users Association had been formed in 1903 because of almost constant litigation among private canal companies. In 1917 the association took over the operation of Roosevelt Dam, and by the 1950's it had paid off the mortgage on the dam. After 1920, several more dams were built on the Gila and Salt watersheds to impound water and to provide hydroelectric power.

On the Colorado River the Laguna Dam was built to divert water into canals on both the Arizona and California banks. The first great storage project was the Hoover Dam, built during the 1930's for hydroelectric power and flood control. Since then other dams have been built along the Colorado to provide water for irrigation.

The water of the Colorado has long been a subject of dispute among the seven states that cover parts of the river basin. In 1922, representatives of the seven states drew up the Santa Fe Compact, under which fifteen million acre feet of annual flow was evenly divided between the Upper Basin (Utah, Colorado, Wyoming, and New Mexico) and the Lower Basin (Arizona, California, and Nevada). The states of the respective basins were to work out the allocation of their share. It is now suspected that the fifteen million acre feet may have come from a series of unusually wet years not matched since. Not until 1944 did Arizona agree to cooperate. Since then the Central Arizona Project has evolved to provide water pumped from Lake Havasu on the Colorado River to Phoenix and Tucson. It is stipulated that this water is to be used exclusively to meet growing urban demands.

In 1973 approximately 1,424,000 acres, or 1.96 per cent of the area of the state, was under irrigation.

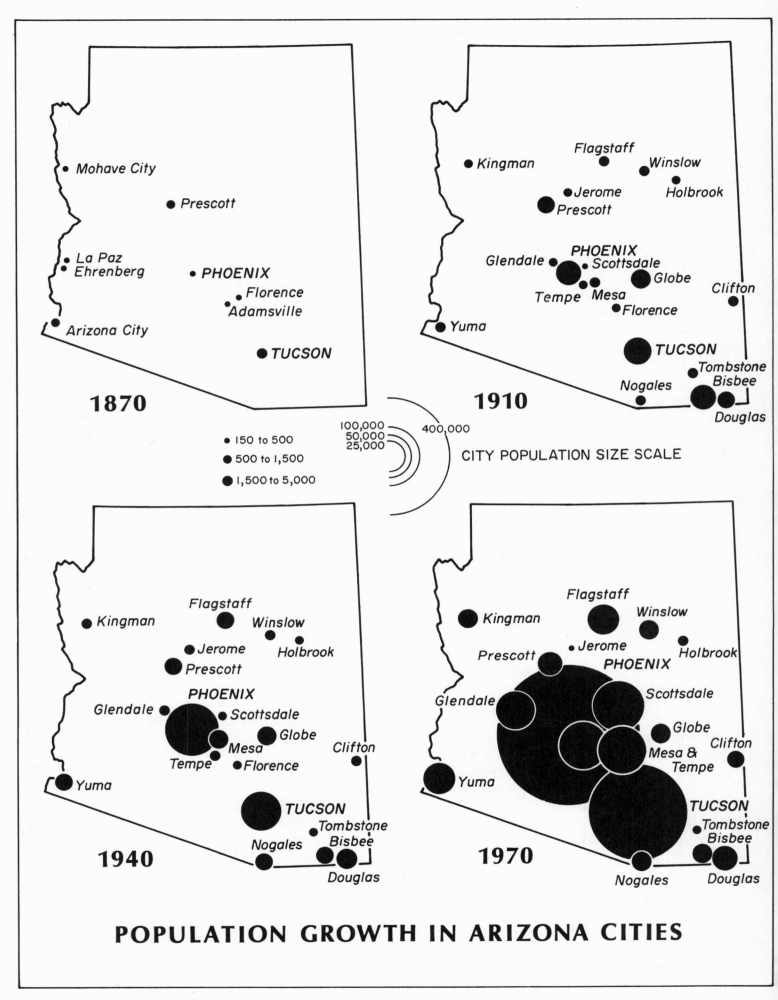

POPULATION GROWTH IN ARIZONA CITIES

1870

1910

1940

1970

CITY POPULATION SIZE SCALE

- 150 to 500
- 500 to 1,500
- 1,500 to 5,000

100,000
50,000
25,000
400,000

60. POPULATION GROWTH IN ARIZONA CITIES

IT IS DIFFICULT to set a date for the establishment of a town or city, even within several years. There often was a period of some length between the arrival of the first settler in a district and the arrival of enough settlers to form a recognizable community. It may have been several more years before the townsite was platted, the village incorporated, or a post office opened.

The first official census of Arizona was taken in 1860, when Arizona County (Map 29) was part of the territory of New Mexico. Before that time, population figures were pure estimates. Between 1846 and 1853 Tucson was estimated to have about 500 souls. In 1857 Tubac was credited with 500 inhabitants. The 1860 census showed that Tucson, with 620 people, was by far the largest settlement and that Tubac, with 163, was the second largest. In both cases outlying settlements were enumerated separately. For example, San Xavier, eight miles south of Tucson, had 99 inhabitants, and various mines and farming communities that used the Tubac post office accounted for 141 persons.

According to the first territorial census, taken in 1864 (Map 30), Tucson had grown to 1,568, roughly one-third of the population of the territory. At the same time, the number of residents of Tubac had declined to 118.

Because many of Arizona's towns and cities were closely connected with mining, they sometimes reached their peak population between decennial censuses as shown on the table below. Changes in mining activity also indirectly affected the growth of cities. In 1880 Tucson had 7,007 inhabitants, but with the collapse of silver mining in the southern part of the state the city's population declined to 5,150 by 1890.

						POPULATION						
COUNTY	1870	1880	1890	1900	1910	1920	1930	1940	1950	1960	1970	1975 (est.) *
Apache	—	5,283	4,281	8,297	9,196	13,196	17,765	24,095	27,767	30,438	32,304	42,200
Cochise	—	—	6,938	9,251	34,591	46,465	40,998	34,627	31,488	55,039	61,918	76,000
Coconino	—	—	—	5,514	8,130	9,982	14,064	18,770	23,910	41,857	48,326	65,000
Gila	—	—	2,021	4,973	16,348	25,678	31,016	23,867	24,158	25,745	29,255	32,800
Graham	—	—	5,670	14,162	23,999	10,148	10,373	12,113	12,985	14,045	16,578	19,600
Greenlee	—	—	—	—	—†	15,362	9,886	8,698	12,805	11,509	10,330	11,900
Maricopa	—	5,689	10,986	20,457	34,488	89,576	150,970	186,193	331,770	663,510	969,425	1,230,000
Mohave	179	1,190	1,444	3,426	3,773	5,259	5,572	8,591	8,510	7,736	25,857	36,600
Navajo	—	—	—	8,829	11,471	16,077	21,202	25,309	29,446	37,994	47,559	55,800
Pima	5,716	17,006	12,673	14,689	22,818	34,680	55,676	72,838	141,216	265,660	351,667	452,000
Pinal	—	3,044	4,251	7,779	9,045	16,130	22,081	28,841	43,191	62,673	68,579	84,500
Santa Cruz	—	—	—	4,545	6,766	12,689	9,684	9,482	9,344	10,808	13,966	18,100
Yavapai	2,142	5,013	8,685	13,799	15,996	24,016	28,470	26,511	24,991	28,912	36,837	49,600
Yuma	1,621	3,215	2,671	4,145	7,733	14,904	17,816	19,326	28,006	46,235	60,827	71,000
TOTAL	9,658	40,440	88,243‡	122,931§	204,354	334,162	435,573	499,261	749,587	1,302,161	1,773,428	2,245,100

* 1975 population estimates are from the *Arizona Statistical Review*, 31st ed. Valley National Bank of Arizona, Phoenix, 1975.

† Greenlee County was authorized by the legislature in 1909, but was not in fact in existence until 1911.

‡ Indians were not enumerated in the 1890 general census, but were counted at 28,623 in a special Indian census. Population by county totals 59,620, plus 28,623 Indian population, equals 88,243.

§ The San Carlos Indian Reservation was enumerated as a unit separate from those portions of Graham, Gila, and Apache counties, in which it existed. Population by county totals 119,866, plus 3,065 for the San Carlos Reservation, equals 122,931.

The history of the city of Globe illustrates some of the difficulties of establishing a municipality. The town was incorporated in 1880, but that fact seems to have been forgotten, because the town was again incorporated in 1905. The inhabitants found the corporation to be too expensive and disbanded it within a year. Finally, in 1907, it was incorporated as a city.

In the early days of Arizona's development the military outnumbered the civilians in the population of a number of communities. For example, the 1860 census of Arizona County of the Territory of New Mexico shows forty-three civilians and ninety-two military personnel at Fort Buchanan. The first territorial census of 1864 listed eight civilians at Calabasas and 173 soldiers from two companies of California Volunteers.

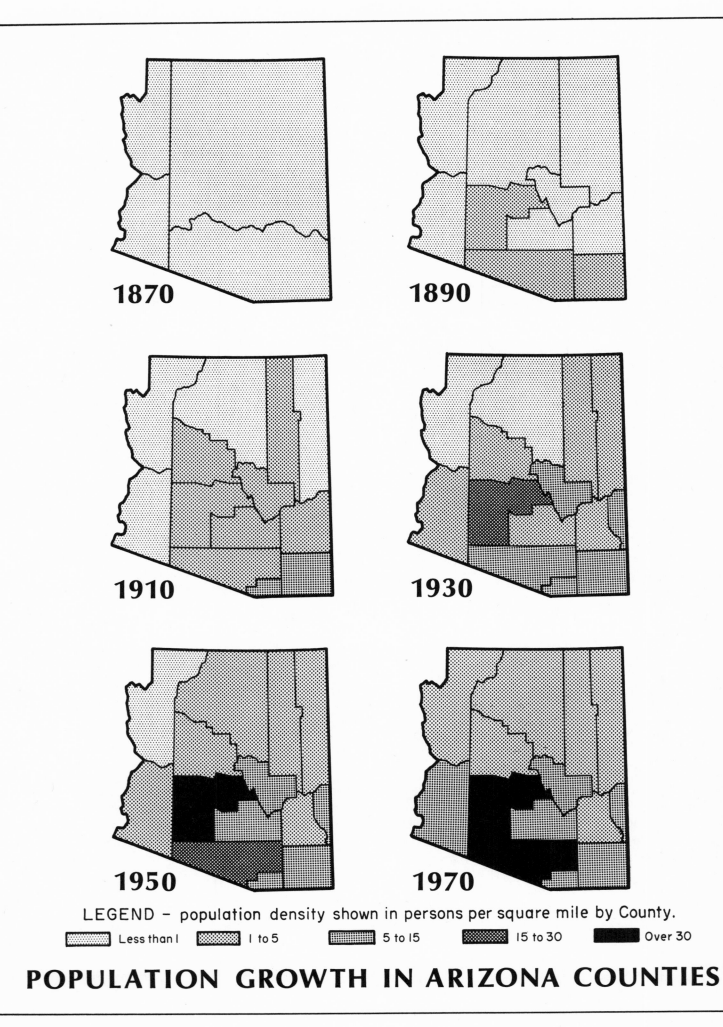

1870

1890

1910

1930

1950

1970

LEGEND – population density shown in persons per square mile by County.

Less than 1   1 to 5   5 to 15   15 to 30   Over 30

POPULATION GROWTH IN ARIZONA COUNTIES

ARIZONA'S POPULATION has grown steadily throughout the century beginning in 1870 and now boasts the third highest rate of growth among all the states of the nation. However, there has been marked variation in the rate of growth of its counties, as indicated by the table below.

In some cases the decrease in the number of inhabitants is clearly attributable to the formation of new counties. Apache County lost about 20 per cent of its population when Navajo County was erected in 1895. The establishment of Greenlee County in 1909 cut into the population of Graham County, and the latter has not yet exceeded the figure set in 1910. Pima County suffered two losses. The first came in 1881 when Cochise County was formed around Tombstone, then the largest city in the territory. The second occurred when Santa Cruz County was erected in 1899. It was not until 1910 that Pima County passed the figure set in 1880.

The sudden increase in the number of inhabitants of Santa Cruz County in 1920 and the drop by 1930 can be accounted for by the inclusion of the garrison of Camp Stephen D. Little at Nogales. The 3,261 soldiers were members of National Guard units from many states that had been ordered to the Mexican border in 1916–17.

The greatest setback to a record of steady growth for four of the counties was the depression of the early 1930's. The price of copper slumped so drastically that most of Arizona's copper mines closed down or heavily curtailed production. In 1929 some 830 million pounds of copper had been produced, but in 1932 that figure had dropped to 182 million pounds. Gila County lost 23 per cent of its people in the 1930's. Greenlee county suffered most heavily when it lost 35.6 per cent of its inhabitants. Cochise County's loss amounted to 11.8 per cent between 1920 and 1930 and another 15.5 per cent in the following decade. The closing of the United Verde Extension Mine and its smelter at Jerome in 1938 adversely affected the growth of Yavapai County, and the decline continued through the next decade

with the gradual reduction of activity in the United Verde Mine, which finally closed in 1953.

Another factor that influenced growth in counties that relied heavily on mining was the shift from underground mining to open-pit operation. The latter system yields a much lower man-hour per ton ratio.

In general, those counties which were primarily agricultural until the close of World War II showed the steadiest rate of growth. Since the late 1940's the rate of growth of the whole state has been little short of phenomenal. Between 1940 and 1950 the population of the state increased by about 50 per cent. In the next decade the rate of growth was about 72 per cent, and in the decade of the 1960's it was some 38 per cent. Most of this growth has been concentrated in Maricopa and Pima counties and was brought about by the influx of light industry and the arrivals of many retired persons from throughout the country.

	POPULATION				
CITY	1864	1870	1910	1940	1970
Adamsville	—	400	—	—	—
Bisbee	—	—	9,019	5,853	8,328
Clifton	—	—	4,874	2,668	5,087
Douglas	—	—	6,437	8,623	12,462
Ehrenberg	—	223	less than 150	—	—
Flagstaff	—	—	1,633	5,080	26,117
Florence	—	218	807	1,383	2,173
Glendale	—	—	1,000	4,855	36,228
Globe	—	—	7,083	6,141	7,333
Holbrook	—	—	609	1,184	4,759
Jerome*	—	—	2,393	2,295	290
Kingman	—	—	900	2,956	7,312
La Paz	352	255	—	743	—
Mesa	—	—	1,692	7,224	62,853
Mohave City	—	159	—	—	—
Nogales	—	—	3,514	5,135	8,946
Phoenix	—	246	11,134	65,414	581,562
Prescott	—	676	5,092	5,018	13,134
Scottsdale	—	—	260	743	67,823
Tempe	—	—	1,473	2,906	63,550
Tombstone†	—	—	1,582	822	1,241
Tucson	1,568	3,224	13,193	36,818	262,933
Winslow	—	—	2,381	4,577	8,066
Yuma	151	1,142	2,914	5,325	29,007

* Peak population in 1929, about 15,000.
† Peak population 1882–84, probably about 10,000.

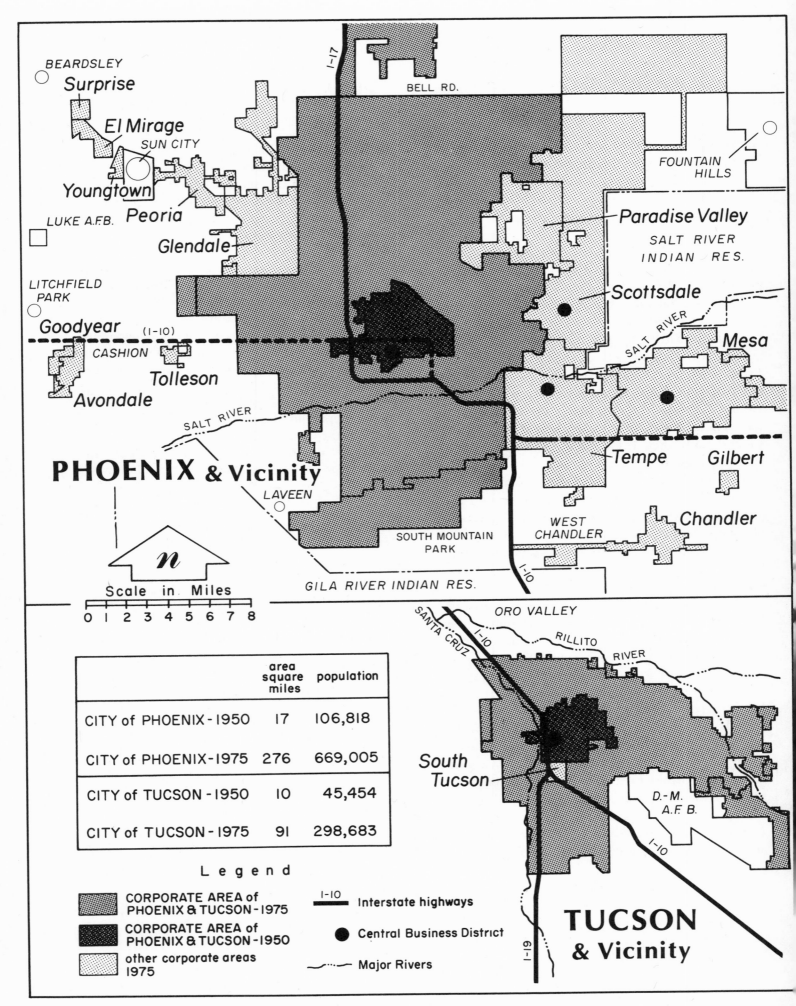

BEARDSLEY
Surprise
El Mirage
SUN CITY
Youngtown
Peoria
LUKE A.F.B.
Glendale
LITCHFIELD PARK
Goodyear (I-10)
CASHION
Tolleson
Avondale
SALT RIVER

I-17
BELL RD.

FOUNTAIN HILLS

Paradise Valley
SALT RIVER INDIAN RES.
Scottsdale
SALT RIVER
Mesa

Tempe   Gilbert

PHOENIX & Vicinity

LAVEEN

WEST CHANDLER
Chandler

SOUTH MOUNTAIN PARK

I-10

GILA RIVER INDIAN RES.

n

Scale in Miles

0 1 2 3 4 5 6 7 8

	area square miles	population
CITY of PHOENIX - 1950	17	106,818
CITY of PHOENIX - 1975	276	669,005
CITY of TUCSON - 1950	10	45,454
CITY of TUCSON - 1975	91	298,683

Legend

CORPORATE AREA of PHOENIX & TUCSON - 1975

CORPORATE AREA of PHOENIX & TUCSON - 1950

other corporate areas 1975

I-10 Interstate highways

● Central Business District

Major Rivers

ORO VALLEY
SANTA CRUZ
I-10
RILLITO
RIVER

South Tucson

D-M. A.F.B.

I-10

I-19

TUCSON & Vicinity

ARIZONA HAS two metropolitan centers, large cities with even larger dependent suburban areas. In point of age, Tucson is the senior city. Established as a Spanish presidio in 1775, it remained no more than a frontier village throughout the Spanish and Mexican periods. When Brevet Lieutenant Colonel Philip St. George Cooke passed through in 1846, he estimated the population to be "perhaps five hundred inhabitants." Following the Gadsden Purchase, Anglos began to arrive, and there set in a period of slow and somewhat erratic growth.

When the first territorial governor, John N. Goodwin, visited the town in 1864, he proclaimed it to be an incorporated municipality, the only one in Arizona at that time, and appointed William S. Oury as mayor. A year later the population was estimated to be about fifteen hundred. Goodwin's proclamation was premature, if not illegal. It was not until 1871 that official surveys were completed. It was another three years before Tucson received its patent from the General Land Office in Washington. Finally, in 1877, Governor A. P. K. Safford signed the act incorporating Tucson as a Charter City.

The transfer of the territorial capital from Prescott in 1867 infused life into the city, which by 1871 was claiming three thousand inhabitants, a newspaper, several saloons, and one bathtub. When the capital was returned to Prescott in 1877, Tucson had become the supply center for the rejuvenated mining industry in the southern part of the state and for the army posts and Indian agencies of the area. Thus, Tucson had an economic base that was not affected by the whims of parochial politicians.

The decline of mining, especially silver mining, in the decade of the 1880's caused Tucson's population to drop from 7,007 to 5,150. By 1900 it had only reached 7,531. It held the position of the largest city in the state until 1920, when its population of 20,292 was exceeded by the 29,053 residents of Phoenix. The population of Maricopa County, around Phoenix, had passed Tucson's Pima County two decades before.

The greatest boom in Tucson's growth followed World War II, when many men who had received military training in the state decided to settle in the area. Another factor was the increase in industry desiring to take advantage of the warm climate and relatively smogfree atmosphere. Between 1950 and 1975 the population rose from 45,654 to 298,683.

The first settlement in the area where the city of Phoenix arose seems to have been a hay camp for Fort McDowell, some thirty miles up the Verde River. In 1867 Jack Swilling, late of the Confederate Army, began to reopen a prehistoric irrigation ditch to provide water for farms. The name Phoenix seems to have been given the new settlement by an Englishman, trained in the classics, who noted a new civilization rising on the ruins of an older one. An election precinct of Yavapai County was established there in 1868, and in the following year a post office was opened.

With a population of about three hundred in 1871, the first town lots were sold, and a year later the town was made the county seat of newly established Maricopa County. The first United States census to note the existence of Phoenix was that of 1880, which counted 1,708 inhabitants.

The struggle between the northern and southern parts of the territory, as represented by Prescott and Tucson, for possession of the territorial capital was finally settled by compomise when Phoenix, about halfway between the two, was selected as the permanent capital. Since then the growth of the city has been steady and rapid. As in the case of Tucson, the aftermath of World War II brought to Phoenix a vigorous growth of industry and a large increase in the number of inhabitants. By 1975 there were some 669,005 people in the city, while the metropolitan area included more than half the population of the state.

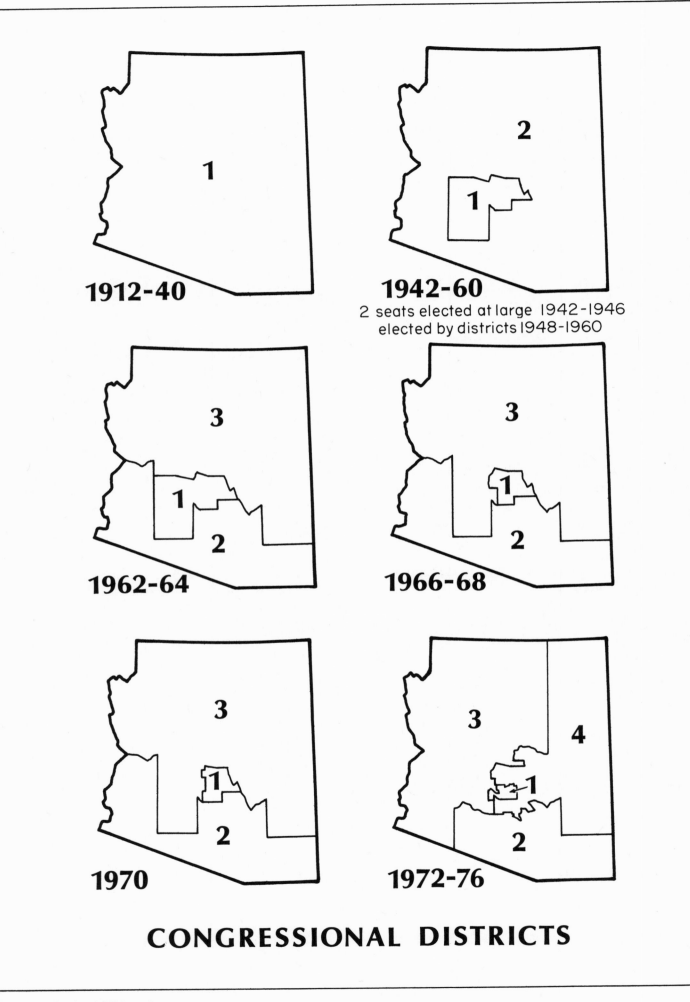

1912-40 1

1942-60 2 1
2 seats elected at large 1942-1946
elected by districts 1948-1960

1962-64 3 1 2

1966-68 3 1 2

1970 3 1 2

1972-76 3 4 1 2

CONGRESSIONAL DISTRICTS

63. CONGRESSIONAL DISTRICTS

WHEN ARIZONA was at last admitted to the Union as a state in 1912, its first two senators were Marcus A. Smith, who had already served eight terms in Congress as Arizona's delegate, and Henry F. Ashurst. Because of the state's small population, it was allowed only one congressman-at-large. Carl Hayden won the first election and went on to serve seven terms before moving to the Senate in 1926. Senator Hayden retired from active politics in 1968, having served for fifty-six years in Congress.

By 1942 Arizona's growing population was recognized when she was allowed two congressmen-at-large in the election of that year. In 1947 the Eighteenth State Legislature marked out congressional districts for the first time. District One consisted of Maricopa County, a reflection of the growth of metropolitan Phoenix. District Two covered the rest of the state.

Based on the 1960 census, Arizona gained a third seat in Congress, which was first filled in 1962. The First Congressional District again consisted of Maricopa County. The Second District comprised Cochise, Pima, Pinal, Santa Cruz, and Yuma counties. The Third District, lying largely in the northern part of the state, covered Apache, Coconino, Gila, Graham, Greenlee, Mohave, Navajo, and Yavapai counties.

The districts were modified in 1966 when District One was reduced to the eastern portion of Maricopa County (Metropolitan Phoenix) while the western part was added to District Three. There was another minor change for the election of 1970, which shifted small parts of Maricopa County from District One to District Three.

The 1970 census showed that Arizona was entitled to a fourth congressman in the 1972 election. As Maricopa County contained approximately two-thirds of the population of the state, District One was further reduced in size. Because of the requirement that congressional districts have very nearly the same number of inhabitants, the lines between districts in the center of the state cut across county lines to an extent never before seen.

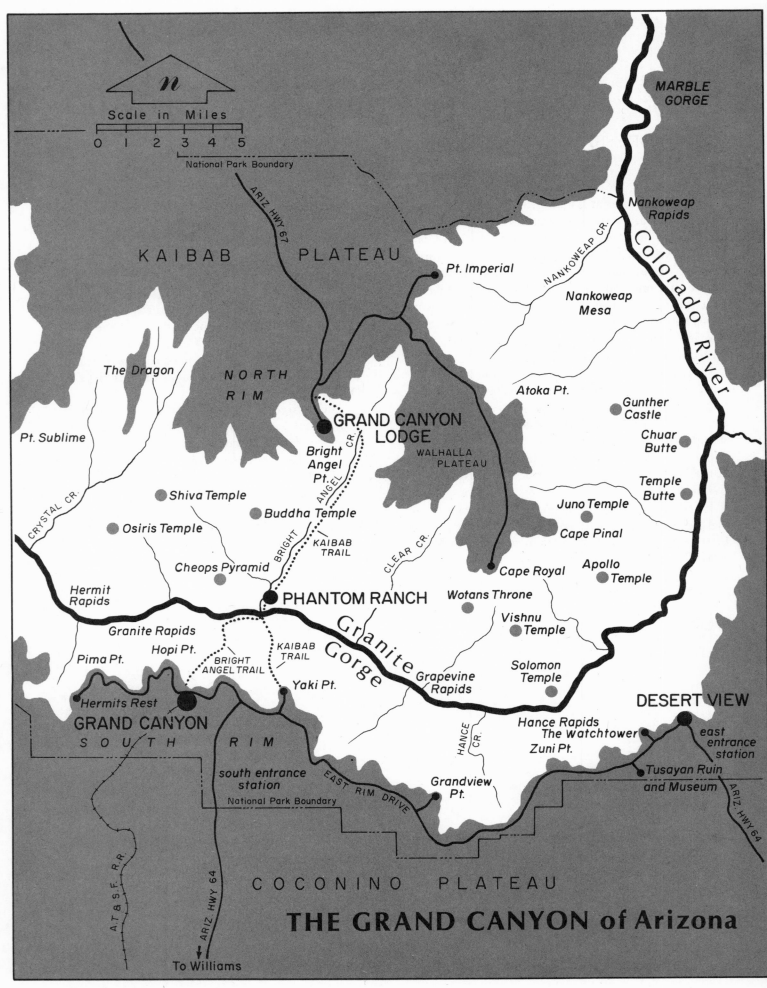

THE GRAND CANYON of Arizona

Scale in Miles

0 1 2 3 4 5

National Park Boundary

KAIBAB PLATEAU

MARBLE GORGE

Colorado River

ARIZ HWY 67

Pt. Imperial

NANKOWEAP CR.

Nankoweap Rapids

Nankoweap Mesa

NORTH RIM

The Dragon

Pt. Sublime

GRAND CANYON LODGE

Bright Angel Pt.

WALHALLA PLATEAU

Atoka Pt.

Gunther Castle

Chuar Butte

Shiva Temple

Buddha Temple

ANGEL CR.

Temple Butte

Juno Temple

Osiris Temple

CRYSTAL CR.

BRIGHT

KAIBAB TRAIL

CLEAR CR.

Cape Pinal

Apollo Temple

Cheops Pyramid

Hermit Rapids

PHANTOM RANCH

Cape Royal

Wotans Throne

Vishnu Temple

Granite Rapids

Granite Gorge

Hopi Pt.

BRIGHT ANGEL TRAIL

KAIBAB TRAIL

Solomon Temple

Pima Pt.

Yaki Pt.

Grapevine Rapids

Hermits Rest

GRAND CANYON

SOUTH RIM

HANCE CR.

Hance Rapids

DESERT VIEW

The Watchtower

Zuni Pt.

east entrance station

south entrance station

EAST RIM DRIVE

National Park Boundary

Grandview Pt.

Tusayan Ruin and Museum

ARIZ HWY 64

COCONINO PLATEAU

A.T.& S.F. R.R.

ARIZ HWY 64

To Williams

EVER SINCE García López de Cárdenas first saw the Grand Canyon of the Colorado River in 1540, this great chasm has been an object of wonder and a barrier to travel. Cárdenas and his men spent three days trying to find a way to descend into the canyon. Finally, three volunteers spent a whole day climbing in the canyon only to report that they had descended only one-third of the distance.

In 1776 Fathers Silvestre Vélez de Escalante and Francisco Atanasio Dominguez sought to lay out a trail from Santa Fe, New Mexico, to California. After traveling through southwestern Colorado and southern Utah, they reached the brink of the great gorge. There, just north of the Arizona line, they found one of the few practical crossings, El Vado de los Padres (Crossing of the Fathers). In the same year Father Francisco Garcés visited the Havasupai Indians in their tributary canyon and gave the main river its name—Río Colorado.

Some of the mountain men, such as James Ohio Pattie and Jedediah Strong Smith, saw sections of the canyon in their travels through the southwest. In 1858 Lieutenant Joseph C. Ives penetrated the lower end in his steamboat *Explorer*. However, it was not until 1869 that a thorough exploration was undertaken. On May 24 of that year Major John Wesley Powell and a party of nine men left Green River, Wyoming, in four boats. After many hair-raising experiences, the trip ended on August 30 at the mouth of the Virgin River. As a result of this trip the Smith-sonian Institution sponsored a number of years of explorations by Powell of the whole Grand Canyon area, especially the North Rim country.

As word of the canyon, one of the great natural wonders of the world, spread, tourists and scientists in ever increasing numbers came to visit. The first Bright Angel Hotel was built in 1896. In the early 1900's Fred Harvey, the great restaurateur of the southwest, built the El Tovar Hotel and Bright Angel Lodge on the South Rim. Connection with the Atchison, Topeka and Santa Fe Railroad at Williams was by stagecoach beginning in 1895. In 1908 the Grand Canyon National Monument of 958 square miles was established to prevent exploitation of the natural resources. As early as 1881 small mines had been opened in the canyon and some of its branches. The famous Bright Angel Trail was built to provide access to some of these mines. In 1901 a railroad was built from Williams to Grand Canyon Village.

As interest in the area grew, the Grand Canyon National Monument was raised to the status of a national park in 1919. Downstream from the national park the Grand Canyon National Monument extends protection along the northern rim until it meets the Lake Mead Recreation Area. Along the South Rim is located the Hualapai Indian Reservation. North and south of the park is the Kaibab National Forest, while to the east lies the Navajo Indian Reservation.

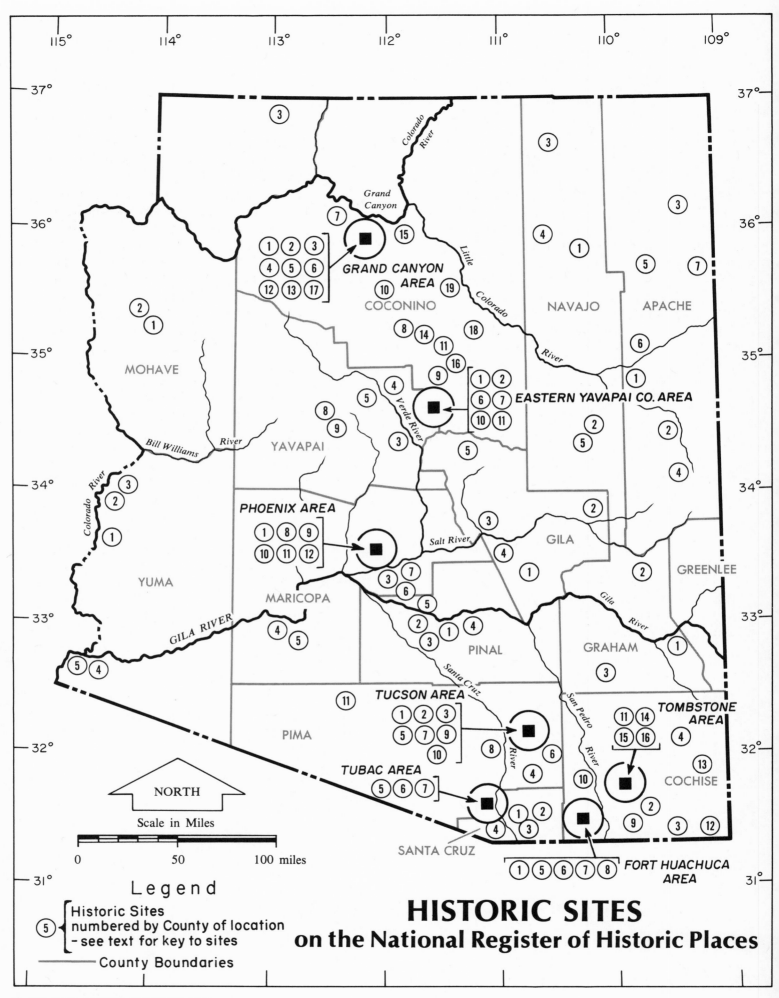

HISTORIC SITES
on the National Register of Historic Places

65. HISTORIC SITES ON THE NATIONAL REGISTER OF HISTORIC PLACES

Apache County

1. Agate House Pueblo (Petrified Forest National Park)
2. Barth Hotel (St. Johns)
3. Canyon de Chelly National Monument
4. Casa Malpais Site
5. Hubbell Trading Post
6. Painted Desert Inn (Petrified Forest National Park)
7. St. Michael's Mission

Cochise County

1. Coronado National Monument
2. Double Adobe Site
3. Douglas Municipal Airport
4. Fort Bowie
5. Garden Canyon Archaeological Site
6. Garden Canyon Petroglyphs
7. Lehner Mammoth-Kill Site
8. Old Fort Huachuca
9. Phelps Dodge General Office Building, Bisbee
10. Quiburi
11. St. Paul's Episcopal Church, Tombstone
12. San Bernardino Ranch
13. Stafford Cabin
14. Tombstone City Hall
15. Tombstone Courthouse (Cochise County Courthouse)
16. Tombstone Historic District

Coconino County

1. Bucky O'Neill Cabin (Grand Canyon National Park)
2. El Tovar Hotel, Grand Canyon
3. El Tovar Stables
4. Grand Canyon Railroad Station
5. Grand Canyon Village Historic District
6. Grandview Mine
7. Hermit's Rest Concession Building
8. Lowell Observatory
9. Mayhew's Lodge (Thomas House)
10. Merriam, C. Hart, Base Camp Site
11. Old Headquarters, Walnut Canyon
12. Rangers' Dormitory (Grand Canyon National Park)
13. Superintendent's Residence, Grand Canyon
14. The Homestead, Flagstaff
15. Tusayan Ruins
16. Walnut Canyon National Monument
17. Water Reclaim Plant, Grand Canyon
18. Winona Site
19. Wupatki National Monument

Gila County

1. Gila County Courthouse
2. Kinishba Ruins
3. Roosevelt Dam
4. Tonto National Monument
5. Zane Grey Lodge

Graham County

1. Kearny Campsite and Trail
2. Point of Pines
3. Sierra Bonita Ranch

Maricopa County

1. Arizona State Capitol Building
2. Brazaletes Pueblo Site
3. Farmer-Goodwin House
4. Fortaleza
5. Gatlin Site
6. Hackett, Roy, House
7. Hohokam-Mormon Irrigation Canals, Mesa
8. Hohokam-Pima Irrigation Sites
9. Phoenix Carnegie Library and Library Park
10. Pueblo Grande Ruin
11. Rosson, Dr. Ronald, House
12. Taliesen West

Mohave County

1. Bonelli House
2. Camp Beale Springs
3. Pipe Spring National Monument

Navajo County

1. Awatovi Ruins

2. Flake, James M., Home
3. Navajo National Monument
4. Old Oraibi
5. Smith, Jesse N., Home (Pioneer Memorial Home)

Pima County

1. Cordova House, Tucson
2. Desert Laboratory
3. El Tiradito (Wishing Shrine), Tucson
4. Empire Ranch
5. Fremont House
6. Manning Cabin
7. Old Main, University of Arizona
8. San Xavier del Bac Mission
9. The Old Adobe Patio (Charles O. Brown House)
10. Velasco House
11. Ventana Cave

Pinal County

1. Adamsville Ruin
2. C. H. Cook Memorial Church, Sacaton
3. Casa Grande Ruins National Monument
4. First Florence Courthouse
5. Snaketown

Santa Cruz County

1. Calabasas

2. Finley, James, House
3. Guevavi Mission Ruins
4. Kitchen, Pete, Ranch
5. Old Tubac Schoolhouse
6. Tubac Presidio
7. Tumacacori National Monument

Yavapai County

1. Clear Creek Church
2. Clear Creek Pueblo and Caves
3. Fort Verde District
4. Hatalacva Ruin
5. Jerome Historic District
6. Loy Butte Pueblo
7. Montezuma Castle National Monument
8. Old Governor's Mansion, Prescott
9. Prescott Public Library
10. Sacred Mountain (Ida Ruin and White Hill)
11. Tuzigoot National Monument

Yuma County

1. Old La Paz
2. Old Presbyterian Church (Mojave Indian Presbyterian Mission Church)
3. Parker Jail
4. San Ysidro Hacienda, Yuma
5. Yuma Crossing and Associated Sites

BIBLIOGRAPHY

General

Bancroft, Hubert H. *History of Arizona and New Mexico,* new ed. Albuquerque, Horn & Wallace, 1962.

Granger, Byrd H., ed. *Will Barnes' Arizona Place Names.* Tucson, University of Arizona Press, 1960.

Wagoner, Jay J. *Arizona Territory, 1863–1912: A Political History.* Tucson, University of Arizona Press, 1970.

————. *Early Arizona: Pre-history to Civil War.* Tucson, University of Arizona Press, 1975.

Wyllys, Rufus K. *Arizona: The History of a Frontier State.* Phoenix, Hobson & Herr, 1950.

Map 1. *Location of Arizona*

Bartholomew, John, ed. *The Times Atlas of the World.* Boston, Houghton Mifflin, 1957.

Miller, Joseph, ed. *Arizona: The Grand Canyon State.* New York, Hastings House, 1966.

United States Geological Survey. *The National Atlas of the United States of America.* Washington, D.C., 1970.

Map 2. *Base Line and Principal Meridian*

Hecht, M. E. *Township and Range Index of Arizona.* Tucson, Bureau of Business and Public Research, University of Arizona, 1963.

Van Zandt, Franklin K. *Boundaries of the United States and the Several States.* Geological Survey Bulletin No. 1212. Washington, D.C., 1960.

Map 3. *Generalized Relief*

United States Geological Survey. Map "State of Arizona." 1:500,000 (1955).

Map 4A, Map 4B. *Physiographic Provinces and Surface Water Study Areas*

Atwood, Wallace W. *The Physiographic Provinces of North America.* Boston, Ginn and Company, 1940.

Hecht, Melvin, "The Physical Environment." In *Arizona: Its People and Resources.* 2d ed. Tucson, University of Arizona Press, 1972.

Forrester, J. D., *et al. Mineral and Water Resources of Arizona.* Arizona Bureau of Mines Bulletin 180. Tucson, 1969.

Map 5. *Landforms*

U.S.G.S. Map "State of Arizona."

Map 6. *Major Drainage*

U.S.G.S. Map "State of Arizona."

Map 7. *Climate*

Sellers, William D. "The Climate." In *Arizona: Its People and Resources.* 2d. ed., Tucson, University of Arizona Press, 1972.

Ligner, J. J., *et al.* "Water Resources," In *Mineral and Water Resources of Arizona.* Arizona Bureau of Mines Bulletin 180. Tucson, 1969.

Map 8. *The Sonoran Desert Region*

Dunbier, Roger. *The Sonoran Desert: Its Geography, Economy, and People.* Tucson, University of Arizona Press, 1968.

Hastings, James R., and Raymond M. Turner. *The Changing Mile: An Ecological Study of Vegetation Change with Time in the Lower Mile of an Arid and Semi-Arid Region.* Tucson, University of Arizona Press, 1965.

Shreve, Forrest, and Ira L. Wiggins. *Vegetation and Flora of the Sonoran Desert.* 2 vols. Stanford, Stanford University Press, 1964.

Map 9. *Life Zones*

Lowe, Charles H., ed. *The Vertebrates of Arizona.* Tucson, University of Arizona Press, 1964.

Hastings. *The Changing Mile.*

Map 10. *Economy*

Arizona Statistical Review. Phoenix, Valley National Bank, 1972.

Faculty of the University of Arizona, "Arizona's Economy." In *Arizona: Its People and Resources.*

Map 11. *Prehistoric Civilization*

McGregor, John C. *Southwestern Archaeology.* 2d ed. Urbana, University of Illinois Press, 1965.

Martin, Paul S. *The Last 10,000 Years: A Fossil Pollen Record of the American Southwest.* Tucson, University of Arizona Press, 1963.

Turney, O. A. "Prehistoric Irrigation," *Arizona Historical Review,* Vol. II (1929–30).

Map 12. *Indian Tribes circa 1600*

Bolton, Herbert E. *Rim of Christiandom: A Biography of Eusebio Francisco Kino, Pacific Coast Pioneer.* New ed. New York, Russell and Russell, 1969.

Spicer, Edward H. *Cycles of Conquest: The Impact of Spain, Mexico, and the United States on the Indians of the Southwest.* Tucson, University of Arizona Press, 1962.

Map 13. *Routes of Spanish Explorers*

Bolton, Herbert E. *Spanish Exploration in the Southwest, 1542–1700.* New York, Scribner's, 1916.

Ewing, Russell C. "The Spanish Past." In *Arizona: Its People and Resources.*

Map 14. *Spanish and Mexican Missions and Presidios*

Ewing, "The Spanish Past." In *Arizona, Its People and Resources.*

Fontana, Bernard L., "Biography of a Desert Church:

The Story of Mission San Xavier del Bac," *Smoke Signal No. 3.* Tucson Corral of the Westerners, Spring, 1961.

Kessell, John L. *Mission of Sorrows: Jesuit Guevavi and the Pimas, 1691–1767.* Tucson, University of Arizona Press, 1970.

Brinckerhoff, Sidney B., and Odie B. Faulk. *Lancers for the King: A Study of the Frontier Military System of Northern New Spain.* Phoenix, Arizona Historical Foundation, 1965.

Map 15. *Spanish and Mexican Land Grants*

Mattison, Ray H. "Early Spanish and Mexican Settlement in Arizona," *New Mexico Historical Review,* Vol. XXI (October, 1946), 273–327.

———, "The Tangled Web: The Controversy over the Tumacacori and Baca Land Grants." *Journal of Arizona History,* Vol. VIII (Summer, 1967), 70–91.

Powell, Donald M. *The Peralta Grant: James Addison Reavis and the Barony of Arizona.* Norman, University of Oklahoma Press, 1960.

Map 16A., Map 16B. *Interior Provinces of New Spain and the Louisiana Purchase*

Almada, Francisco R. *Diccionario de Historia, Geografía y Biografía Sonorenses.* Chihuahua, Ruiz Sandoval, 1952.

Bancroft, Hubert H. *History of the North Mexican States and Texas.* 2 vols. San Francisco, The History Company, 1889.

Brooks, Philip C. *Diplomacy and the Borderlands: The Adams-Onis Treaty of 1819.* Berkeley, University of California Press, 1939.

Loomis, Noel M. "Commandants-General of the Interior Provinces: A Preliminary List," *Arizona and the West,* Vol. XI (Autumn, 1969), 261–86.

Map 17. *Anglo Penetration: The Mountain Men*

Cleland, Robert G. *This Reckless Breed of Men: The Trappers and Fur Traders of the Southwest.* New York, Alfred A. Knopf, 1963.

Kroeber, A. L. "The Route of James O. Pattie on the Colorado in 1826," *Arizona and the West,* Vol. VI (Summer, 1964), 119–36.

Wheat, Carl I., and Dale L. Morgan. *Jedediah Smith and His Maps.* San Francisco, California Historical Society, 1954.

Weber, David J. *The Taos Trappers: The Fur Trade the Far Southwest.* Norman: University of Oklahoma Press, 1971.

Map 18. *Routes of the Mexican War*

Cooke, Philip St. G. *The Conquest of New Mexico and California.* New ed. Albuquerque, Horn & Wallace, 1964.

Dobyns, Henry F., ed. *Hepah California: The Journal of Cave Johnson Couts.* Tucson, Arizona Pioneers Historical Society, 1961.

Emory, William H. *Notes of a military Reconnaissance from Fort Leavenworth . . . to San Diego, Sen. Exec. Doc. 7, 30 Cong., 1 sess.*

Golder, Frank A., ed. *The March of the Mormon Battalion.* New York, Century Company, 1928.

Map 19. *The Disturnell Map of 1847 and The Boundary Controversy, 1848–54*

Faulk, Odie B. *Too Far North—Too Far South.* Los Angeles, Westernlore Press, 1967.

Rittenhouse, Jack D. *The Story of Disturnell's Treaty Map.* Santa Fe, Stagecoach Press, 1965.

Map 20A., Map 20B. *Mexican Cession of 1848* and *Proposed State of Deseret, 1849*

Arrington, Leonard J. *Great Basin Kingdom: An Economic History of the Latter-Day Saints.* Cambridge: Harvard University Press, 1958.

Creer, Leland H. *Utah and the Nation.* Seattle, University of Washington Press, 1929.

Faulk, *Too Far North—Too Far South.*

Smith, Justin H. *War with Mexico.* New ed. 2 vols. Gloucester, Mass., Peter Smith, 1963.

Map 21. *Gadsden Treaty Proposals*

Garber, Paul N. *The Gadsden Treaty.* Gloucester, Mass., Peter Smith, 1959.

Schmidt, Louis B. "Manifest Opportunity and the Gadsden Purchase," *Arizona and the West,* Vol. III (Autumn, 1961), 245–64.

Map 22. *Gadsden Purchase, 1854*

Garber. *Gadsden Treaty.*

Schmidt. "Manifest Opportunity."

Map 23. *Routes of American Explorers and Surveyors*

Goetzmann, William H. *Army Explorations in the American West.* New Haven, Yale University Press, 1959.

Bailey, L. R. *The A. B. Gray Report.* Los Angeles, Westernlore Press, 1963.

Map 24. *Indian Tribes* circa *1860*

Executive Orders Relating to Indian Reservations, 1855–1912. Washington, 1912.

Goodwin, Grenville. *The Social Organization of the Western Apaches.* New ed. Tucson, University of Arizona Press, 1969.

Spicer. *Cycles of Conquest.*

Swanton, John R. *The Indian Tribes of North America.* Washington, 1953.

Map 25. *Territory of New Mexico, 1850 and Territory of Arizona, 1863*

Bancroft, Hubert H. *History of Arizona and New Mexico.* New ed. Albuquerque, Horn & Wallace, 1962.

Sacks, B. *Be It Enacted: The Creation of the Territory of Arizona.* Phoenix, Arizona Historical Foundation, 1964.

Map 26. *Military Posts, 1849–64*

Brandes, Ray. *Frontier Military Posts of Arizona.* Globe, Ariz., Dale Stuart King, 1960.

Hart, Herbert M. *Old Forts of the Far West.* Seattle, Superior Publishing Company, 1965.

————. *Old Forts of the Southwest.* Seattle, Superior Publishing Company, 1964.

Prucha, Francis P. *Guide to the Military Posts of the United States.* Madison, The State Historical Society of Wisconsin, 1964.

Map 27A. *Military Telegraph 1873–77*

Rue, Norman L. "Pesh-Bi-Yalti Speaks: White Man's Talking Wire in Arizona," *Journal of Arizona History,* Vol. XII (Winter, 1971), 229–62.

Map 27B. *Heliograph System, 1890*

Volkmar, William J. *Report of General Practice of the Heliograph System, Department of Arizona, in May, 1890.* Washington, ca. 1890.

Map 28. *Mormon Settlement*

McClintock, James M. *Mormon Settlement in Arizona: A Record of Peaceful Conquest of the Desert.* Phoenix, Manufacturing Stationers, Inc., ca. 1921.

Peterson, Charles S. *Take Up Your Mission: Mormon Colonizing along the Little Colorado River, 1870–1900.* Tucson, University of Arizona Press, 1973.

Wyllys, Rufus K. *Arizona: The History of a Frontier State.* Phoenix, Hobson & Herr, 1950.

Map 29. *County Boundaries 1855 and 1860*

Sacks. *Be It Enacted.*

Map 30. *County Boundaries 1864–65*

Bancroft. *History of Arizona and New Mexico.*

Kelly, George H. *Legislative History: Arizona, 1864–1912.* Phoenix, Manufacturing Stationers, 1926.

Wagoner. *Arizona Territory.*

Map 31. *County Boundaries 1871, '75, '77, '79*

Bancroft. *History of Arizona and New Mexico.*

Kelly. *Legislative History.*

Wagoner. *Arizona Territory.*

Map 32. *County Boundaries, 1881, '89, '91, '99, 1909*

Bancroft. *History of Arizona and New Mexico.*

Kelly. *Legislative History.*

Wagoner. *Arizona Territory.*

Map 33. *County Seats*

Journals of the Legislative Assembly of the Territory of Arizona, 1864–1912.

Journals of the House, Legislature of the State of Arizona, 1912–1970.

Journals of the Senate, Legislature of the State of Arizona, 1912–1970.

Map 34. *Proposed Arizona Counties*

Journals of the House.

Journals of the Senate.

Journals of the Legislative Assembly.

Map 35. *Boundary Disputes*

Journals of the Legislative Assembly.

Naegle, Conrad K. "The Rebellion of Grant County, New Mexico, in 1876," *Arizona and the West,* Vol. X (Autumn, 1968), 225–40.

Map 36. *Judicial Districts*

Murphy, James M. *Laws, Courts, & Lawyers: Through the Years in Arizona.* Tucson, University of Arizona Press, 1970.

Map 37. *Military Posts, 1865–1920*

Brandes. *Frontier Military Posts of Arizona.*

Hart. *Old Forts of the Far West.*

Prucha. *Guide to the Military Posts.*

Map 38. *Major Points of Indian-White Contact*

Heitman, Francis B. *Historical Register and Dictionary of the United States Army.* New ed. Urbana, University of Illinois Press, 1967.

Thrapp, Dan L. *Conquest of Apacheria.* Norman, University of Oklahoma Press, 1967.

Utley, Robert M. *Frontiersmen in Blue: The United States Army and the Indian.* New York, Macmillan, 1967.

Map 39. *Colorado River Ports & Major Supply Routes*

Mills, Hazel E. "The Arizona Fleet," *American Neptune,* Vol. I (1941), 255–74.

Yates, Richard & Mary Marshall, *The Lower Colorado River: A Bibliography.* Yuma: Arizona Western College Press, 1974.

Woodward, Arthur. *Feud on the Colorado.* Los Angeles, Westernlore Press, 1955.

Map 40. *Major Trails*

Jackson, W. Turrentine. *Wagon Roads West.* New Haven, Conn., Yale University Press, 1965.

Walker, Henry P. "Wagon Freighting in Arizona,"

Smoke Signal No. 28, Tucson, Corral of the Westerners, 1973.

Map 41. *Main Stagecoach Lines*

Hinton, Richard J. *The Handbook to Arizona, 1877.* New ed. Glorieta, N.M., Rio Grande Press, 1970.

Theobald, John and Lillian Theobald. *Arizona Territory: Post Offices & Postmasters.* Phoenix, Arizona Historical Foundation, 1961.

Map 42. *Development of Indian Reservations, 1859–72*

Kappler, Charles J., comp. "Indian Affairs: Laws and Treaties," Vols. I–II, *Sen. Doc. 452,* 57 Cong., 1 Sess. (Serials 4253–54) .

————, *ibid., Sen. Doc. 719,* 52 Cong., 2 Sess. (Serial 6166) .

————, *ibid., Sen. Doc. 53,* 70 Cong., 1 Sess. (Serial 8849) .

————, *ibid., Sen. Doc. 194,* 76 Cong., 3 Sess. (Serial 10458).

Spicer, *Cycles of Conquest*

Map 43. *Development of Indian Reservations; 1873–1912*

Kappler, "Indian Affairs: Laws and Treaties"

Spicer, *Cycles of Conquest*

Map 44. *Indian Reservations: Apache, Hopi and Navajo*

Kappler, "Indian Affairs: Laws and Treaties"

Spicer, *Cycles of Conquest*

Ownership and Administration of Public Lands in Arizona, Phoenix, Planning Division, Arizona Dept. of Economic Planning and Development, 1971

Map 45. *Indian Reservations*

Kappler, "Indian Affairs: Laws and Treaties"

Ownership and Administration of Public Lands in Arizona, Phoenix, Planning Div., DEPAD, 1971.

Map 46. *Railroad Development*

Myrick, David F. *A Brief Survey of the Histories of Pioneer Arizona Railroads.* Golden, Colorado, Railroad Museum, 1968.

————, *Railroads of Arizona, Vol. I, The Southern Roads.* Berkeley, Calif. Howell North, 1975.

Trennert, Robert A. "A Vision of Grandeur: The Arizona Mineral Belt Railroad," *Arizona and the West,* Vol. XII (Winter, 1970), 339–54.

Map 47. *Railroads*

Myrick, *Brief Survey of Arizona Railroads*

Trennert, "Vision of Grandeur."

Map 48. *Mining*

Dunning, Charles H. *Rock to Riches,* Phoenix, Southwest Publishing Co. 1959.

Elsing, Morris J. and Robert E. S. Heineman. *Arizona Metal Resources.* Arizona Bureau of Mines Bulletin 140, Tucson, 1936.

Forrester, J. Donald, *et al. Mineral and Water Resources of Arizona.*

Wilson, Eldred D., *et al. Gold Placers and Placering in Arizona.* Arizona Bureau of Mines Bulletin 168. Tucson, 1961.

Map 49. *Notable Mines*

Dunning, *Rock to Riches*

Elsing and Heineman, *Arizona Metal Resources*

Forrester, *et al, Mineral and Water Resources*

Alenius, E. M. J. *A Brief History of the United Verde Open Pit, Jerome, Arizona.* Arizona Bureau of Mines Bulletin 178. Tucson, 1968.

Wilson, Eldred D., *et al. Arizona Lode Gold Mines and Gold Mining.* Arizona Bureau of Mines Bulletin 137. Tucson, 1967.

Map 50. *Major Copper Mines*

Joralemon, Ira B. *Copper.* Berkeley, Calif., Howell North Books, 1973.

Dunning, *Rock to Riches.*

Map 51. *Major Lost Mine Legends*

Conrotto, Eugene L. *Lost Desert Bonanzas.* Palm Desert, Calif., Desert Southwest Publishers, 1963.

Mitchell, John D. *Lost Mines of the Great Southwest.* Glorieta, N.M., Rio Grande Press, 1970.

Polzer, Charles W. "Legends of Lost Missions and Mines," *Smoke Signal 18.* Tucson Corral of the Westerners, 1968.

Weight, Harold O. *Lost Mines of Old Arizona,* Twenty-nine Palms, Calif., Calico Press, 1959.

Map 52. *Federal Land Excluding BLM-Administered Land*

Carstenson, Vernon, ed. *The Public Lands: Studies in the History of the Public Domain.* Madison, University of Wisconsin Press, 1963.

Robbins, Roy M. *Our Landed Heritage: The Public Domain, 1776–1936.* New ed., Lincoln, University of Nebraska Press, 1962.

Ownership and Administration of Public Lands.

Seventh Arizona Town Hall. *Public Land Use, Transfer and Ownership in Arizona.* Phoenix, 1965.

Map 53. *Federal Land: Bureau of Land Management Land*

Peffer, E. Louise. *The Closing of the Public Domain: Disposal and Reservation Policies, 1900–1950,* Stanford, Stanford University Press, 1951.

Henderson, Patrick C. "The Public Domain in Arizona, 1863–1891." Ph.D. dissertation, University of New Mexico, 1966.

Ownership and Administration of Public Lands.

Map 54. *National Forests*

Ames, Charles R. "A History of the Forest Service," *Smoke Signal 16*, Tucson Corral of the Westerners, Fall, 1967.

Ownership and Administration of Public Lands.

Seventh Arizona Town Hall. *Public Land Use.*

Valley National Bank. *Arizona Statistical Review,* 1971.

Map 55. *National & State Parks*

Seventh Arizona Town Hall. *Public Land Use.*

Leaming, George F. "Tourism and Recreation." In *Arizona: Its People and Resources.*

Ownership and Administration of Public Lands.

Map 56. *Military Posts, 1921–76*

Seventh Arizona Town Hall. *Public Land Use*

Ownership and Administration of Public Lands.

Map 57. *State-owned Land*

Seventh Arizona Town Hall. *Public Land Use.*

Ownership and Administration of Public Lands.

Map 58. *Privately Owned Land*

Seventh Arizona Town Hall. Public Land Use.

University of Arizona Faculty. *Arizona: Its People and Resources.*

Ownership and Administration of Public Lands.

Map 59. *Irrigated Land and Major Dams*

Mann, Dean E. *The Politics of Water in Arizona.* Tucson, University of Arizona Press, 1963.

Ownership and Administration of Public Lands.

Map 60. *Population Growth in Arizona Cities*

Valley National Bank. *Arizona Statistical Review,* 1971.

United States Bureau of the Census, *Reports,* 1850–1970

Map 61. *Population Growth in Arizona Counties*

Valley National Bank. *Arizona Statistical Review.*

United States Bureau of the Census, *Reports,* 1850–1970.

Sen. Doc. 13, 89 Cong., 1 Sess. (Serial 12668–1) .

Map 62. *Growth of Phoenix and Tucson*

Valley National Bank. *Arizona Statistical Review,* 1971.

McLaughlin, Herb, and Dorothy McLaughlin, eds. *Phoenix, 1870–1970, in Photographs.* Arizona Photographic Associates, 1970.

Pederson, Gilbert J. "The Townsite is Now Secure," *Journal of Arizona History,* Vol. XI (Autumn, 1970) , 151–74.

Map 63. *Congressional Districts*

Arizona Revised Statutes—Annotated. St. Paul, Minn., West Publishing Co., 1956–72.

Map 64. *Grand Canyon of Arizona*

Granger. *Will Barnes' Arizona Place Names.*

Faculty of the University of Arizona. *Arizona: Its People and Resources.*

Map 65. *Historic Sites on the National Register*

National Register of Historic Places, Department of the Interior, Federal Register. Washington, 1977.

INDEX